The Civilization of the American Indian Series

(Complete list on pages 255–259)

The Chronicles of Michoacán

THE
CHRONICLES
OF
MICHOACÁN

Translated and Edited by
Eugene R. Craine
and
Reginald C. Reindorp

UNIVERSITY OF OKLAHOMA PRESS : NORMAN

BY EUGENE R. CRAINE

Treatise on Fossils (Maryville, Tenn., 1938)

The Story of Fort Robardeau (Altoona, Pa., 1940)

Historical Analysis of Maya Culture Change (Hays, Kan., 1950)

Coal-Oil Canyon: A Preliminary Report (editor) (Topeka, Kan., 1960)

The United States and the Independence of Buenos Aires (Hays, Kan., 1961)

The Chronicles of Michoacán (with Reginald C. Reindorp) (Norman, 1970)

BY REGINALD C. REINDORP

Metodología de las lenguas vivas (Peru, 1945)

Royal Road to Friendship (El Salvador, 1946)

La Décima de Nuevo México (El Salvador, 1946)

Idiomas, Cultura y Educación (Quito, Ecuador, 1954)

Let's Talk with our Latin American Neighbors, Books I–IV (with Trugen Hudson) (Hattiesburg, Miss., 1959–61)

The Chronicles of Michoacán (with Eugene R. Craine) (Norman, 1970)

International Standard Book Number: 0–8061–0887–8

Library of Congress Catalog Card Number: 69–16726

Foreword

THE *Description of the Ceremonies, Rites, Population, and Government of the Indians of the Province of Mechuacán,* better known as the *Relación de Michoacán,* is the basic work for the study of Tarascan prehistory. It was compiled between the years 1539 and 1541, presumably by Fr. Martín de Jesús de la Coruña, who with five Franciscan companions went into Michoacán in the year 1525 or early 1526.

The author personally presented the original manuscript to the Viceroy Don Antonio de Mendoza on the occasion of the Viceroy's second visit to the city of Michoacán (Tzintzuntzan) in 1541, an event recorded by an Indian artist in a drawing which is the first of forty-four sketches that appear in the manuscript. (See Plate 1.) In spite of the fact that the author found "among these people . . . no virtue other than generosity" and "hardly a single moral virtue . . ., rather recriminations, idolatries, drunkenness, death and war," he does give the only survey of their government, customs, and traditions drawn from the Indians themselves at the time of the Conquest. The writer obtained his material from informants and from one he called the brother-in-law of the Cazonci, Don Pedro, who was governor of the city of Michoacán. The writer's effort to present his informants' accounts in their own form of expression, with parenthetical comments of his own, presents a chronicle which, at times, is difficult to follow and is sometimes confused with the priest-interpreter's own religious beliefs and customs entering the narrative.

The origin of the Tarascans remains another enigma of ancient

Mexico. Who they were or where they came from either did not intrigue the author of the *Relación*, or he was satisfied that the Indians themselves did not know the answers. In one respect it is unfortunate that their conquest by the Spaniards was a relatively peaceful one as compared to the defeat of other Mexicans, such as the Aztecs, because no interpreters and no proud Tarascans wrote with nationalistic fervor of the extent or composition of the Tarascan state. Unlike the Aztecs there has been no Ixtlilxochitl or Tezozomoc.

Since no pre-Conquest codices or historical records of any type exist for Michoacán, and specifically for the Tarascans, the *Relación de Michoacán* achieves a position of significance as the primary source of post-Conquest sources. It is the only one which traces the historical development of Michoacán and which attempts to give some detail of the rites, ceremonies, government, law, social and religious institutions, and imperialism which existed in the area before the arrival of the Spaniards. Other post-Conquest sources may be found that examine, to some degree, pre-Conquest times. These are in the claims and depositions made by Tarascans in the Spanish courts and in the testimonies of the conquistadores of Michoacán, which may be found in the Archivo Generál de Indias, Sevilla, under the sections "Patronato," "Justicia," and "Audiencia de México." There are also occasional references to Michoacán in various codices, such as the *Códice Ramírez* and the *Códice Mendocino*.

From a number of remarkable documents, primarily the chronicles of the early Franciscan and Augustinian friars, it is possible to glean considerable information about pre-Columbian Tarascan culture and something of the later pre-Conquest political history. From a purely ethnographic viewpoint, the Franciscan reports are most useful. Members of this order were the first to penetrate the Tarascan empire, establishing in 1526 their first convent, Santa Anna, in Tzintzuntzan, and during the Colonial period they were particularly associated with the towns geographically most properly called focal in the sense of a Tarascan culture area.

The earliest and most revealing of these documents is the *Relación de las ceremonias y ritos y población y gobernación de los indios de la provincia de Mechuacán*. The manuscript of the *Relación* is in the Real Biblioteca de El Escorial in Madrid, where it is generally known as Códice C–IV–5 and is sometimes called the *Códice del Escorial*. It contains 140 sheets, with three additional sheets on the Tarascan calendar and forty-four illustrations. In a critical note written for the Revista Mexicana de Estudios Historicos [Vol. I, 1927, 191–213] entitled *La Relación de Michuacán*, Nicolas Leon maintains that the original is lost and the Escorial manuscript is a copy. While this definitely affects the problem of orthography found in the comparison of the Madrid and the Morelia editions, it does not change the fact that all published editions are based on Códice C–IV–5. Three other manuscript copies exist: the Peter Force copy in the Library of Congress, a copy in the Obadiah Rich collection in the New York Public Library designated there as "Rich 42," and a copy in the Aubin collection in the Bibliothèque Nationale in Paris. The *Relación* was first published in Madrid, in 1869, as Volume 53 of the *Coleción de Documentos Ineditos para la Historia de España*. There was also a fraudulent reissue in 1875. Probably the best edition was the one translated here, the Morelia (Mexico) edition of 1903, which was based upon the 1869 Madrid edition compared with the Peter Force copy.

The basis of this translation is the printed Morelia edition of 1903. When translating, we adhered to the original Spanish as closely as the English idiom permitted. It has been convenient to break up the lengthy sentences, make paragraphs, and shorten the priest-translator's long descriptive chapter headings. No attempt has been made to identify all the proper names of persons and places that occur in the text. Where the Morelia edition was in error in identifying the sketches, we used the captions given in C–IV–5. A very real difficulty in this study is the different orthography used for names of both persons and places, not only between the Madrid and the Morelia copies but also within the Morelia edition. In most cases it is impossible for us to know what the correct spelling should be; therefore, other spellings found in the manuscript will appear immediately following such a name and in brackets. Since the purpose here is to present a readable translation of the *Relación* in a single volume, additional notes have not been included.

Two comments should be emphasized. First, the Indians called themselves Purépeche, the name Tarascan having been applied to them by the Spaniards, a name which the Indian believed "shamed him" and which he did not like. Furthermore, the so-called Tarascan culture at the time of the conquest was not a true Purépeche culture but rather one that had undergone strong acculturation from the invading Chichimecas. In fact, if the manuscript is correct, when the Spanish arrived, the entire leadership of the ancient peoples of the lakes was Chichimecan. We have added a map, a glossary, a list of the feasts as they appear in the book, and a list of suggested readings as a guide to interpretive studies that have been made of the *Relación* and to some of the more recent anthropological and geographic studies which have been made of Michoacán. This bibliography is intended only to direct the reader to specific studies of the *Relación* and Michoacán, not to be a complete guide to historical literature dealing with early Mexico.

Important, particularly for post-Conquest data, is the *Crónica de la Provincia de los Santos Apóstoles S. Pedro de Michoacán* of Pablo de la Purísima Concepción Beaumont, written at the end of the eighteenth century, first published in Mexico in 1874 and republished in 1932. Useful information is also found in the *Crónica de la Orden de N. Seráfico P. S. Francisco, Provincia de San Pedro y San Pablo de Mechoacán en la Nueva España*, by Fray Alonso de la Rea (1882). In Book I, Chapter 5, Rea makes vague reference to lost information stating that "according to the paintings and traditions preserved in the *archives of the times* ....." (translators' italics), but the only item from such "archives" found to date has been the *Lienzo of Tucutacato*. The *Lienzo* (drawing on linen), discovered in the 1870's by Dr. Don Crescencio García de Cotija, recounts the movement of the Tarascans and eight other nations from Aztlán, the "Seven Caves of the West," to their home in Michoacán and is the only known document that attempts to locate the place of origin of the Tarascans. Less detailed but still valuable as a document is the *Historia Eclesiástica Indiana* of Fray Gerónimo de Mendieta, written at the end of the sixteenth century and first published in 1870.

The paucity of information in literature is matched by the lack of archaeological studies. Michoacán has been consistently ignored by archaeologists, and until recently all the artifacts of western Mexico were jauntily indexed, shelved, or displayed as Tarascan. It is not possible to state what the total archaeological content of any one site might be, nor has any stratigraphy been developed which would make possible establishing the proper chronological relationships between and among the items found.

Although some interest was evidenced in the pre-Conquest Tarascans as early as 1852 when Don Ignacio Trespeña completely destroyed one of the *yácatas* and in 1886 when the Englishman Charles Hartford and the priest Domingo Reyes Corral excavated some buildings. It was not, however, until the modern Mexican artists, such as Diego Rivera, began to make large collections of high-quality Tarascan objects that any real interest was created. Further impetus came in the 1930's as a result of the concern of Lázaro Cárdenas, president of Mexico, and the work of Alfonso Caso, Eduardo Noguera, Rubín de la Borbolla, and others who, using the writings of Beaumont as a guide, excavated in the areas of Zacapu, Zamora, Pátzcuaro, Jacona, and Ihuatzio. Archaeologists took notice, some surveys were carried out, and finally the entire problem was placed on the agenda of the Fourth Round Table on Anthropological Problems of Mexico and Central America held in Mexico City in 1947. The conference did not clarify the confusion which exists in the Tarascan area, but it did emphasize the fact that a great amount of study is needed if we are ever to know and understand the pre-Conquest Tarascans.

Placing the Tarascans in time and space gives one the strange feeling that history was marking time by waiting for one group of actors to exit, a process slowly taking place, and another group to enter. It is even stranger when one realizes that, for the most part, the actors were completely unaware of the others, and yet their destinies are linked. It soon becomes apparent that man has learned little about getting along with his fellow man, for, at the time of the arrival of the Tarascans in Michoacán, the predominant state of affairs, not only of Mexico but also of the world, was war. However, other events were occurring.

The eleventh century in Europe witnessed the Capetian kings tightening their hold through a series of internal and external wars on the country which became France. The English state was just beginning to develop after conquest by William I, both internal and external wars were in vogue, and man was getting a new introduction to taxation by means of the Domesday Book. Spain, destined in a short time to bring to an end the newly developing nations of Mexico, was at the beginning of her long war against the Moors and the founding of the Spanish Empire. This was the period of the cruel, selfish, and proud Cid, whose activities became legend and the man himself the great national hero of Spain. In China it was the period of the Sung Dynasty, the golden age of landscape painting and Chinese essayists.

In Mexico the old powers were also in decline. The Classic period of the Olmec, Maya, and Zapotec had passed, and the Maya Renaissance was doomed to fail. The glory that had been Teotihuacán was gone, although its influence still lingered throughout all of Mesoamerica; the great Toltec center, Tula, now at its peak, was within a few years of an invasion that would leave the center destroyed and its inhabitants fleeing southward. Carrying their culture with them, they left their mark throughout all Mexico, from Tula in the north to Chichén Itzá in the Yucatán peninsula. In a limited sense chaos existed before the fall of Tula, but with the sacking and destruction of the Toltec capital in A.D. 1156 by the invading Aztec warriors, chaos became a reality throughout all of Mexico.

The fall of the old centers, as a result of internal struggle or of invasion by outsiders, led to a general decentralization throughout Mexico. There developed a tendency for small groups to

XII

establish their own government, distrusting anyone not of their
family, clan, or tribe, and this became characteristic of tenth-
and eleventh-century Mexico. For reasons unknown there was
also a movement of nomadic groups from the northwest into the
central plateau, which not only caused further movement of
peoples but also brought newcomers into the region.

Among these late-comers a small group calling themselves
Purépeche, under the leadership of Iré Thicátame or Hireticátame, settled in and around Zacapu in what is now the state of
Michoacán. Some believe they were a conglomerate of nomads
and refugees who had been living in the area for some time. In
the tenth century they developed a militant political conscious-
ness and, under the influence of ambitious leaders, desirous of
prestige and power, began to create an empire. According to their
own traditions, as has already been mentioned, they emerged
along with their contemporaries, the Aztecs, from the "Seven
Caves of the West," but elected to remain in Michoacán rather
than continue the journey into the valley of Mexico. Anthro-
pologists have generally discounted the idea of common origin
with the Nahuas on the basis of language differences, as the
Tarascan tongue is completely distinct from the Nahuatl. It
might, in time, also be proved that religious concepts as well as
social and political institutions were quite different.

Unfortunately for the Indian the new culture, which had its
beginning in Zacapu, was not truly a new culture. Indeed, in
many respects it was a strange society which developed in the area
between the Río Lerma in the north and the Río Balsas in the
south and from approximately the boundary between the modern state of Mexico and Michoacán on the east to a line roughly
drawn from Lake Chapalla south to the Río Balsas on the west.
Perhaps the key to their culture as it developed in the years between the tenth century and the arrival of the Spaniards is to be
found in the term *eclecticism*. Apparently the Tarascans were
borrowers, not inventors. This is reflected in the artifacts of the
area, which range from stirrup-handled "teapots" with a distinct
flavor of Peru or Ecuador to the presence of the Chac-mool, which

was a definite influence of Tula. As with most peoples of Mesoamerica, the Tarascans were excellent craftsmen in obsidian, clay, stone, bone, and shell. The leaders of their society were easily identified by the beautifully carved obsidian earplugs and delicate lip-rings of laminated gold and turquoise which they wore. They produced polychrome ceramics, rock-crystal beads for necklaces, anthropomorphic and spiraled clay pipes, spiraled spindle whorls, silver tweezers, gold rings, and brightly varnished gourds. They were unsurpassed in their beautiful featherwork.

Unusual, however, for Mesoamerica, was their work with metal, for the Tarascans knew and used the more advanced and complex methods of metal-working processes such as welding, alloying, casting, annealing, soldering, and plating. Beautiful copper masks come from the area, as well as bracelets of copper, copper needles, bells with copper gilding, and laminated gold and silver objects. It is generally believed that metalworking as an art developed in Peru, but it is also agreed that the most important inventions were made in Colombia. These discoveries were casting *a cire perdue*, gilding by the *mise en couleur* process, and the gold-copper alloy known as *guanin* or *tumbage*. All were used by the Tarascans, and it would appear that as far as Mexico is concerned it was the Tarascans who developed metallurgy.

Presumably the developing Tarascan state was composed of migrants or refugees from many diverse areas, or their trade was indeed extensive and varied. The probability is great for a combination of the two with a borrowing and manufacturing of those things which pleased them. It is interesting to note that their language reflects this same wide influence, for many of their words are Quechua, the language of Peru, and even some of their tombs are the same bottle-shape type found in Peru. If the Aztecs could claim they were the heirs to the Toltec culture, then the Tarascans could well claim they were the heirs to the arts of all Mesoamerica and a large part of South America as well. Unfortunately, they did not add to or strengthen their heritage; they merely borrowed and continued the same skills.

Political centralization of Michoacán came late and was not

accomplished by Hireticátame. He did successfully complete a
number of military campaigns against various peoples and Tarascans who had settled on the shores of Lake Pátzcuaro, but his
career was cut short by assassination. He was succeeded by his
son Sicuirancha, who established himself in a beautiful palace on
an island in Lake Zirahuén in the region known today as Quiroga.
The dynasty which he established ruled for many years.

The real founder of the Tarascan state was Tariacuri, son of
the daughter of a Jaracuaro fisherman and Pavacume, a Tarascan
chief. Tariacuri, with a combination of machiavellian duplicity
and the aid of his son Hiqugage and two nephews, Hiripan and
Tangaxoan I, conquered the Sierra of northwestern Michoacán
and northern Guerrero, a part of which is known as the Tierra
Caliente. Since the Aztec state was developing at the same time,
it was necessary for the Tarascans to maintain strong military
outposts on their eastern and southwestern border, therefore
instigating the conquest of northern Guerrero. The Tierra
Caliente was needed because it was a major source of supply for
copper, gold, honey, wax, cinnabar, cacao, cotton, feathers, hides
and skins, gum, copal, and vegetable fats.

When Tariacuri died, the state was divided, with his son
Hiqugage ruling in Pátzcuaro, Hiripan in Cuyacán, and Tangaxoan I in Tzintzuntzan. Hiqugage and Hiripan died without
heirs, and so the state was again united under Tzitzic Pandacuare,
the son of Tangaxoan I. This leader conquered southeast Jalisco
and Colima and proved Tarascan military prowess by defeating
the Aztec Axayacatl in the bloody war of 1469–78. The extent of
the Tarascan state waxed and waned during the years, but the
boundary between their state and that of the Aztecs was successfully defended until the arrival of the Spaniards. The last reign-
ing Tarascan was the weak Tangaxoan II. Bewildered by omens
and myths about the coming of "new" men and disturbed by a
plague which swept through his kingdom, he failed to send his
powerful armies against the Spaniards under Cristóbal de Olid
and finally surrendered himself and his kingdom to Nuño
Beltrán de Guzmán. Guzmán took his gold, dispersed his armies,

and had Tangaxoan II dragged behind a horse through the streets of his capital city, Tzintzuntzan, until dead. The native Tarascan state collapsed and was never rebuilt.

We wish to express our gratitude to the staff of the Real Biblioteca de El Escorial for their labors on our behalf and for their permission to use the sketches that appear in the *Códice del Escorial*, and to José de Prado Herranz, photographer at the Real Biblioteca de El Escorial, for the photographs of those sketches. The Institutional Research Committee of Fort Hays Kansas State College assisted in defraying the cost of transcribing the original manuscript, and Robert W. Hill, Keeper of Manuscripts, New York Public Library, was very courteous and kind in answering questions in the early stages of this work. We are indebted to many who lent assistance: John Ray, Wright State University, for the map of Michoacán; and our secretaries, Josephine Soukup, Linda McKee, and Edith Davidson, who spent many long hours typing the manuscript and checking "two-inch-long" names.

EUGENE R. CRAINE
REGINALD C. REINDORP

January 9, 1970

Contents

Plates

The Chronicles of Michoacán

Introduction

to

Morelia Edition

THIS book, which is now being published by order of the progressive governor of this Federative entity, Mr. C. Aristeo Mereado, and by initiative of the undersigned, is commonly known in the scientific world by the title of "Relación de Michoacán."

The manuscript is preserved in the Library of the Escorial, and, in Madrid, in 1875, a printed copy was made of that priceless document whose true title is the one that appears on the front of this book. That printing was full of errors which have been corrected in the present edition; the original spelling has been preserved and its worth will be appreciated by the reader when he learns that a copy of the old manuscript of the above mentioned "Relación" is to be found in the Library of Congress in Washington, U.S.A. This last copy was the property of Colonel Peter Force and is referred to by the Abbot (Abbé) Brasseur de Bourbourg in his *Histoire des Nations Civilissées du Mexique et de l'Amérique Centrale.* In 1888, Dr. Nicolas Leon, through the great influence of the unforgettable diplomat, D. Matías Romero, then Minister of Mexico to the United States, succeeded in getting Mr. Albert S. Gatschet to correct the erroneous copy printed in Madrid in accordance with the authoritative manuscript in Washington. Mr. R. L. Ridgway copied the color plates that go with it; together they resulted in a faithful reproduction of the manuscript in the archives of the Michoacán Museum, which is published in this first printing.

For these reasons it is hoped that it will be well received and will awaken a lively interest among students of the early history of our country, especially the little known history of Michoacán.

MANUEL MARTÍNEZ SOLÓRZANO
Director of the Michoacán Museum

Morelia
Michoacán, Mexico
April, 1903

Prologue
to
Morelia Edition

Your Excellency.

IT is a common saying that everybody naturally wants to learn and that to acquire knowledge many years are spent delving in books, long hours in study, and in much travel, learning many languages for the sake of inquiry, and knowing how the gentiles lived as is narrated and recounted in greater detail by the blessed San Gerónimo in the Prologue to the Bible. Naturally, there came to me, as to others before me, a desire to investigate these new Christians and learn what kind of life they lived as infidels, what their beliefs were, how they lived and were governed, and where they came from. Many times I thought about it and wondered why I did not investigate it myself, but I did not feel qualified for the task. Neither did I have access to the means to reach the goal and the end that I desired; on the one hand, because of the great lack of records among these people, and on the other, the lack of living witnesses to the events, and finally, because of the great amount of work and trouble involved in such matters, for we religious have other purposes, namely implanting the faith in Christ and to train and develop these people in new customs, and to reform them if it be possible into people of reason after God. I had already lost faith in this my desire when I was encouraged by your Holy Excellency who, upon coming the first time to visit this province of Mechuacán, asked me two or three times why I did not put to good use my administration over these people. Realizing that your Holiness had the same idea as I, it became clear to me that Your Most Excellent Holiness would look upon my wish with favor.

For the sake of doing some good, yet hesitating to attempt to express in writing something of the recollections of the oldest and most ancient residents of this province for the purpose of showing your Lordship a sample, as it were, of the customs of these people of Mechuacán so that your Lordship may favor them, governing them through the good qualities they used to have and separating them from the bad. In this entire document hardly a single moral virtue will be seen, rather recriminations, idolatries, drunkenness, death, and war. Among these people I have found no virtue other than that of generosity, for in their time the Masters held it to be an offense to be stingy. I say there were hardly any other virtues among them, for they had no names for any of them, and it seems that they did not function inasmuch as, for example, the only way they could say "chastity" in their language was by paraphrase. The same was true of other virtues as temperance, charity, and justice, for even though they may have some of the words, they do not understand them since they have no books. They would have done well in many things had they been governed by the dictates of reason, but since everything was so chaotic among them and confused by their idolatries and vices, they occasionally did some good by accident. May our good Lord provide them with religious who, leaving Castile with its cloisters and spiritual ease, may be inspired to come here and get down to business, not only to preach according to their ability but even more to teach them to read. Not only this but also they must simplify everything for their childish minds and be all things to all of them as the apostle St. Paul said of himself. In this fashion they will be provided each day with someone to show them the moral virtues as was provided by Your Illustrious Holiness for the administration, government, and regulation of this new world. All this I say without the slightest intention of flattery because such intentions are not becoming to the religious as is well known to everybody.

Truth is not to be hidden because your Seigniory appears to be chosen of God to govern this land, to maintain peace and justice, to listen to the little fellow as well as the big man, and to remedy injustices, and the proof thereof is well established. Your door is always open to the lowly as well as to the grandee, and everyone comes to you in full confidence while you sacrifice your Lordship's recreation and pastime, give audience all day and even into the night to one or another, to such an extent that we religious are amazed by the constancy of Your Excellency; and we can say of you that we do more to sustain and preserve what was conquered than was done in the original conquest, because the latter was achieved in a matter of days while the present work is a matter of many years. In the beginning courage and daring were praised; now the kindliness toward all, the great talent for governing, the prudence in all things, your affability without loss of authority and respect as required by the office, your zeal to implant our Christian religion among these people are all praised. And for all these reasons may our Lord permit these people to respond in kind with the love, fear, and reverence that everyone feels toward Your Excellency in this province and in all the others of this New Spain; the mere words of Your Excellency are held to be commandments in view of the manner in which Your Excellency treats the people, protects them and maintains peace and order which was not so easily accomplished in their infidelity, because the slightest disobedience of their Masters cost them their lives, and they were sacrificed. What they were unable to accomplish in such rigor to make them obedient, Your Illustrious Holiness accomplished now with gentleness for which thanks should be given to our Lord. We are amazed by the great courage and spirit of Your Excellency as you are enlightened by the Holy Spirit and share your talents so openly and tangibly that both great and lowly benefit.

Sir, this document and history are presented to Your Illustrious Lordship by the older residents of this city of Mechuacán, and by me also in their name, not as the author but rather as their interpreter, from which you will note that the signs or symbols (*synas*)[1] are appropriate to their style of speech, and I intend to

---

[1] Probably an abbreviation of *sentencyas* ["sentences"] according to a note by Alfred S. Gatschet. We suggest that it was meant to be *señas*. Spanish for signs,

preserve this while making note of it, but as a faithful interpreter I have not wanted to change this manner of speaking so as not to lose the true nature of their language. This I have attempted in the entire interpretation with the possible exception of a few words and some that would be lacking or unintelligible if something were not added. Some signs [words, symbols] are explained so that the reader will understand this manner of speaking, [for example] *no cuche-he-puhu-carixacan* means literally, in our romance language, we do not have our heads with us. They do not give it the meaning that we do, but, in their day, they meant that they were in deep trouble or feared they would be the captives of their enemies who would cut off their heads and mount them on long poles. Their meaning, then, was that their heads had already been cut off, for which reason they would say they had lost their heads. In their manner of inverting words [sentences?], it is worthy to note that they do not use as many words with equivocal meanings as in our language. In this connection I repeat that I serve as the interpreter of the old men, and please take note that they are telling the story to Your Most Illustrious Lordship and to the readers, giving an account of their life and ceremonies, their government and land. Illustrious Sir, Your Lordship told me that I should write of the administration of this province for the benefit of those religious who may undertake their conversion, that they may learn also where their principal gods came from and the feasts that were celebrated in their honor, all of which I described in Part I. In the second part, I discussed the manner in which the ancestors of the Cazonci colonized and governed this province, and, in Part III, how they governed themselves in this province until the Spaniards arrived and up to the death of the Cazonci. Please, will Your Lordship

---

marks, tokens, etc., since even Spaniards of the time placed great stock in writing, especially words, as representing or actually being the object or person for which they stood. There was some belief in magic attached to written words. Sentences as construed today were not nearly so important, for the concept still needed further development. When this document was written, it had been only a few years since the first modern grammar was written by Antonio de Nebrija and presented to Queen Isabel in 1492.

8

amend, correct, and promote this writing, for it was be[
your name and by your commandment, so that this langua[
style may be accepted with favor by readers and not releg
oblivion that which was so laboriously translated into pure (
ian. Most of all I wish to warn the reader that he should
full use of the question marks in this writing and should
in the manner in which these people talk if their manner of
ing is to be understood, because, for the greater part, he
speaks negatively does so in the form of questions.

The Chronicles
of
Michoacán

IT has been told, in the first part, how the Gods of the Heavens informed the God Curicaveri that he was to be king and was to conquer the entire earth; that there would be someone to represent him for the purpose of ordering wood for the temples. Afterwards people would say that the Cazonci is the representative of Curicaveri. After the time of Zizispandagre, Grandfather of the Cazonci, this province of Michoacán was united into one seigniory as his father had ordered. This situation was maintained until the Spanish came: for the God Curicaveri was King and the Cazonci his human representative, governor, and captain-general in war.

The Kingdom was divided into four parts and a very principal lord placed in each part. In each village the Cazonci placed leaders whose duty was to oversee the bringing of wood. There were other important persons, called Achaechas, who maintained a palace for the Cazonci and who were continually in his company as were the chiefs of the province, called Carachacapachas. There were others, called Ocambecha, each in charge of an assigned district, who were charged with the collection of tribute, counting the people, and calling them together for public works. At the beginning of Don Pedro's administration as Governor, he assigned to each one of these principals twenty-five houses. They did not count these houses as homes or residences but counted instead the number of persons included in a family. According to custom, there might be two or three residents with their relatives in some houses, and in others only a husband and wife, in

11

another a mother and son, and so on. It was not customary for these principals, called Ocambecha, to exact more than wood and a seed plot for this office. Others made huts for them, but now the Ocambechas often demand too much in the name of tribute from the people in their charge, and they frequently keep this tribute from the people, especially gold or silver.

Over all of these principals there was another deputy who was next in line after the Cazonci: this one collected the tribute from all the principals.

There was another, called Pirovaquen-vandari, who was in charge of collecting all the blankets and cotton which the people gave as a tribute and all this he kept in his house. He also had charge of collecting the mats and matting from officials for common needs.

Another representative, called Tareta Varatati, was over all those who were in charge of the Cazonci's seed plots; he was a major major-domo or principal supervisor assigned over all the seed plots [in the province], for there was another supervisor over each seed plot in each of the villages, who had it seeded, weeded, and harvested for the wars and for offerings to their gods.

Another supervisor was in charge of the more than 2,000 officials whose work was building houses, with another thousand for the renovation of the temples they constructed. Often they did nothing but build houses and temples ordered by the Cazonci; many of these still exist.

One called Cacari was the principal supervisor of all stone masons and quarries. He had other helpers, and there are still many of these with their supervisors in charge of them.

There was another one called Quanicoti, chief of all the hunters, who brought in deer and rabbits for the Cazonci. There were also bird hunters in case he should want this kind of game.

There was one called Curru Apindi, who supervised hunting of ducks and quail, and he gathered up all the birds for the sacrifices at the feasts of the goddess Xaratanga. After the feast the Cazonci and his lords ate all this game.

There was a person called Varuri in charge of all the net fishermen who supplied fish to the Cazonci and to all the lords. The fishermen did not eat the fish but took it all to the Cazonci and the lords, for they ate nothing but fish. Neither did they eat their chickens but had them only for the feathers with which to make adornments of their gods. The office of Varuri still follows the custom of getting fish from the fishermen but not in the same quantities as before.

Cavaspati was a supervisor over all those who harvested for the Cazonci, while other supervisors were in charge of all the seeds, such as pigweeds of many kinds, kidney beans, and others. (See Plate 2.)

There was a principal assigned to receive and store the corn and bee honey brought to the Cazonci.

There was an official tavern keeper, called Atari, to receive all the maguey wine that was made for the feasts.

Cuzuri was the chief leather dresser from Valdres, who made warcoats of leather for the Cazonci. This official still plies his trade.

An official called Uscuarecun was an overseer of all the feather workers who made adornments from feathers for their gods and for the dancers. This specialty has come down to the present. They used to bring many parrots in a variety of colors and sizes to the villages for their feathers. Others brought in the feathers of herons and other kinds of birds.

The one who was in charge of all the forest guards, of those who cut wooden beams [vigas], and made boards and other lumber from the forests was called Pucuricuari. He had under him his own principals and those of other lords. These Pucuricuari still serve here in Michoacán. There was also one who, with his workers, made canoes.

There was a chief treasurer who was responsible for all the silver and gold which they used during their feasts for their gods, and he had others under him as assistants who kept the accounts of the jewels. These consisted of mitres, silver bracelets, gold wreaths, and so on.

An official called Cheriguenquei [Chereguequauri] supervised the making of cotton doublets for the wars. He was assisted by many principals.

The making of bows and arrows was assigned to one called Quaricoguauri [Quarnicoguauri], whose responsibility it was to store them also, since large quantities of them were needed. It was a part of the daily work of the city dwellers to make them out of cane. (See Plate 3.)

The round shields were in the charge of and stored by the plumage workers who made them of rich feathers of birds including parrots and white herons.

There was a chief major-domo called Quengue, who supervised all the corn on the ear that was brought to the Cazonci and placed in very large granaries.

There was a chief canoe maker called Hicharuta Vandari, along with a chief boatman called Paricuti to whom people were assigned as rowers. People still work at this occupation today.

Even the wartime spies had a chief over them.

All messengers and couriers were stationed in the Cazonci's patio, ready to go when needed and were under the supervision of a deputy titled Vaxanoti. Today they serve as letter carriers.

For the time of war there was a chief ensign and others who carried flags made of bird feathers attached to long canes.

These offices were all held by the incumbents by succession and inheritance, for, when one died, a son or a brother took his place, assigned by order of the Cazonci.

There was another one who was the guardian of the eagles, both great and small, and other birds. There were more than eighty birds, including royal eagles and other small ones kept in cages, and they were usually fed chickens taken from the common storehouse. The feeding of the lions, jackals, tigers, and wolves was in the charge of others; when the animals were full-grown they were shot and replaced by small ones. There was one man over all the Cazonci's medicine men, and another placed over all the gourd plate painters whose name was Vrani Atari. This craft is practiced today. All the painters were under a man whose title was Chunicha, while the potters were under a different man, and still another called Hucaziquauri over those who make jars, plates, and bowls. The Cazonci also appointed a deputy over all the sweepers in his house and one over those who make flowers and wreaths for his head.

There was a supervisor over all the dealers who gather gold, plumages, and stones for the Cazonci by exchange or barter.

Some valiant men who were as lords to him, called Quangariecha, accompanied the Cazonci, wearing their gold or turquoise rings in the underlip and their golden earrings.

The day after the feast all the women gather around a fire made in the village where they get drunk and eat parched corn dipped in honey. Some would do a dance called Paracala Vazange, dancing in the patio, which was fenced with boards, or in the houses of the chief priests. The priestess of the goddess, wearing an artificial snake around her waist and a paper butterfly, would also dance.

2. THE FEAST OF SICUINDIRO

Five days before this feast, the priests and the goddesses from the above mentioned villages would arrive. Dancers called sescuasecha and two priests called Huaripiapecha [Hauripiupecha] would enter the houses where they fasted until the day of the feast. On the eve of the feast the priests mark the chests of two delinquent slaves who are to be sacrificed the next day. At the appropriate time the dancers perform, wearing round, silver shields on their backs and gold crescents around their necks. Two principals who came to that dance represent white, yellow, red, and black clouds, disguising themselves to represent each one in turn. When they represent the black cloud, they dress in black and likewise for each of the other colors. They dance with the other four priests representing other goddesses who are with Cuesariaperi, and they sacrifice the slaves who have been marked. When they take out the victims' hearts, they perform the customary ceremonies with them and while the hearts are still warm they are taken from the village of Cinapecuaro [Cinapequaro] to the hot springs of the village of Araro, where they are thrown into a small hot spring and covered over with boards. Then they throw blood into all the other springs in the village that are dedicated to other gods. These springs give off a vapor of their own, and they say that from them the clouds rise to give rain and that the goddess Cueravaperi is in charge, that she sends it from the east and that out of reverence for her they throw the blood into the springs. After performing the sacrifice, those two, called Hauripiupecha, which means hair pullers, come out and follow the people, both men and women, and cut off their hair with some locally-made knives. The people would then go about painted red with minium and wearing light shawls on their heads. They place some of the hair they cut off in the blood of those who have been sacrificed and then put it in the fire. The next day they dance dressed in the skins of the sacrificed slaves and they stay drunk for five days. In the month of [the feast of] Charapuzapi [Charapu Zapi], they make offerings on behalf of the sacrificed slaves. In another feast called Caherivapansquaro [Caheri Upanscuaro], they dance with cornstalks on their backs. This goddess, with her priests, goes to two feasts in the city of Mechuacán, the feasts of Cuingo and Corindaro [Curindaro], and there the people would give her two slaves as an offering.

This goddess [Cuesariaperi] sometimes suddenly enters into someone who then falls as if dead, and afterwards that person voluntarily goes to be sacrificed. They give this person quantities of blood to drink beforehand. She enters into many men and women and those she singles out in this manner are sacrificed from time to time with the understanding that she herself has chosen them. She is held in great esteem in the entire province and is mentioned in all their fables and prayers in which she is held to be the mother of all the gods of the land. Legend also has it that she sent the gods to live on earth and to bring ripe wheat and seeds. There are temples to her in the village of Ariro [Araro] and also in other villages, and their principal idol is in a temple in the village of Cinapequaro [Cinapecuaro], on top of a hill where its ruins may be seen today. The people believe that this goddess sends the famines to the land.

16

3. THERE WERE THE FOLLOWING PRIESTS IN THE TEMPLES

There is a greatly revered chief priest called Petamiti, who rules over all the priests. (See Plate 4.) It has already been told how this priest dresses himself and that, with other adornments, he had on his back a gourd set with turquoise and carried a lance with a flint point. There are many other priests who hold an office called Curitiecha, and they act as preachers, officiate at ceremonies, and go about the province making certain that the wood is gathered as has already been described. Each has a gourd on his back, and they say that they bear all the people on their backs. In each *cu* or temple, there is a chief priest who serves as a bishop assigned over all the priests. All these priests are called parish priests, which means grandfather; all are married, hold their offices by inheritance, and know the histories of the gods and their feasts. There are other priests called Curicitacha, or Curipecha, who, on appropriate occasions, are in charge of putting incense in the braziers and fonts at night. Today they supply branches and cypress for the feasts.

Other priests are called Tininiecha, who carry their gods on their backs, and, dressed in this fashion, they go to war. They are known by the name of the god which they carry on their back.

The Cazonci and the Knights, being held in high esteem, are among the priests called Axamiecha who perform the human sacrifices. Priests called Opitiecha hold the victims to be sacrificed by the hands and feet when they are on the sacrificial stone. There is an official over all these priests. The bodies of those sacrificed are dragged to the place where their heads are raised on long poles by priests called Quiquiecha.

The sextons and guards of the gods are known as Pasantiecha [Pasartiecha], and, as mentioned previously, there are kettle-drummers and others who play trumpets and bugles.

When the nation is to go to war, priests known as Hiripacha are in charge of making prayers and exorcisms with fragrances called andamuqua beside the fires in the houses of the chief priests. There is a principal in charge of all the hatapatiecha, who sing and march ahead of the captives being brought back from the war.

4. INDOOR SERVICES IN THE HOUSE OF THE CAZONCI

All the servants in the Cazonci's house are women, and no one serves in his house except women. There is one, above all the others, called yreri, and she is closer to the Cazonci than the others and is as a mistress over them as well as his common-law wife. In his house there are many in confinement, such as the daughters of principals, who do not emerge except to dance with the Cazonci on feast days. They make the shawls and the bread used for offerings to their God Curicaveri, and it is said that they are the wives of Curicaveri. The Cazonci has many children by them, and many of them are his relatives. They all share the duties of his house, and later he marries some of them to principals. One of them, known as Chuperipati, with many women assigned to her as assistants, is in charge of keeping all the Cazonci's jewels, such as gold or turquoise lip-rings and gold ear-loops. There is a head chambermaid with assistants who serve as pages and hand him clothes. One woman is in charge of keeping his cotton war doublets and his doublets of bird feathers.

His cook, with her assistants, makes bread for the Cazonci, and I do not say for his table because they do not eat on tables. The woman page of the cup is called Atari, Yyamati makes his sauce, and another serves as chief waitress and serves his food. One called Siguapubri is in charge of all his light blankets, while another woman is in charge of all the wristlets made of stones, turquoise, and feathers worn by the Cazonci. A woman known as Pazapeme is over all the women slaves in his house, and all these women serve him with their breasts exposed.

Other women are in charge of seeds, all his footwear, all the fish brought to his house, the making of his corn-pulp, keeping the large blankets called *quapimequa*, which are offerings for the gods, and keeping all the salt which is brought to his house and put into chests. In charge of all these women was another woman called Quateperi, and finally over all the women is an old man.

Each of his children has a house for himself from the time they are given over to be raised, and the parents of the child's mother come to make seedbeds and blankets for him. The Cazonci gives the child both male and female slaves, individuals who were captured in the wars but not sacrificed, and they are called terapaquabahecha.

Assigned to overseers are many people who make seedbeds for peppers, kidney beans, and corn, both early and irrigated, and who bring fruit called acipecha—all for the Cazonci.

The lords and ladies of the villages had servants of this kind, and today their descendants still perform the same services. They are relatives of the slaves taken in the wars, or they were ransomed because of their hunger and were loaned some corn; or perhaps they were caught with stolen goods in the seed plots, or they are slaves purchased from merchants and assigned as domestic servants to serve in the seed plots.

There were many buffoons who said witty things to entertain the Cazonci, and there were some called Vanaonciquarecha, who were in charge of other diversions referred to as novelties.

When a lord talks with the Cazonci, he removes his shoes, puts on some old blankets, and addresses him from a distance.

The Cazonci frequently goes to the wars carrying his bow and arrows in his hands, and if he becomes ill the valorous men and lords bring him back in a hammock. At times he goes deer hunting, and at other times he sends the people. He has his hot baths where he bathes with all his women.

The ministry of the Cazonci consists of overseeing the feasts of the gods, ordering wood for the temples, and sending people to the wars. All the lords have no virtue other than generosity, for they hold it insulting to be niggardly. When messengers sent by the chief of some village enter the house of the Cazonci, he orders that blankets and shirts be given to them. Frequently he distributes blankets to the people attending the feasts and banquets given for the lords.

19

5. CONCERNING THE FORAYS INTO ENEMY VILLAGES

About the time of the feast of Hancivas quaro [Hancinas-quaro][1] and before the people depart for war, the Cazonci has wood brought for the temples throughout the entire province, and during the vigil of the feast all that wood is stacked in large piles in the patio. Then a priest called Hiripati, with five of the sacrificers and five other priests called Curitiecha, gather in an apartment in the house of the Cazonci, where they make little balls of fragrances[2] and attach them to oak branches. Later they place all the balls of fragrance in some gourds which are carried by the sacrificers and the Curitiecha; five other priests called Tininiecha take some earthen bowls which they carry on their shoulders; some of them are smoking pipes, and dressed in this fashion they all go to the houses of the chief priests.

The sacrificers hang their gourds at the entrances to the houses of the chief priests and then station themselves at those doors at midnight. The priests who carry the gods on their backs and play the trumpets in the high temples, after looking at a star in the sky, build huge fires in the houses of the chief priests and place near those fires their gourds and some branches. Then the priest called Hiripati approaches the fire, takes some of the balls of fragrances, and offers the following prayer to the God of Fire: "Thou God of Fire who hast appeared in the midst of the houses of the chief priests, perhaps there is no virtue in this wood which we have brought to the temples and in these fra-

---

1 The name of this feast appears in the Escorial manuscript C–IV–5 as it is within the brackets. While there is considerable debate on whether Hacinasquaro preceded or followed the feast of Hicuandiro, we feel that the *Relación* implies that Hacinasquaro served as a preparatory feast. War is related in relationship to the feast of Hicuandiro.

2 The use of "balls of fragrance" seems to have been a trait held in common in much of Mesoamerica, and modern writers use the term copal in this regard. The Tarascans gathered resin from various tropical trees, which they made into little balls for use in their religious ceremonies and apparently at any time an important decision had to be made. At times the balls were also made of tobacco. These little balls, when placed in fire, burned slowly and gave off an odor that was pleasing to the gods.

grances which we have here to give thee—receive them thou who art called primarily Morning of Gold and to thee Uredecuave-cara, God of the Morning Star, and to thou who hast the Reddish Face, see how contrite the people are who have brought this wood for you." As soon as he finished this prayer, Hiripati called out the name of each of the lords of his enemies and said: "Thou Lord, who hast in charge all the people of such and such village, receive these fragrances and let there be a few of your vassals for us to take in the war." Then he names the priests and sacrificers of the villages of his enemies, for they say that they carry all the people on their shoulders. When Hiripati finishes his very long prayer, having named all the lords beginning with Mexico City and including all the frontiers, the other priests and sacrificers draw near the fires. They take in their hands those little balls of fragrances and perform the war ceremony while the priests called Curipecheo are putting incense in the braziers with the ceremony and the organization that was described for the feast of Sicuindiro for Curicaveri. (See Plate 5.) These ceremonies are performed so that their gods will cause illness in the villages of the enemies they are to conquer, and they offer the following prayer: "Oh Gods of the Fourth Heaven, you did not hear us from where you are because you are the only Kings and Lords, only you dry the tears of the poor." The incense ceremony is performed two nights, and they say these same words to the four quarters of the world and to the Inferno. After they have finished their prayers, they throw all the balls of fragrances on the huge fires burning before the temples. The prayers by the priest Hiripati are offered at the same hour throughout the province by other priests of this office called Hiripacha.

When the feast of Hanzinas quaro [Hancinasquaro] finally arrives, the Cazonci adorns himself and sends the couriers called Vaxanocha throughout the province with orders for the people to come. Upon arriving at the villages, the Vaxanocha gather the people, admonish them to obey the Cazonci, not to ignore his order, and tell them that everybody should get ready. Everyone was expecting these couriers, and that night they all perform the war ceremony, put incense in the braziers, and the priests called Tininiecha carry the chief god of the village to the temple.

The next morning the chief, serving as captain, departs with his people, taking his principals to count the people and apportion them to go to the frontiers. No woman goes with them; all are men who carry their provisions for the march: the leather coats, flour to drink in a beverage, cotton doublets, round shields, and arrows. Some go to the frontier of Mexico and make war on the Otomis who are brave men, which was the reason Montezuma assigned them to the frontiers; others go to the boundaries of Cuynaho. Each chief follows his course and takes along his squadron with its gods and ensign. In this manner they arrive at the main thoroughfare, called *curuzetaro*, of the village that they are going to conquer.

The spies know where the rivers are, as well as all the entrances, exits, and dangerous points of the village. When camp is made, the spies draw a clear map on the ground tracing all these features for the captain-general who shows it to the people. Before they fight their enemies, they send the spies secretly into the village with eagle feathers, two bloodied arrows, and some of the little balls of fragrances to hide in some seed plots, or beside the house of the lord, or in the temple to bewitch the village. Then after the spies have returned without being detected, each one in the squadron charges and attacks the people in the seed plots or in the forest. To keep the victims from shouting warnings, they tie their mouths with something like a hackamore for work animals and in this manner bring them back to the camp. Then they take the captives to the city, and the priests called Curitecha and others called Opitiecha, with gourds on their backs and spears on their shoulders, would come out to receive them at the entrance to the city where there are two altars on which they place the war gods they brought back from the war. These priests greet and praise the captives, who are tied by the neck to canes, and begin to sing with them until they are brought before the Cazonci and given food. Afterwards they put them in a jail called *curuzegro*, where they stay until the feast when they are to be sacrificed. The foregoing is the manner of their forays.

6. HOW THEY DESTROY OR ATTACK VILLAGES

At the time of the feast of Hicuandiro, the Cazonci sends general orders throughout the province for wood for the temples. In ten days it is stacked in the patios, and all the chiefs of the province come to the city with all the gods of their villages. Customarily the priests adorn themselves, for they have their gods on their backs, and they go up to the temples. All the men of valor adorn themselves, blackening their bodies and putting wreaths made of deer skin or bird feathers on their heads. To each one of these brave men is commended a district as a captaincy, and with each district there is a principal who keeps the accounts for it and who knows the residents in it. Those who are going to this conquest are the people from Mechuacán with Chichimecas and Otomis, whom the Cazonci had subjected, the Maltalzincas, the Vetamaocha, and the Ychontales, who were joined by those from Tuspa, Tamazula, and Capotlan. The Cazonci sends his captain-general, accompanied by a lieutenant, with all these people. He commands the people to take all the needed victuals, bows, arrows, round shields, flour or bread made of pigweed, and offerings which the Cazonci sends for the gods who are going to war. Each village takes its own victuals and, thus provisioned, the people from all the villages depart. The villages through which they pass give them a great deal of additional food as they go by. Before reaching the point where they are to camp, all the people get together, along with the priests who carry the gods, and they blacken and dress themselves. Some put on white plumes from white herons, others, eagle feathers, and still others, colored parrot feathers. The people of the city take two hundred flags made of white feathers pertaining to their God Curicaveri, and from Cuyacán, forty, and from Pátzcuaro, forty. They get forty heavy, pointed, wooden sticks that are two fathoms long and have hooks on them; these sticks are carried by the brave men. All the

23

people carry oak clubs, some put sharp, copper barbs on the heads of those clubs, and they take their round shields made of the feathers of many birds, some from white herons which belong to Curicaveri, some from red parrots, and others from little gold- and green-colored birds. All the valiant men dress themselves in cotton doublets while the common people wear cotton breast-plates. The lords and valiant men put on doublets made of rich bird feathers and have a holiday with a good deal of boasting.

They make a very wide royal road for the people and the lords from Mechuacán who arrive where their camps are set up and sleep there that night. The next morning all the war people ar-rive, and the captain-general of the Cazonci adorns himself, put-ting a great plumage of green feathers on his head and a very large, round silver shield on his back. A tiger-skin quiver, some golden ear-loops and golden bracelets with a red cotton doublet, an Indian suit of serrated leather on the shoulders and gold bells down the legs, a tiger skin four fingers wide on his wrist, and a bow in his hand complete his costume. All the chiefs are there, each with all the people he has brought from the villages. They leave a space in their midst for the five adorned priests of Curi-caveri, who come along with four priests of Xaratanga, and all the valiant men of Mechuacán come ahead of the captain-general, all appropriately adorned. After them come the afore-mentioned captain-general, and everybody salutes him, and he settles him-self in his seat in the midst of them all and speaks the following exhortation: "You Chichimeca Lords of the family name of Eneani, Zacapuhiretin, and Vanacacin who are here—now we have brought our God Curicaveri this far, putting the wood and branches on him for we have made his dais of branches at this point on the road. Now our God Curicaveri and Xaratanga have issued judgment against our enemies. Since the Gods called First Born and those called Viranecha have come, does it not appear to you as Chichimecas that Curicaveri and the gods have handed down their sentence? They must have since we gave them so many offerings while we were in the villages; we brought them much wood for the bonfires, along with fragrances which the priests cast on the fires to bid farewell to the gods who were coming here to war. So the Gods of the Heavens are to come to the map[3] of the village we are to conquer, here where there is wood for the fires which represent the four parts; here will come the Royal Eagles, which are the principal gods, the small Eagles, which are the lesser gods, the hawks, falcons, and other fast carrion birds called *tintivapema*. Here the Gods of the Heavens will favor us, this is so. You people of the villages who are here note that the Cazonci, our King, is counting the days waiting for us to give battle to our enemies—how are we to gainsay him? The lords hold it to be evil to lose the wood that was brought for the temples, for we are here voluntarily. You chiefs, you who are here from the frontiers and you principals from the cities of Mechuacán, Pátzcuaro, and Cuyacán, listen to these chiefs, for you are here because I am charged to assign the wood for the temples, and I have here the maps of the villages which are to be conquered. This is what they told our God Curicaveri when they begot him—that he go with his Captaincies in formation by day, that our Goddess Xaratanga should go in the midst, that the First Born Gods should go on the right hand and the Gods called Viravanecha on the left. All shall go by day, in the place appointed for each one, with the people from his village. You common people, see to it that you do not break these commandments and do not desert your squadrons, because if you are absent or we contradicted the commandment of the Cazonci, your chiefs who are the Captains will have to suffer. This is what I say to you, you chiefs and common people; now I have complied with the orders and the words that I brought with our God Curicaveri." Having finished his exhor-

[3] Before going to war, spies were sent out to examine carefully the village to be attacked. They checked all roads and paths that could be used for the enemy to escape or to slip out and come up behind the attacking Tarascan forces. Everything about the village was noted by these men: the number of houses and their location; the location of the Principals' houses and those of the chief priests; the location of the food-producing fields; the number of people in the village and the most efficient way to attack. This information was then pooled, and the various "commanders" were informed by means of a detailed "battle map" which was drawn on a cleared spot on the ground. The map gave them precise up-to-date information. The plan of attack was then worked out with all participants knowing exactly what they were to do.

tation he seated himself, after which all said that it was very well spoken.

Then the lord from Cuyacán got up and spoke to all the people: "Now you have heard him who stands in the place of Curicaveri, and he has done his duty with what he has told you, see that you respect it, all you from Mechuacán, Cuyacán, Pátzcuaro, and you chiefs of all the four parts of this province, you Matlalzincas, Otomis, Ocumiechas, and you Chichimecas. In this that I say, I do no more than approve what has been said by him who represents our God Curicaveri, namely, the Cazonci. If you turn back because of fear of our enemies, don't forget that our King prayed in the house of the chief priests; remember that we shall not all return to the villages, for some shall die in this battle, others will have poles and stones tied to their necks, and the rebellious ones will be killed on the road if they do not respect what they have been told. For these reasons prepare yourselves, you chiefs, to suffer where we are to die. Let it be here that we die, and here only, because the death we die in the villages is a great sorrow; let our death be here where you can have your liprings of turquoise and rawhide wreaths and necklaces of precious fishbones. Be strong in your hearts, do not look backwards over your shoulders to your houses; remember that it is a great boon for us to die here as brothers. You people of the villages, take to heart this that I tell you," and he sat down. The lord from Pátzcuaro got up and spoke to the people: "You have already heard what was spoken by the representative of the Cazonci and what the lord from Cuyacán told you. I approve of what they have told you because our God Curicaveri has his seigniory in three parts; look you chiefs that you are not a mockery in this battle, remember that you are not alone, for you have your people with you. Perhaps our enemy may be braver men; let what I have told you suffice," and he sat down.

After this one, the lord from Xacona, which is on one of the frontiers, stood up and spoke to the people: "You have heard the representative of the Cazonci and these lords. This which we tell you now is not from us but from the Cazonci, the one who

26

brought wood for the temples to this place. You have brought
our lord and King Curicaveri because we consider it a blessing
to be at his back. Look at the suffering and the work of the spies,
going without sleep and wading in the dew to look for the trails
which are to be followed by our God Curicaveri to give battle to
this village. See that you do not become a laughing stock but
rather capture or kill the enemy. Let it be forgotten that you
were with the women in the villages for the sake of the sins you
committed with them and because you did not go to prayer in
the house of the chief priests; you did not enter voluntarily to do
penance, for you thought it more important to join the women.
See that you do not look back to your villages, do not turn back,
for if you turn back or do not keep faith with what you have
been told, be prepared to suffer; do not look back at your women
to whom you are married nor at your old parents; strengthen
your hearts, let us die for all death is the same—whether we die
in the villages or here in the battle. This is why you are men; do
not break faith with these words. The spies have seen all the
measures that are to be taken in the villages of the enemy; this is
what I was to say to you and I am free of it." Upon finishing his
exhortation, he walked over to the plan for the village which the
spies had seen and mapped. There he showed all the lords and
people who were gathered around how the villages which they
were to conquer were laid out. After explaining the map, the
captain-general arrayed the people in a specific order. In front
he placed all the valiant men from the city of Mechuacán and
the priests who carry Curicaveri and Xaratanga and all the other
major gods. Two processions were lined up on opposite sides.
Each group of six squadrons established ambushes with their
gods and flags, and in the midst of the ambushes there was a
squadron of four hundred men and a god of the runners called
Pungarancha. All these go to the village with their bows and
arrows and set fire to the houses. Then they begin to draw back,
pretending to run away and pretending that they are sick; others
pretend to be lame and some act as if they could not stand up,
falling on the ground, and so, running away and falling, they

entice their enemies out of the village and lead them into the ambush. When the enemy reaches the ambush, a smoke signal or a trumpet releases the attack. The captains say, "Up! Everybody!" Then they join from both sides of the ambush and catch all the enemy from the village in the middle and take them captives. Those who are in the forefront enter the houses, capture all the women, children, and the aged, and then sack and set fire to the houses. (See Plate 6.) They capture eight thousand or sixteen thousand, causing great fright among the enemy; and they bring all these captives back to the city of Mechuacán where they are sacrificed in the temples of Curicaveri, Xaratanga, and in other temples of gods in that city and throughout the province. They keep the children and raise them to work in the seed plots. The aged, the babies, and the wounded are immediately sacrificed, and their flesh is cooked and eaten.

7. THE DESTRUCTION AND BURNING OF A VILLAGE

When a village is to be destroyed, the Cazonci sends throughout the province for wood for the temples, and all the chiefs, with the people from their villages, come and make a broad road as far as the place where they are to encamp. All the lords and their people from Mechuacán travel this road, while the people from other villages go through the brush. Thus all the people of the villages arrive at the place where the maps of the enemy village have been traced [on the ground]. They array all the squadrons, and the more principal gods take positions on the road that goes straight to the village that is to be destroyed. All the other nations with their gods surround the entire village, and at a certain signal, all attack as one, setting fire to the village and sacking it with all its subjects. They take all the people, men, women, children, and babies in their cradles, count them, and separate all the aged, the babies, and those wounded by arrows, and they sacrifice them, as has been told. (See Plate 7.) They place guards on all the roads and trails, and right there they take from the people all the gold, silver, rich feathers, and precious stones that they captured in the raid and all the spoils. They do not allow them to keep any of the blankets, copper, ornaments of gold and silver, jewels, or feathers. They destroy the village and are pleased with their success. Afterwards, when other enemies see how they were treated, they go to receive them and say, "Let us all be one, and let us augment Curicaveri's arrows for they say the Chichemecas are very generous." They bring a gift of gold and silver to the Cazonci, who receives them, saying: "Lords, you are welcome; if you are true, we shall be brothers," and they honor all of them and send them back to their villages. The Cazonci sends a valiant man and an interpreter with the lords who, upon arriving at the village, call all the people together and tell them about the generosity of the Cazonci and how he has received them as brothers and that they shall people their villages again.

8. CONCERNING THOSE WHO DIE AT WAR

If some of the lords happen to die at war, the Cazonci is very sad, saying, "The gods killed some of our people to deprive us of support," and he gives blankets to the widows who tear their hair and wail at home. (See Plate 8.) They wrap the heads of their dead in blankets and cover those bundles with blankets. At night they place them in order before the temples and beside the big fires while trumpets and snail horns are played. They also place beside those bundles their bows and arrows, their leather wreaths, their colored plumages, and many offerings of bread and wine. Then they burn them. There must be two hundred or more of them without counting those of the common people who carry on in a similar manner. They put the ashes in pots, after which all the relatives of the dead man gather at his house and console each other and speak in this manner: "As the gods have willed it, he has already died; they unleashed it, he died in the war; it is a handsome and valorous death and that is the way he left us." Since he will come again, they say to his poor wife, "He is and lives in this house a few days, and you will be widowed a few days, since your husband travels, do not marry." This is how they would console the woman: "Sweep the patio so no weeds will grow, do not disinter your husband again by giving people cause to talk about you. If you are bad, they will talk because your husband is well known, and he made you known through him."

9. CONCERNING THE ADMINISTRATION OF JUSTICE BY THE CAZONCI

The administration of justice in the case of the wrongdoer was touched upon in Chapter 2, but it was incomplete. For that reason this chapter has been prepared, and that explanation will be completed here.

If a woman is taken from among the women of the Cazonci by a principal, he is killed along with his children, his wife and relatives, and all those in his house. (See Plate 9.) The members of his family are held to be traitors and derelicts, because not one had reported what the principal was doing. All his wealth and seed plots are confiscated for the granary and the treasury of the Cazonci, and he is deprived of the insignia of a valiant man.

In the case of a less serious sin, the guilty party serves a jail sentence for a few days; if it is more serious, he is exiled and deprived of his insignia as a valiant man, such as the lip-ring and other items. The clothes are taken off his wife, leaving her naked, and the clothing becomes the property of the representative sent by the Cazonci to administer justice in the villages.

If a *mazagual*, a chief, or a principal in the province has committed a crime, they take him to the chief priest who, in turn, reports him to the Cazonci for sentencing. If the accusation is true, others are killed in the same village where the crime was committed. The Cazonci sends a messenger, called *vaxanoti*, which is a separate office, who stains himself all over, takes a staff and goes to the delinquent's house, taking him prisoner and depriving him of his lip-ring and gold ear-loops. The prisoner asks, "Why do you treat me this way, sir?" The messenger answers, "I don't know the cause, for the complaint was not brought to me. I am sent because the King has issued sentence." Thereupon the culprit is killed by a blow on the back of the neck with a bludgeon. The Cazonci orders others to be dragged until dead and some of these are buried, while others are left to be eaten by the jackals and buzzards in accordance with the Cazonci's orders. Sometimes the priests are required to administer justice.

In the case of a witch, the death sentence is administered by butchering his mouth with knives, then dragging him until he is dead. After death, he is covered with rocks.

If a son or brother of the Cazonci does not live right, if he is always drunk, he is sentenced to death. The Cazonci inherits the seigniory and gathers wood for the temples, because he is more steadfast in the service of the gods and does not get drunk so much. The son who is sentenced to death loses all his goods through confiscation, as in the case of other principals who are sentenced to death. The governors and nurses who had raised the son are killed, as are his servants, because they had taught him those bad customs.

Adulterers and thieves are also sentenced to death in accordance with their crime when the Cazonci is in his right mind. At other times he may be drunk and hand down the death sentence for a principal when one of them complains of these things. Later, when he is in his right mind again, he regrets it and scolds those who executed the sentence.

10. CONCERNING THE DEATH OF THE CHIEFS AND THE SUCCESSION

When a chief dies in a village of the province, his brothers and relatives report it to the Cazonci, and they bring him the dead man's gold lip-ring, ear-loops, bracelets, and necklaces of turquoise which are the insignia of rank that the Cazonci had given him when he raised him to the lordship. As they bring in these adornments, they put them beside those of the Cazonci, who intones, "The poor fellow is dead, let it be as the gods will for the fact that the people remain is as nothing. Let his wife sweep the house and keep herself dressed as if he were alive. So that the people of his village may not become divided nor dispersed, let another prove himself worthy of the office."

The Cazonci must now choose a new chief from among five or six relatives—brothers, sons, and nephews of the dead man—and the Cazonci asks, "Who among these shall it be?" (See Plate 10.) They reply, "Thou art the one to command," and he commends the office to the most discreet, *the one who has the most sorrows* as was his manner of saying, for this one has had the most experience and is the most obedient. Then the Cazonci brings together the priests called Curitiecha and tells them to take the new chief and count out for him the people he is to have in charge. The Cazonci then orders that he be given a new lip-ring, an ear-loop of gold, and bracelets. He tells him to take these as the insignia of the honor he bears and admonishes him concerning his duties, speaking to him in this manner: "Hear what I have to tell you, be obedient and bring wood for the temples so that the common people will remain faithful, for if thou dost not bring wood, what is to become of them if you are bad? Go into the houses of the chief priests for your prayer, and retain the vassals of our God Curicaveri so that they shall not go elsewhere. Do not eat your meals alone, but call the common people and give them some of what you have. In this manner you will keep the people and rule over them. Do not mistreat the people, but rather cause them to reverence you. Now you have heard this that I have told you, remember these words, and let this which I have spoken to you suffice, brother; go thou to thy house." The newly raised chief replied: "So be it, Sire, as you order; I want to see how well I can fulfill my responsibility." After the Cazonci finishes his exhortation, the local governor or the chief priest says to the new chief: "Go, brother; you have heard the King and do not forget what he told you: do not take the women of the dead chief and remember that you are to manage the wars; give more attention to this than to women." He answers: "So be it, Grandfather, I shall go." A priest goes with him, one of those called Curitiecha, to install him in the seigniory, and he gives blankets to the Cazonci and skirts to his wife. When they arrive at the village, all the people gather and greet the priest and the new chief, and the priest, while standing, speaks to them in this manner: "Hear me people of the village, your poor chief who was in charge of you is dead, having been killed by something. No person killed him as he died a natural death from his illness. The King learned about it and sent this one here, who is to have charge of all of you, for it is not the fashion now to set aldermen over the common people which was an old custom. Look you well that you do not disobey this chief because of his youth, for he will report to the Cazonci, who sentences you to death if you are not obedient. Obey him and enter into the houses of the chief priests to tend to your candles and stick to your hoes, which is to say, make seed plots for him. Do not be lazy in war, and remember that you are never to fail to accompany our God Curicaveri in war when he is to travel to other places, for he has his dwelling here. Take care that you need not repent after what may happen to you for having been lazy. Having taken care of this, do not join with other principals because you will be taken and killed by them as will those of you who may be adulterers and witches.

"You see, you are of many opinions, common people, this is a fact. Do not forget that the office of chief was not made up just now but was decreed and ordered by the ruling woodhaulers, Hiripan and Tangaxoan, who had great stores of wood for the temples. They began it without pretense so that there would be chiefs in this house of the lords in the past. It was not so easy then to make chiefs, only those were qualified who worked hard with the hoes and made the seed plots for the Cazoncis and were very obedient. Work! How will you rule if you do not see that the people make seed plots? What food will you give those who may enter your house?" The priest turns to the principals: "Do not fail the chief, you principals," and then he turns and says to the chief, "Do not mistreat the people." At this everybody replies that it will be done.

The new chief stands up after the priest has spoken to the people and says: "You have heard this priest who is our Grandfather and what he says is what the King ordered at the time of our departure. It is not just this priest you have heard, but the Cazonci himself who is the King over all. Remember that I shall not be able to suffer nor have any courage of heart if you are all of different opinions, in which case I shall report to the King. You have already heard what he has told you, and remember that I shall be your Father and your Mother and I shall rule over all of you. If you are obedient and if you respect me, we shall live in peace in this wonderful village, and we shall outdo ourselves sometimes. We shall help each other in the wars to defend our God Curicaveri. If you do not help me, what can I do alone? Who will be with me? Remember that we have the hoes and let us make seed plots for the wars. And you women, make blankets so that we may supply the gods. This is why we were conquered, and this is what we promised in the past—the hoes and the squadrons for war, and we are to supply the offerings for Curicaveri since we are to carry his stores to the wars. For this reason honor me by helping me, and I shall return the favor to you by ruling over you. Know you that I will not be lying around sleeping all day in the corner. You old men who are very ancient and have knowledge of the past, you know that in this village there were no lazy chiefs or lazy people. So be it now. You well may complain if I were to be that way and not what I ought to be, if I should not take your advice. This is true, old men, understand this that I have told you. Remember that I have succeeded to this office and that I am here willingly."

When the chief had finished, an old man who was acting chief stood up and spoke to the people: "Hear me, people of the village, what I shall say unto you. You have already heard the words they have brought us from the Capital and the city of Mechuacán, where the King stands in place of our God Curicaveri. Hear and obey them so that you need not repent of what would otherwise happen to you. Mark you well that the new chief is a youth and that he will not dissemble, but complain to the King who has charge of everybody." Then he turned to the new chief: "May it please the gods to let you come in truth; if not, you shall see us die here for we are already old, and we do not know how long we are to live. We shall be your Fathers and we shall counsel whatever you charge us with." Turning to the people, he said: "What do you say, you people who are here, we have found Mother and Father again, and you principals account to him for the people and count them out to him all you who have charge of the districts in which you live, and do not conceal the people. Remember the chief will not dissemble but will kill either me or you. Make seed plots for him so that he may give food to whosoever may come to his house. He shall enter his house as no one else here ever has before. Remember that the Cazonci will send messengers and priests. How will the chief hide his embarrassment? What will he give them to eat? Assign women to his house to make corn-pap for our God Curicaveri. The chief will eat the leftovers, for they will make it for him to eat after he has made offerings to Curicaveri, and you women will make blankets for Curicaveri so that he may clothe himself. Then you will make some for the chief to wear and keep Curicaveri from being cold at his side. This is what I have told you, and may it please the gods that you understand it. Old man that I am, I do nothing but approve the words of the King." He sat down, and they all began to eat.

The new chief goes with all the people to the houses of the chief priests to pray for four days and four nights. Then he goes with all the people to get wood for the temples, and to the priest who had installed him in the seigniory he gives blankets, gourd plates, and wreaths made of the thread used by the priests. The priest then returns to the city of Mechuacán and reports to the chief priest and to the Cazonci, and the latter says: "So be it. Let him try. If he does not do well, we shall remove him from the office and another one shall be given an opportunity to see how well he can discharge it."

35

11. CONCERNING THE MANNER OF MARRIAGE
OF THE LORDS

The marriage of Don Pedro is described here as being typical of the general custom since he is the governor.

If the Cazonci decides to give a daughter or sister in marriage, he has her dressed in new clothes typical of the kind used by these people, including turquoise necklaces, many pendants, and drop earrings. He calls one of the priests called Curitiecha, who is accompanied by other priests, and tells him to take his daughter, sister, or relative to such and such a lord, telling him also what he is to say. (See Plate 11.) Many women accompany the lady, as well as many other people who carry her jewels, little baskets, and reed mats. Upon arriving at the house of the lord who is to receive her, many new reed mats are put out, along with food, and all the relatives are there to welcome them. They all sit down, placing the lady and the groom in front, and the priest speaks: "Behold this Lady whom the King has sent. I bring her to you. Do not quarrel, be good spouses, bathe each other, [to the Lady] prepare food for this Lord and make him blankets. If someone enters your house, give him blankets, says the King, for whatever you may give, it is he who gives it. Your duty is to give blankets and do favors for the chiefs, Lords, and other people, for the Cazonci cannot remember all of them. Your Lord, who holds you to be a brother, tells you not to break with his words and to accept this which he has ordered told to you. To whom else should we tell it? That is why you, who are his brother, are here. All the people of Mechuacán are here. The Cazonci says that as brothers and because the Spaniards have come, both of you will be ready to carry messages to do whatever may be required of you." Then the groom answers, saying, "So be it as our Lord says, for no one speaks more generously than our Lord and King. Behold this woman who is our daughter and mistress and is given us for wife. She is not given to us for wife but so that we may bring her up and that we may be governors to her. I have already heard you;

may it please the gods to let us serve her. As for the King, being what we are, perhaps we shall not be what we ought to be. What the King has just now done, he does only because of the confidence he has in us. Here is my older brother, how could we separate from him? It is for us to be vassals, and we shall froth at the mouth in our efforts to undertake whatever the Spaniards may order us as their serfs, as we are to be their brothers. For, in the beginning, we were conquered by their ancestors and we Islanders are their slaves. We take their meals to the Kings on our backs, along with axes for cutting wood in the mountain, and we carry their water jars from which they drink. For these reasons they call us brother because we govern for them, and we attend to that which the Kings order us where it is customary for the Kings to speak for themselves and not to have representatives. It is our responsibility to attend to the offices, because the old men decreed long ago that there should be officials and that the Kings should not have to attend to everything.

"You are welcome, Grandfather, and upon your return you shall say that it was so to our Lord the King; may it please the gods that you may have been understood by this Lady and her mothers here present. Who is to be more obedient, my brother or I? Since we are to live according to the things invented against us by the Spaniards because they have brought the Lords with them, for now we have prisons, jails and beatings, and bastings with lard. With all this we only hope to die but let us not separate from him, for if they kill him we shall die with him. Be seated, Grandfathers, you will be given food. Let us look at one another a little while, for tomorrow you shall go and report to the King." Everybody began to eat, and the next morning the old men returned.

Principals of lower rank go through a different ceremony. While the Cazonci is getting drunk, he says, "Let John Doe and such and such a woman be married, because I have need of their help and efforts." He gives her a trousseau and the priests take her to the groom.

37

12. MARRIAGE AMONG THE LORDS

This is an old custom that comes down from their ancient old men whose ashes were saved because they were the first, according to these people, for man made gods from ashes, as was explained in the first part. They began to marry their relatives to benefit each other, and because they were all one related family, they still have this custom handed down by them.

If the son of a lord or a chief wants to marry the daughter of another lord, a messenger is sent to ask the lord or the girl's mother for the girl's hand on behalf of the lord's son or other relative. The messenger carries gifts, and upon arriving at the house of the lord or principal, he explains what brings him, saying, "I am sent by John Doe, such and such Lord or principal, to ask for your daughter." The father extends a welcome, to which the messenger rejoins, "It shall be as you have said. My Lord says for you to give him your daughter for his son." The lord is agreeable and says, "It shall be done as he says; for many days I have intended to give her to him because I am a member of that family and of their stock, a dweller of that district. Welcome. I shall send someone who will take her, and you shall report this to him." So the messenger takes his leave, and having gone, the lord confers with his women and says to them, "What are we going to do about what they have come to tell us?" The women reply, saying, "What are we to say, Sir? You decide it alone." To which he replies, "Be it as you say, since our seed plots are not over there." They dress up the woman and bundle up her dowry. She takes blankets and short shirts with wide sleeves for her husband, axes to cut wood for the temples, along with mats and cinches, all of which she carries on her back. All the women who accompany her dress up and gather all her jewels, mats, and cotton which they have spun. She departs with her relatives, the women, and one or more priests, and in this fashion she goes to the house of her husband. He is already outfitted and has prepared his wedding bread, which consists of some very large tamales stuffed with ground pinto beans. There are also gourd plates, blankets, water jugs, large earthen jars, corn, peppers, pigweed seeds, and kidney beans in the granaries. He also has at hand a pile of skirts and adornments for the women. All the relatives are gathered together and they greet the priest, saying to him that he brings good fortune. They put the daughter in the middle of the room and the priest says: "Lord so and so sent this woman, his daughter, and we pray to the gods that you were sincere when you asked for her, that you will each be a good husband and wife, and that you may possess wealth. Remember that we willingly establish here our dwelling place, let us not belittle it nor do wrong so that we may not be defamed lest they gossip about the Lord who gave his daughter. So, be productive, make clothing, do not be of low esteem so that neither vice nor adultery may come into this house; do right and be well married. Look, let no one be killed because of some adultery or injury that you may commit. Beware, let no one put the cudgel to your neck to kill you, and let you not be covered with rocks for some crime." Then he turns to the woman, "Let thee not be found in the road talking with some man, for they will seize thee, and then we shall be the talk of the village. Be what you ought to be, for I have come to point out the dwelling that you are to have here and the life that you are to make." To the husband the priest adds: "And you, sir, should your wife be guilty of some adultery, leave her gently and send her home without hurting her for she will blame no one except herself. If she should do wrong, it cannot be helped; may it please the gods that you understand this that has been spoken to you." Then the father of the husband speaks: "Our brother has done us a great favor; may it please the gods that everything may be as he has said and that you pay attention to us as I shall not admonish these my children. Our brother has now given us his daughter because we have our roots here and belong here and our antecedents, the Chichemecas, left us here." Then he names his forebears who had lived there and finally says to the priest, "You have now done your duty, Sir, report it to our brother."

Having finished all the talks, everybody eats at once and they are given some of the previously mentioned large tamales and other foods. The father-in-law points out the seed plots they are to plant. Blankets are given to the priest and to the women who brought the bride, and they return home. The father of the groom sends a gift to the bride's father. This is the way the lords marry among themselves; they always marry their relatives and take wives of the stock they sprang from, and they do not mingle the lineages as do the Jews.

13. MARRIAGE AMONG THE LOWER CLASS PEOPLE

When lower class people are to be married, the relatives of the man who is to be married talk with the parents and relatives of the woman, and they come to an agreement among themselves. The priest does not enter into this ceremony. They give their dowries, and the father of the girl admonishes his daughter in the following manner: "Daughter, do not leave your husband asleep at night and go off somewhere to commit adultery. Remember, do not be bad, do not do this evil thing to me; beware that you will be an omen and you will not live long. Mark you that you alone will seek your death; perhaps your husband will enter the temples at prayer time and you alone will seek your death for they will not kill anyone but you. Remember that your father does not act that way, that you will make me weep, dragging me into your evil trade and that they will kill both of us." It was the custom that for the evil doings of anyone his parents or relatives should die. Thus he sends her to the house of the husband or they simply live together. Others marry for love without informing their parents, and they make an agreement among themselves. Other girls from the time they are little are promised in marriage. Some men take the mother-in-law first while the daughter is little, and when the girl has come of age, they leave the mother-in-law and take the daughter in marriage. Others marry the woman they love after her husband has died. Again they marry

40

their relatives as has been told, and they leave them and take other women if they do not make blankets for them or commit adultery.

14. OTHER MATRIMONIAL CUSTOMS

When a man marries a second time, after giving the new wife the dowry and after she has entered into his house, it is customary for him to spend four days gathering wood for the temples before he approaches her or knows her carnally. During those days she sweeps her house and the road for a great distance in the direction from which one comes to her house. (See Plate 12.) This is their way of praying to be a good husband and wife and to have a long married life. The sweeping is symbolic of the life they are to have in the future. Afterwards, they are joined as one. If she is a lady, their servants will cover both of them. If she is a woman of the lower class, the husband tells his wife to cover him, and thus they become man and wife. Others do not wait so many days but know each other on the second day; others wait longer, and some not so long.

15. MARRIAGE FOR LOVE

If a young girl who has parents is attractive to a young man, they enter into an agreement, and he knows her. Afterward he sends a female relative or some other woman to ask for her hand in marriage. The father and mother, frightened by the turn of events, ask their daughter where the young man met her. She replies that she does not know. Her father asks whether her suitor has property. Will he work a seed plot to provide food for her? Would he make use of it and take care of her old father? By this the father means that he has a trade or occupation, but because of his age he can no longer practice it and that the would-be son-in-law should save him that work by doing it for him. For this reason he says that he will wait a few days to see what is to come. If the daughter does not admit that the young man has known her, the father takes a club and beats the girl who brought the message because she told an untrue story about his daughter. At the same time the young man sends a message three or four times asking for the girl in marriage. The parents then believe that he has known her and they reprimand her for what she has done, and they say to her, "I, who am your father, do not do this kind of thing that you have done; you have dishonored me greatly, you have thrown dirt in my eyes. I do not dare appear among people, nor am I able to face them because everybody will throw it up to me and will insult me because of what you have done." And he continues, saying to his daughter: "When I was young I married this woman, your mother; we have a home and they gave me a dowry of corn and blankets and they gave me a house. Whom are you like in what you have done? Why do you want that profligate? He is a rake and he wants to dishonor you." Her mother also reprimands her, and they go to the house of her corruptor and take away from him all he has in his house, such as blankets, grinding stones, and the seed plot which he made for himself. They dishonor themselves if they decide to give her to him, in which case her parents discuss it among themselves, and they say: "Now, why do we want our daughter any more? How can we make her a virgin again, for she is already corrupt? They have affected each other's heart and have talked to each other." Then, accompanied by her relatives, they take her to his house and deliver her to him, explaining that they are from a district that gives married people, for otherwise they would not give her to him.

16. MATRIMONIAL REPUDIATION

When a married couple do not conduct themselves appropriately, this information is relayed to the chief priest called Petamiti. This priest admonishes them to be a good husband and wife, asking them why they quarrel, and he says to them, "You must stop. Since you do not have a house, you must make an effort to obtain one. Remember that you have children now." He scolds the one who is to blame and sends them away. Should they complain three more times, Petamiti tells them: "Now you two must separate for you have complained too many times." To the husband he says, "You have taken another woman, saying that you have not been good married people because you are mistreated. Now, you and the new woman get together and remember that you cannot leave each other." If the wife is caught in adultery, the husband complains to the priest and she is killed. If the husband goes with other women because he does not want to live with his wife, her parents take her away from him and marry her to another. If the husband who has taken a second woman complains that they are not living together, they are both incarcerated in the public jail, and they may not be divorced.

If one man has two women, one of the women goes to the doctors called Xurimecha who, with their charms, say they will separate him from the one and unite him with the other. To accomplish this, the Xurimecha use the following ceremony: they take a gourd dish of water and place two grains of corn in the water; if those grains sink together and unite on the bottom of the gourd dish, it is a sign that the married couple are to be together; if one of those grains separates, it is a sign that the man should be joined with the other woman.

Today, couples will live together without marriage, but promising matrimony and promising that they will be as one until they die. Others say they are poor and go into the house of the woman, this act constituting a marriage without a word. In these marriages they do not ask the woman whether she wants to marry, as it is enough that the parents or relatives come to an agreement about it. Furthermore, in the clandestine marriages today, they never speak in the present tense but in the future. "I shall marry you," and their present intention is copulation because this is the way they speak their language. Later they marry the girls with whom they have had relations. Some marry after becoming Christians, one party being of the faith and the other being baptized afterward, and they remain married as before. They observe no relationship of any degree in their customs nor of consanguinity except that of the first degree. Marriage among all the other relatives is legal, including that of mother and son. Marriage never takes place between brothers and sisters or father and daughter, or nephew and aunt, but a niece may marry an uncle.

One may also marry a woman who has a daughter with the intention of living with the woman; sometimes the marriage with the mother is only temporary until the daughter is of age, at which time she is taken for wife, the man leaving her mother.

The men who are priests do not marry.

One who has been an infidel before marriage and who then becomes a Christian after the death of his wife may not marry a woman with whom he has copulated and promised to marry, nor may he marry his wife's sister. He has acquired affinity, albeit in infidelity.

17. CONCERNING THE DEATH OF THE CAZONCI AND THE BURIAL CEREMONY

During the life of the Cazonci, the son who is to succeed him in the Kingdom begins to rule in accordance with their custom, but he is not given full powers. When the old Cazonci is ill, all his doctors make attempts to cure him. He sends for doctors to come from all over the province, and they make every effort to cure him. Since it is known that he is in danger of dying, he is visited by all the chiefs, lords, valiant men, and governors from the entire province, even those who have been commissioned by the Cazonci. Anyone who does not come is held to be a traitor. All greet him and present their gifts to him if he is strong enough to receive them. When he is near death, not even a lord is allowed to enter his room. In that event they all stay in the patio in front of his house, and the gifts which he cannot receive are placed in the vestibule with his insignia and his chair.

As soon as the lords who are in the patio know that the Cazonci is dead, they lift their voices in a great weeping, open the doors of his house, enter his room, and adorn him. First, all the lords who are present bathe him very carefully as do the old men who are next in line according to rank; then come all those who are to accompany them. After this they dress him in the following manner: Next to his body they put on a short, very thin undershirt, such as that worn by the lords, and next to this a leather war coat; around his neck they put some white fishbones, which are highly prized among them, small golden bells on his legs, turquoise stones on his wrists, a braid of feathers and a turquoise collar around his neck, some large gold earrings in his ears, two gold bracelets on his arms, and a large turquoise lip-ring. They make a bed for him of many varicolored blankets that are piled high. The blankets are placed on some very wide boards, the body is placed on top, tied with braids and covered with many more blankets as if he were in bed. Finally, poles are placed under the bed. They wrap his head in many blankets, place it on top, and adorn it with a large plumage of very long, green feathers, some golden earrings, his turquoise collar, his bracelets of gold, a very good braid of hair, his leather war jacket, his bow and arrows, and his tiger-skin quiver. All his wives cry and weep for him.

The people who march in the procession consist of the men and women who his son has indicated are to dwell with him. There are seven lords and the following women: one to carry all of his golden lip-rings and his turquoise, tied in a cloth and fastened to her neck; his chambermaid; the keeper of his turquoise collars; his cook; a fifth, who serves him his wine; still another who hands him the finger bowl and holds the cup for him while he drinks; the seventh is his urinal bearer, and there are other women who serve in all these same capacities. Of the men, one carries blankets on his back, a second is in charge of making clover-wreaths for him, another is in charge of braiding, a fourth carries his chair, a fifth carries the light blankets on his back, another carries his copper axes, a seventh carries a large fan, an eighth carries his footwear and war jackets, and another carries his cane-tubes of fragrances. There are also an oarsman, the sweeper of his house, and another man who burnishes his little rooms, a superintendent of the women, a feather dresser from among those who make his plumages, a silverworker from among those who make his lip-rings, an arrow maker, a bow-maker, two or three beaters, some of the doctors who could not

45

cure him, a novel reciter or storyteller, a jester, and an innkeeper. In all there are more than forty, adorned and appropriately made up, wearing white blankets and each one carrying with him all that is related to his craft that might serve the dead Cazonci. There are also a dancer, a kettledrummer, and a maker of drums. Other servants who want to go are not allowed to do so, and they say that they had eaten his bread and that perhaps they would not be treated as well by the new Master. They all put clover-wreaths on their heads, paint their faces yellow, and lead the procession, playing on crocodile bones and turtle shells. The lords and their sons carry his bier on their shoulders and are the only ones permitted to do so. All the relatives with the family name of Heneani, Zacapuirio, and Banacaci march in the procession, and as they accompany him they sing one of his songs that begins this way: *"Utayne, Uze, Yoca, Zinalayo,"* but since it is unintelligible, it is not translated here. All the valiant men wear their insignia and the procession starts at midnight. Some large torches precede the procession lighting the way, two trumpets are blown, and all the marchers who carry lethal weapons lead the way, intoning: "Lord, thou art to go this way, lose not thy way," and many people station themselves beside the road. In this fashion they take him to the patio of the great temple, where they have already placed a large heap of dry wood arranged in layers of pine one upon another. Four times the procession marches around the pyre blowing their trumpets. Then they put him on top of the pile of wood just as he is, his relatives begin singing their song, and the wood is set on fire. (See Plate 13.) When it begins to burn all around, those who had carried the jewels are caused to become drunk and are beaten to death with cudgels and buried behind Curicaveri's temple, on their backs and with all the jewels they were carrying, three by three and four by four. When dawn comes, the Cazonci is completely cremated. While he was burning, all the lords who had come with him were stoking the fire. They gather up all the remaining ashes, some small bones, and the melted gold and silver, and they take it all to the entrance of the house of the chief priests. There they make a bundle, all wrapped in blankets, of all the melted gold and silver, a turquoise mask, his gold earrings, his feather braid, a large plumage of many very rich green plumes on his head, his gold anklets, his turquoise collars, some sea shells, a round gold shield at the back and at the side his bow and arrows, the tiger skins for the wrists, his leather war jackets and the gold leg bells. At the foot of and under the first step leading to Curicaveri's temple, they dig a grave more than two and a half fathoms wide, and rather deep, and they line the walls with new reed mats and on the floor they put a wooden bed. One of the priests, all having carried the gods on their backs, takes the ashes and the bundle that has been made up and transports it on his back to the grave which has already been lined with round gold and silver shields. Many of the Cazonci's arrows are placed in the corners, and they put in many large earthen jars, smaller jars, wine, and food. On top of the bed and looking eastward, they place another large earthen jar in which the priest placed the bundle containing the head. On top of the jar and bed they place many blankets, mats, feathers which he used in dances, gold and silver shields, and many other things. They crisscross many beams over the grave, place boards on top, and plaster it all over. Since the other people who came along had been thrown in their graves, they cover them with dirt and everyone then goes to bathe, that is, all those who have gone near the dead Cazonci and everybody else too, so that they will not contract his disease.

All the lords and people go to the patio of the house of the dead Cazonci, and huge quantities of food that had belonged to the dead Cazonci are brought out—food that has been prepared for the occasion—in the form of corn cooked white. Each person is given a small amount of white cotton to serve as a napkin, and they all eat. After eating, each one on his own account turns sad and downcast, and for five days no one in the city grinds corn between stones nor lights a fire in his home; no one plays music during those days, nor barters, and no one goes about the city. All the people are sad and stay in their houses. The chiefs of the province and the lords meet one night in the houses of the chief priests, where they hold their prayer and vigil.

47

18. THE SELECTION OF A MASTER
AND RELEVANT ORATORY

The day after the Cazonci was buried, all the chiefs of the province came together in his patio with all the most principal lords from Cuyacán, all the old and valiant men and lords who were at the four frontiers of the province, and relatives of the Cazonci. (See Plate 14.) They gathered by one accord and began their deliberations: "What shall we do, gentlemen, how can this house remain deserted, dark and foggy and uninhabited? If we concealed [buried] our Master to come here we cannot return to our houses leaving these same conditions. What news shall we take back? You came here opportunely and in good season, gentlemen; would it not be good for one who is present to try out at being Master? How can this house be abandoned?" Then the son of the Master spoke loudly, saying it should not be he: "Let it be my uncle, who has had more experience, for I am a boy." The brother of the deceased objected: "I am an old man, you may try your hand at it, Sir. Why do you not want to accept being a Lord? How can this house remain abandoned? Who is to speak in the words of Mother Cueravaperi and of the Gods who generated the heavens and of the Gods of the Four Parts of the world, and of the God of the Inferno, and of the gods who come together from all places, and of our God Curicaveri, and of the Goddess Xaratanga, and of the First Born Gods, and the poor people? Who will take charge of the seigniory, Sir? Try it for you are of age now and have discretion." They spent five days talking this over and importuning the son of the dead Cazonci to accept, which at long last he did. Then he who is to be the Cazonci and Master would speak, saying: "You chiefs and Lords who are here and have deliberated and determined that I accept this charge, take heed and do not leave me nor be rebellious. I shall try to fill this charge and should I not be successful in ruling I beg of you not to kill me violently, but gently separate me from the office and take away from me the braid which is the insignia of the Master. Should I not be what I should be, should I not rule the people well, and should I do evil or wrong after getting drunk, throw me out of this house gently, for this has been the usual custom. May it please the gods that I shall rule the people and hold them all. I have listened to all of you and done what you wanted; take heed that you chiefs do not leave me. If you should go away and be rebellious, if you fail in your wood account for the temples, or if you break the squadrons and Captaincies of the wars, I shall not excuse you from death." The conference broke up and everyone went to his lodgings.

Five days later they all went to the home where the newly chosen Cazonci had lived first. The chief priest and all the principal lords and chiefs were there too. Upon arriving at his house, they greeted him saying *Quanga*, which means strong and valiant man, and he returned the greeting. They would say, "We have come for you so that you may enter the house of your father," and he would reply: "I am happy to go, Grandfather," for that is the way they address the priests, and he made ready. He put a tiger-skin wreath on his head, a quiver of tiger skin or other colored animal skin full of arrows on his shoulder, a piece of leather four fingers wide on his wrist, some bracelets made of deer skin with the hair on, and some deer hoofs on his legs, all of which were the insignia of a lord, and all the lords bedecked themselves in a similar manner. They left the house with the chief priest, going ahead of him accompanied by ten bishops or supervising priests who were over the others, dressed as was their custom with gourds and spears on their shoulders. Behind them came the king-to-be, followed by all the chiefs and lords of the province who had come for him. The people of the city already were in the patio, and gathered together outside were all the war spies, all the runners and messengers, and all had blackened themselves. They were arrayed in proper order, the priests in their places as were the spies and the officials of the temples. When the Cazonci came to the patio, he was greeted first by the priests who called him *Quanguapapagua*, which means Majesty, then he passed through their lines greeting them all. They brought him a new chair, putting it on the porch where his father customarily sat, and he seated himself. As he sat down, he was surrounded by the lords, chiefs, and all the people. This was the signal for the speech-making to begin.

19. THE PRESENTATION

"You chiefs and Lords who are gathered here: we now have brought the King and installed him in his house—how was this house to be left unprotected, dark, foggy, and cloudy? We lost our Master so-and-so who died; now we have installed in his house and in his place his own son. This custom comes down to us from long ago, from the Kings who wanted lots of smoke here, which is their way of speaking, and it means that when the Masters are at home they put a great deal of wood on the hearth and great clouds of smoke go up. This cannot be when he dies, for then everything is deserted, dark and as in a fog. For this reason it is customary to have a lot of smoke because this keeps the houses smoky and the straw will not rot." The priest continues: "Well, you chiefs who are here from all parts, let us not desert him and let us help him in the charges we have, by holding to and awaiting his commands in our villages, for the wood he may order us to bring to the temples of Mother Cuervaperi, of the celestial and engendering gods, and of the Gods of the Four Parts of the world, of the Gods of the Right Hand and of the Left Hand, along with all the others, including the God of the Inferno, for he is to be in charge in the name of Curicaveri, along with his brothers and the Goddess Xaratanga. Take heed, chiefs, and do you not break faith with him in any of this, but be on the alert when he communicates with you. The King will supply the war people with wood which will be placed on the fires as a prayer and a supplication to the gods that they may help us in the wars. This is not the only responsibility of our King, for he has many other duties so that he must delegate some to us his Lieutenants and Governors of the chiefs. When we are not in the villages, be attentive and await the King's orders which will concern many things. Let it be thus as you have been told, chiefs, and do not abandon the King, but be obedient. You Lords of Mechuacán, Cuyacán, Pátzcuaro, and chief of the south of the Province, be prepared to obey. Now, Lords, go all of you to your houses. You know now that we have a King and that I have put him in this house; go happily and in contentment to your villages."

Having finished his speech, he sat down, and a very principal lord stood up, who must have been their governor (see Plate 15), and he in turn admonished "all the Lords and chiefs to obey the Cazonci, that they should be ready for whatever orders might be sent to them, and that they should not transgress them for the reason that he is King and is the representative of their God Curicaveri," and he sat down. The lords spent an entire day exhorting the people to obey the new Cazonci, especially the lords who were assigned to frontier posts, admonishing them to fight and hold off their enemies, and to advise and encourage the people throughout the villages to be obedient to the Cazonci. After all the lords had spoken, the new Cazonci stood up and said: "Now, Lords and chiefs, you have heard our Grandfather, who was over all the priests, you have heard what I ordered him to say, may it please the gods that I speak the truth, saying that you will be obedient here and at all times. You have brought me here and I have accepted this responsibility. Be sure that you do not fail to keep up the supply of the wood for the temples. Go then to your houses and gather your people in the villages. While you are there, you shall hear my orders. Remember, do not break faith with any of this, and let it not be only now that you say 'yes,' because I shall not excuse anyone from death. Be assured that you will suffer should you be rebellious; do this as a favor to me. Remember that, should you fail in any of these things, we have the squadrons of war; and you would do well to prepare yourselves to suffer. And you Lords who are stationed on the frontiers and who have war people, do not break faith nor transgress any of what you have been told. Go, then, all of you to your houses."

In this manner he was made king and he extended a general invitation to all the people. That night he went to his vigil at the house of the chief priests of Curicaveri in the company of all the lords and chiefs, and they performed the ceremony of war while the priests burned incense at midnight with their rites. At dawn the Cazonci himself went for wood for the temples, accompanied by the lords and the war spies, the priests who put incense in the braziers, the runners, the other priests called Curitiecha, the ensigns who carried the flags in war, and they brought all their wood to the fires. The Cazonci went to a porch at the front of his house and seated himself on a chair, while all the lords, chiefs, and people gathered around, and he repeated his general invitation. Then all the people, chiefs, and lords presented their gifts: hot climate blankets of cotton, axes of copper, mats for the back, fruits from Taximaroa, bows, and so on according to the possessions of each.

After this ceremony they all took leave of the Cazonci and returned to their villages where they gathered all their people, told them about the new king, and admonished them to be obedient. Later the Cazonci sent his priests called Curitiecha to order the people to gather wood for the temples. The people of the villages required only ten days to gather the wood and stack it in the large patio of the temples. Then the priest called Hiripati entered the house of vigil for his prayer, taking the fragrances which were described before in speaking of the wars, and preached a sermon explaining how their God Curicaveri had ordered the wood. The Cazonci also observes the vigil and the priests perform the war ceremony before him. On the third day he orders them to war and convokes all the lords of his lineage, the ones called Vacuxecha who are Eagles, and they all gather in the house of the Eagle dedicated to their God Curicaveri. Here the new Cazonci speaks to them: "Why do we have all this wood for the temples and the stakes that have been split, the fragrances that the priests have cast on the fires for the prayers and sacrificers, is all this to be wasted? Well, the Goddess Cueravaperi, the celestial gods, the Gods of the Four Parts of the world, and the God of the Inferno have all been consulted, and I have reported the decision to Curicaveri, the First-born Gods, and the gods called Virabanecha." He then orders everybody to war and the assembly is dismissed. The lords returned to their houses, and sent runners and messengers throughout the villages ordering everyone to war with the enemy on all frontiers.

The Cazonci remained in the city two days, after which he said he wanted to go hunting and everybody believed that he wanted to take part in a chase, but what he wanted to do was to make a foray. He was accompanied by the priests who put incense in the braziers, by some of the other people who had remained in the city, and he took the trumpets with him, saying that he was going hunting. He went straight to the frontier near the *Cuynacho* enemies and there he quickly made a foray and took between one hundred and one hundred and twenty captives and returned ahead of the people he had ordered to war. The lords returned later and brought back many captives to be sacrificed.

This was the beginning of his reign and thereafter he was the established Master and King, representing his God Curicaveri. He made sacrifice to the gods of the captives they brought back from the forays and granted favors to all who had captured slaves. He married all the women who had belonged to his father and, with the passing of time, other daughters of chiefs and lords were placed in his house.

20. POPULAR AUGURIES AND PROPHETIC DREAMS

These people say that during the four years before the Spaniards came to the land, their temples were burned from top to bottom, that they closed them and they would be burned again, and that the rock walls fell as their temples were made of flagstones. They did not know the cause of this except that they held it to be an augury. Likewise, they saw two large comets in the sky and thought that their gods were to conquer or destroy a village and that they were to do it for them. (See Plate 16.) These people imitate parts of their dreams and do as much of what they dreamed as they can. They report their dreams to the chief priest

53

who in turn conveys the information to the Cazonci. They say that the poor who bring in wood and sacrifice their ears dream about their gods who are reported as having told them that they would be given food and that they should marry such and such Christian girls. If this were a kind of omen they dared not tell it to the Cazonci. A priest related that, before the Spaniards came, he had dreamed that people would come bringing strange animals which turned out to be the horses which he had not known. In this dream these people entered the houses of the chief priests and slept there with their horses. They also brought many chickens that soiled the temples. He said he dreamed this two or three times in considerable fear for he did not know what it was until the Spaniards came to this province. When the Spaniards reached the city, they lodged in the houses of the chief priests with their horses where they held their prayer and kept their vigil. Before the Spaniards arrived they all had smallpox and measles, from which large numbers of people died, along with many lords and high families. All the Spaniards of the time are unanimous in that this disease was general throughout New Spain, for which reason it is to be given credence. The people are in accord in that measles and smallpox were unknown until the Spaniards brought them to the land.[4] The priest also indicated that the priests of the mother of Cueravaperi, who were in a village called Cinapecuaro, had come to the father of the dead Cazonci and reported the following dream or revelation prophesying the destruction of the house of their gods, an event which actually happened in Ucareo: the lord of the village of Ucareo, whose name was Vigen [Vigel], had a concubine among his other women, and

---

4 This is not the contradiction it appears to be. The argument of the Indian is a good one. The Tarascan Indians maintained that these diseases came to Michoacán ahead of the Spanish, which would make the Spanish statement true as far as it goes. However, they point out that they were brought to Michoacán by Tarascans who, when they first went to Mexico City, contacted Spaniards and Aztecs with the diseases and then brought them back home with them. The *Relación*, as well as other sources, supports the contention that the Tarascans sent people to Mexico City in response to a plea from Montezuma, and, while there, they saw a great amount of death and destruction from war and disease.

the Goddess Cueravaperi, mother of all the earthly gods, came and took that woman from her own house. These people say that all their gods frequently enter their houses and take people to be sacrificed to them. The goddess, without leaving the village, took the woman first a little way toward the road to Mexico City and then directed her to go out of the village on the road to Araro. Then putting the woman down the goddess untied a gourd dish shaped like a bowl, which was tied to her skirt, and after washing it in water, prepared a beverage made of water and something like a white seed. She gave this beverage to the woman who, upon drinking it, grew faint, and the goddess told her to walk on alone, saying: "I am not to take you; there is one, all dressed up, who is to take you; I shall neither harm you nor sacrifice you, nor will he who is to take you. You will be taken where there is a council and you will hear all that is said in that council. Then you shall report it all to the King Zangua [Zuangua], who is over all of us."

The woman walked along the road and soon met a white eagle, whistling and bristling his feathers, and with a great wart over large eyes which indicated that he was the God Curicaveri. The eagle greeted her, telling her that she was welcome, and she returned the greeting, saying, "Lord, may you have good fortune." The eagle replied, "Climb up on my wings and do not be afraid of falling." As soon as the woman was seated, the eagle, whistling, rose with her and took her through a forest where there was a spring heated by brimstone and as dawn was breaking placed her on the top of a very high mountain called Xanoata-jacanzio [Xanoato Huacío].

She saw all the gods seated there, painted and wearing wreaths of colored linen [cotton] on their heads, some wore headbands, others clover-leaf wreaths, a few had temples on the crowns of their heads, and others were dressed in many other ways. They also had many kinds of wine, both white and red, made from maguey, cherries, and honey. They had gifts, many of fruit, which they were taking to another god called Curicaveri, who was the messenger of the gods and whom they all called Grandfather. To the woman it seemed that they were all in a very large house and the eagle told her to be seated and she would hear everything that was said.

By this time the sun had risen and the God Curitacaheri was washing his head with soap. He had removed his braid, but he usually wore a wreath of colors on his head, some wooden ear ornaments, miniature earthen jugs around his neck and was covered with a thin blanket. His brother, called Tiripanienquarencha, was with him and they looked very handsome. All the other gods greeted them and extended a welcome to which Curitacaheri replied: "Well, you have all arrived, be sure that no one has been forgotten or was not called." They replied that they were all present and they began asking among themselves, "Have the Gods of the Left Hand arrived too?" The answer was that all were present, and again Curitacaheri urged them to be sure that they had not forgotten to call someone. Once more they assured him that everyone was there. Then he said, "Let my brother tell you what has to be said, and I do not want to go into the house." Then spoke Tiripanienquarencha, saying : "Come close, you Gods of the Left Hand and of the Right. My brother has told me what to tell you. He went out to the east to spend a few days with Cueravaperi and our nephew Curicaveri was there and so were Xaratanga, Huredequa, Vecara, and Querandangaperi. All the gods were there and the poor fellows tried to contradict Mother Cueravaperi. But those who tried to talk were not believed, their words were rejected, and what they tried to say was not accepted. What they tried to contradict is that some other men have remarried and they are to return to the land.[5] Their efforts were in vain and they were told: 'You First-born Gods and you Gods

[5] Man always feels compelled to justify on philosophic grounds any break with established tradition or anything he does not understand. The arrival of the Spanish caused the Tarascans to do just that. The Tarascans had never heard of or seen anything like the Spaniards, but they did have a vehicle which could give them a satisfactory explanation of what and why they were: religion, belief in visions, and the priests to interpret those visions and perhaps even arrange them. Thus, the old gods die, the old people die, and new gods and new people will control everything. Nothing can change that; it was ordered when the world was established. The Spanish won before putting foot on the soil of Michoacán.

of the Left Hand, gird yourselves for suffering and let it be as it was determined by the gods. How can we contradict what has been established? We do not know what this is about. In fact, was it not decided and ordered in the beginning, that no two of us gods should be together before the light came so that we should not kill ourselves nor lose our deity? It was ordered then that the earth should become calm at once and make two revolutions; that they were to be thus forever, and this which all we gods had agreed upon was not to change before the light came.' Now, we do not know what these words are. The gods tried to contradict this change but under no circumstances were they allowed to speak. Let it be as the gods will it. You First-born Gods and you Gods of the Left Hand, go all of you to your houses and do not bring back that wine you have. Break all those jugs for it shall not be from here on as it has been up to now when we were very prosperous. Break all the wine tubs everywhere, leave off the sacrifice of men and bring no more offerings with you because from now on it is not to be that way. No more kettledrums are to be sounded, split them all asunder. There will be no more temples or fireplaces, nor will any more smoke rise, everything shall become a desert because other men are coming to the earth. They will spare no end of the earth, to the Left Hand and to the Right, and everywhere all the way to the edge of the sea and beyond. The singing will be all one for there will not be as many songs as we had but only one throughout the land. And you, woman, who are here pretending not to hear us, publish this and make it known to Zuangua the King, who is in charge of all of us." All the gods of the council replied, saying it would be so and began to wipe the tears from their eyes. The council broke up and that vision was seen no more.

The woman found herself at the foot of an oak, and there was nothing around her when she awoke except a nearby cliff. Singing and walking through the forest, she returned to her home, arriving there about midnight. One of the sextons of the Goddess Cueravaperi heard her coming, opened the door, awakened the priests and told them to get up for the Goddess Cueravaperi was

57

coming. The sexton said that the goddess had come because these people believed that when the Goddess Cueravaperi chose a person she entered into his or her body and partook of their blood.

When the woman entered the house of the chief priest, all the priests were seated there, naked and painted, and they had clover-leaf wreaths on their heads. She went quickly from one end of the house to the other, took four turns around it, went over to the fire and then lay down on the other side of it. The priests then began to sacrifice their ears and feed her blood as the woman said, "Fathers, Fathers, I am hungry." She swallowed the blood they gave her, getting it all over her lips and the priests began to play their trumpets and kettledrums and put incense in the braziers. A procession was formed and the priests, singing all the time, carried the woman around the house four times, then they bathed and adorned her, putting on her a very good skirt, a blouse, a clover-leaf wreath on her head along with a simulated bird, some bells on her legs, and they brought her a lot of wine to drink.

The priests went to inform her husband, the lord of Ucareo, who at the time was performing the war ceremony and putting incense in the braziers. When he saw the priests coming, he extended a greeting and asked them why they had come to see him. They told him that his wife had just arrived, whereupon he ordered them to report it to the priest of Araro, called *Baricha*, and to the priest of Cinapecuaro, and then to warm the baths. As it was night he then went to his house, took a warm bath, slept and went out again in the morning. The priests who had been sent for had arrived, and he said to them: "They say that the Lady, my wife, has arrived, once more we shall see the Goddess Cueravaperi, let us go greet her." He dressed, for he had already bathed, and the priests took blankets, wine, and incense which they offered to the woman. They undressed her, put new clothes on her and bowed to her, saying: "Be thou welcome," and she returned the salutation. Then they asked her, "Madam, how did the goddess find you?" The Lady answered that she was at home and received her there. Then they asked what message she brought back for it must be reported to the king. She replied: "What would she say to me, Grandfathers? When she saw me there she did nothing to me but an eagle took me to the top of the mountain where there was a council of the gods. They were saying that men will come to the land again." Then she told them all she had heard on the mountain called Xanoato Huacío [Xanoatajacanzio]. The priests moved over a little way on the patio and bowed their heads in a huddle, and the lord of Ucareo said: "Grandfathers, since this woman does not speak out of the evil in her and says that men are to come to the land again, what is to become of the Lords who are here? The Mexicans, the Otomis, or the Chichimecas will come to conquer us. She says the entire kingdom is to be abandoned and become a desert. Go tell the King as I think he will want to have this knowledge. Let him not quarter and draw you alive! nor sacrifice you! Prepare yourselves to suffer. Just now I do not want to go to war, but would rather remain here so they may not kill me in battle. Let whoever is to kill me kill me here; sacrifice me here and let the Goddess Cueravaperi eat me. Go, because the King will reprimand us." The priests departed and in three days they arrived at the city of Mechuacán. At the time the Cazonci, called Zuangua, was at a place near his home called *Arataguaro* and he was drunk. He received the priests and said to them: "Welcome Mothers," [This is their manner of addressing the priests of Mother Cueravaperi] and they returned the salutation. He asked about their journey and they reported everything the woman had seen and heard. Zuangua replied: "Why did poor Vigel [Vigen], Lord of Ucareo, say that? Why is he disturbed? As I am not of low estate nor an orphan, why would I draw and quarter you? Wherever I go I am King just as I am no slave of the captives. And you, who are you? Since we are Lords, the loss of the seigniory is ours, not just yours alone and the more so, I expect of all the Provinces. While I shall not die soon and shall remain a while as King, I shall not listen to the gods for I shall die before their prophecy comes to pass. I have my sons among whom I shall divide the seigniory and they shall be Lords. There is my oldest son Zincicha, then Tirimarasco, Anini, Sirangua, Tanistitimas, Taquiani, Patamu, and Guizico. All these sons I have and I do not know which one our God Curicaveri will choose to be King. He who is chosen will hear all this and the poor fellow will not be Master long for he will be mistreated for four years and then, under the new men, the seigniory will be calm. I shall not witness this for I shall die first. Now, you have told me what you came to tell me and I want to give you something to drink and look for some blankets for you."

The servants produced women's skirts, wreaths of gold, plumages and other adornments for the goddess and Zuangua gave them all to the priests. Then Zuangua said, "I also want to tell you something else; this same news which you have brought was brought to me from the Hot Lands. The people of the Hot Lands say that a fisherman, in his boat, was fishing in the river with a hook and that a very large fish took the hook but the fisherman could not bring him in. An alligator appeared, from I do not know where in that river, snatched the fisherman from the boat, swallowed him and sank into very deep water. The fisherman grappled with the alligator and took the alligator to his very nice home. On arriving at his home, the fisherman bowed to the alligator who then said to him, 'You shall see that I am a god; go to the city of Mechuacán and tell the King, who is over all of us and whose name is Zuangua, that the signal has been given that there are now new men and all who have been born in all quarters of the land are to die. Tell this to the King.' This, Grandfather, is what happened in the Hot Lands and which they reported to me. It is all one and the same, the story you bring me and the report from the Hot Lands." After this conversation the priests left and returned to the lord of Ucareo to report the words of Zuangua.

21. THE ARRIVAL OF THE SPANIARDS

According to Don Pedro, who is now governor, Montezuma sent ten messengers from Mexico City to Taximaroa. They brought a message for the Cazonci, called Zuangua, father of the one who had just died, who was very old and who had been the Master of Taximaroa. When asked what they wanted they answered that they brought a message from Montezuma for the Cazonci in Mechuacán and for him alone. The Master of Taximaroa reported this to the Cazonci who ordered that they be received well but that they should not come at once. When they came before Zuangua they delivered gifts of turquoise, jerky, green feathers, ten round shields with golden rims, rich blankets, belts, and large mirrors. All the lords and sons of the Cazonci disguised themselves and put on some old blankets so that they would not be recognized, for they had heard that the Mexicans had come for them. The Mexicans sat down and the Cazonci called in an interpreter of the Mexican language, by the name of Nuritan, who was his Nahuatl interpreter. The Cazonci asked him what the Mexicans wanted and why they came. The Cazonci was calm, holding an arrow in his hand with which he struck the ground repeatedly. (See Plate 17.) The Mexicans repeated their message. "The Master of Mexico, called Montezuma, sends us and some other Lords with orders to report to our brother the Cazonci about the strange people who have come and taken us by surprise. We have met them in battle and killed some two hundred of those who came riding deer and two hundred of those who were not mounted. Those deer wore coats of mail and carried something that sounds like the clouds, makes a great thundering noise and kills all those it meets leaving not one. They completely broke up our formation and killed many of us. They are accompanied by people from Tlaxcala, because these people have turned against us. We should have killed the people of Tezaico if it had not been for those who help them to keep us besieged and isolated in this city. If your sons had not come to help us, the ones called Tirimarasco, Anini, and Acuiche, bringing their people and defending us, we should have all died there."

Having heard the message Zuangua replied: "It is well, you are welcome. You have made your message known to our Gods Curicaveri and Xaratanga. At the moment I cannot send people because I have need of those whom you have named for they are busy conquering in the Four Quarters. Rest here a day or so and these my interpreters, Nuritan and Pivo, and two others will go with you. They shall confer with the people of whom you speak as soon as everyone has returned from the conquest."

The messengers went out and were given quarters, food, belts, blankets, leather war jackets, and clover-leaf wreaths. The Cazonci called his advisors and said to them: "What shall we do? This message they have brought me is serious. What has happened to us for the sun used to look with favor upon these two Kingdoms, Mexico and ours, and we never knew that there were any other people for we all served the same gods. What purpose would I have in sending people to Mexico for we are always at war when we approach each other and there is rancor between us. Remember that the Mexicans are very astute when they talk and very artful with the truth—I have no need of them as I said. Take heed lest it be a trick. Since they have not been able to conquer some villages, they want to take out their vengeance on us by killing us through treachery. They want to destroy us. As I said, let the Nahuatls and interpreters go for they are not boys to do boyish things and they will learn what it is all about." His advisors replied: "Sire, let it be as ordered by you who are King and Master. How can we contradict you? Let those whom you mention go at once."

He sent for rich blankets, gourd dishes, leather war jackets, for the bloody skirts and blankets of their gods and for some of everything produced in Mechuacán. These gifts he gave to the messengers to give to Montezuma just as Montezuma had sent similar gifts from Mexico for the local gods. The Nahuatls went with them to learn the truth, and the Cazonci sent war people by another road who captured three Otomis and asked them whether they had any news from Mexico. The Otomis replied: "The Mexicans have been conquered; we do not know who the conquerors are, but all Mexico City is foul with the odor of dead bodies. For this reason they are looking for allies who will free and defend them. We know how they have sent throughout the villages for help. It is true that they have gone for we know it. Take us to Mechuacán so they will give us blankets for we are freezing to death and we want to be subjects of the Cazonci." The capture of the three Otomis and the news they brought were reported to the Cazonci: "Sire, it is true. The Mexicans have been destroyed and the entire village smells of dead bodies. They are petitioning all the villages for help. This is what was reported also in Taximaroa for the chief *Capacapecho* verified it." Then the Cazonci spoke, saying: "Welcome; we do not know what may become of the poor fellows we sent to Mexico. Let us wait for their return to learn the truth."

22. THE ASSESSMENT

The Cazonci said to the lords: "It is true that people have come from other lands and the Mexicans are not deceiving us. What shall we do? This is a serious matter. When did Mexico's existence begin? It has been a long time since these two kingdoms, Mexico and Mechuacán, were appointed and the gods looked on them with favor from the heavens and from the sun. Never have we heard of the coming of other people from our ancestors; if Tariacuri, Hiripan, and Tangaxoan, who were Masters, knew anything about it, they did not make it known to us. Where would they come from but from the heavens, for the heavens unite with the sea and that is where they must have come from. And the deer which they are said to possess, what are they?"

The Nahuatls answered: "Sire, those deer must be something like a story we know in which the God Cupanzieri played ball with another God, Achurihirepe, won over him and sacrificed him in a village called Xacona. He also left the latter's wife pregnant with his son Siratatapeci. When the son was born, he was taken to another village to be raised, as if he were a foundling. As a youth he went bird hunting with a bow and on one of those hunts he came upon an *yvaña* which said to him, 'Don't shoot me and I'll tell you something. The one you now think is your father is not because your real father went to the house of the God

63

Achurihirepe to conquer, and he was sacrificed there.' When Siratatapeci heard this he went to the village of Xacona to get vengeance on his father's murderer. He excavated the place where his father was buried, exhumed him, and carried him on his back. Along the way there was a weed patch full of quail which took to flight. In order to shoot the quail he dropped his father, who turned into a deer with a mane on his neck and a long tail like those that come with the strange people. He went east for he had come with those newcomers to this land.''

Then the Cazonci asked: "From whom shall we learn the truth? They also say that a poor old woman tells a story about something that happened in Cuyacán. She was a water peddler and in the savanna she met the gods called Tiripemecha, brothers of our Curicaveri, and one of them said to her: 'Where are you going, Grandmother?' [This is the way they address the old women.] She answered: 'I am going to Cuyacán.' The gods asked her if she did not recognize them and she said that she did not. Then they explained: 'We are the gods called Tiripemecha; go to the Lord called Ticatame and tell him that in a little while we shall move from Cuyacán to Mechuacán, that we shall be there a few years and then we shall move again going to our first dwelling place called Bayameo [which is now Sante Fe]. This we tell you and no more.' This is what the old woman learned, and they say that there were other omens: that the cherry trees, even the small ones, would produce berries, the small magueys would produce stalks, and that little girls would become pregnant while still children. This is what the old people said and now it is being fulfilled. By this we shall be guided, since there was no recollection of this in days gone by nor did the old people tell one another that these people were to come. Let us wait and see. Let them come and try to take us. Let us do our best to hold our own a little longer in order to get wood for the temples.'' Thus ended Zuangua's talk and there were many opinions among the lords. Each one told the fable according to his lights for they all feared the Spaniards.

23. NEWS FROM MEXICO CITY AND THE DEATH OF ZUANGUA

The messengers who had been sent to Mexico City returned, appeared before the Cazonci, greeted him and showed him more gifts of rich blankets and belts sent by Montezuma. Zuangua returned their greeting, saying that it was good to see them again and telling them that "long ago, on another occasion, our ancient ancestors went to Mexico City." Then he asked them about their journey and the messengers replied: "Sire, during the night we arrived by canoe in Mexico City and showed the gift you sent to Montezuma, who welcomed us. We explained your orders that we should go with his messengers, we told him that you had sent your people to the Four Quarters and that we came ahead against the day when the war people could come. We told him that we came to learn about these strange people who have come to our land, in order to be better advised. He welcomed us and said: 'Look at that mountain range over there. Behind it are the people who have come from Taxcala [Tlaxcala].' Then they took us by canoe to show us. We landed in Texcuco [Texcoco] and climbed to the top of a mountain. From there they pointed to a long, flat clearing occupied by the strangers and outlined a plan to us: 'You people from Mechuacán will come from that way over there and we shall go this other way to catch them between us and thus kill them all. Why should we not be successful since everyone flees from you people of Mechuacán, who are such great archers? You have seen them, now take this information to your Master and tell him that we plead with him not to break our agreement. This is what we say to him, our gods have told us that Mexico City will never be destroyed, nor will our houses be burned. Two Kingdoms only are appointed, Mexico and Mechuacán. Take heed for there is much work.' We answered: 'Let us return to Mexico City.' We returned, the lords came out to receive us and we took our leave from Montezuma who said to us: 'Return to Mechuacán for you have seen the land. Let us not desert the land which we wish to give to you. This matter which we beg of your

Master, what answer can he give except that you will all come? Are we peradventure to be slaves? Are they to conquer Mechuacán? Let us all die here first and not let them go to your land. This is what you shall say to your Master. May you all come; there is plenty of food so that the people may have strength for the war; do not pity the people. Let us die quickly, if we do not win, and we shall make our dais of the people who die supposing the cowardly gods do not favor us. It has been a long time since they told our god that no one would destroy his Kingdom, and we have heard of no other Kingdom but this one and Mechuacán. So, return.' We departed and the Mexicans came some distance with us before saying goodby. This is the report we bring back."

Then the Cazonci, Zuangua, spoke: "Welcome back. It has been a long time since our old ancestors went to Mexico City and while I know not why they went, the reason for your going now is important. What the Mexicans said is serious business. For what purpose are we to go to Mexico? Each one of us might go only to die and we know not what they will say about us afterwards. Perchance they will sell us out to these people who are coming and will be the cause of our being killed. Let the Mexicans do their own conquering or let them all come join us with their captaincies. Let the strangers kill the Mexicans because for many days they have not lived right for they do not bring wood to the temples but instead, we have heard, they honor their gods only with songs. What good are songs alone? How are the gods to favor them if they only sing songs? We work much more than is customarily required for the needs of the gods. Now let us do a little better, nay more, bring in wood for the temples, perhaps they will forgive us, for the gods of the heavens have become angry with us. Why would the strangers come without cause? A god has sent them, that is why they came! The people must know their sins; recall them to their memory even though they may lay the blame for their sins on me, the King. The common people do not want to listen to me for I tell them to bring wood for the temples. They heed not my words and they lose count of the war people. Why should not our God Curicaveri and the Goddess Xaratanga become angry with us? Since Curicaveri has no children and Xaratanga has not given birth to any, they complain to Mother Cueravaperi. I shall admonish the people to try to do better because they will not forgive us if we have failed in anything." The lords answered: "You have spoken well, Sire; we shall tell the people this which you order." And they went to their houses and nothing more was learned.

At this time a plague of smallpox and hemorrhaging from the bowels struck all the people in the entire province. The bishop of the temples died, as did the old Cazonci Zuanga [Zuangua], leaving his sons Tangaxoan, otherwise known as Zincicha, the oldest, Tirimarasco, Azinche, and Anini.

Another embassy of ten Mexicans came to ask for help. Unfortunately, for their purpose, they arrived at a time when the people were mourning the death of the old Cazonci. The arrival of the Mexicans was reported to Zincicha [Tangaxoan], the oldest son of the deceased Cazonci who ordered them taken to his father's houses where they were welcomed. It was explained to the Mexicans that the Cazonci was not there, that he had gone to rest. The oldest son called the old men into consultation and asked what should be done about the petition which the Mexicans brought. "We know not what their real intent is. Let them follow my Father to the Inferno and present him with the petition there. Tell them to prepare themselves because this is the custom." The Mexicans were so informed, and they replied that as the Master had ordered it, it should be done, and they asked that it be done quickly, adding that there was nowhere for them to go; they had voluntarily come to their death. The Mexicans were made ready in the customary manner, after being informed that they were taking their message to the dead Cazonci, and were sacrificed in the temple of Curicaveri and Xaratanga.

Whenever the Tarascos came into possession of firearms captured from the Spaniards, the arms were offered to the gods in the temples.

67

24. THE INSTALLATION OF A NEW MASTER

All the old men who were spared by the plague went into a conference concerning the raising of another Master, and they spoke to Zincicha [Tangaxoan]: "Sire, you must be our King. How can this house remain deserted and beclouded? Mark you that we shall grieve our God Curicaveri until we have a King. Have wood brought to the temples." Zincicha answered: "Do not say this, old man; let my younger brothers do it and I shall be as a father to them, or let it be the Master of Cuyacán called Paguingata." They rejoined: "What are you saying, Sire? You must be the King. Do you want your younger brothers to take the seigniory from you? You are the oldest." Then Tangaxoan, as the new Cazonci, said: "Having been importuned, let it be as you say, old men; I want to obey you. If perchance I do not do well, I beg you not to harm me, but gently separate me from the seigniory. Take heed that we are not to dissemble, and listen for what is said about the strange people who are coming, for we do not know who they are. Perhaps the days that I shall have this charge will not be many." Thus he became the Master.

The new Cazonci was induced by a principal named Timas to order his brothers put to death, for he said that they were lying with his women and that they wanted to oust him from the seigniory. Afterward he wept for having killed his brothers, and he blamed the principal named Timas. Then it was learned that Timas had arrived in Taximaroa on a white horse at the feast of Purecoraqua, which is the twenty-third of February, spending two days in Taximaroa and then returning to Mexico City.

Shortly thereafter, three Spaniards on horseback arrived in the city of Mechuacán, where the Cazonci received them graciously and feasted them. To put fear into the Spaniards, he sent all his people to the hunt, a large number of painted people with many bows and arrows. The hunters shot many deer, presenting five of them to the Spaniards who, in turn, gave green plumages to the Cazonci and to the lords. The Cazonci had the Spaniards dress in the same manner as the native gods, putting wreaths of

68

gold on their heads, and hanging round golden shields from their necks. They gave each Spaniard an offering of wine in a large cup and offerings of pigweed bread and fruit. The Cazonci said that these were gods from the heavens and to each Spaniard he gave a round, golden shield and blankets. The Spaniards told him that they wanted to trade the merchandise, plumages and other things, which they had brought with them from Mexico. The Cazonci consented and then gave secret orders that no merchant nor any lord should buy those plumages. The sacristans and the guards of the gods bought everything the Spaniards had with the blankets that the gods had earmarked for the purchase of their adornments. The Spaniards gave the Cazonci ten swine and a dog, telling him that the dog would serve to guard his wife. Then the Spaniards packed up their loads and the Cazonci gave them blankets, gourd dishes, and leather war jackets, and they returned to Mexico City.

As the Cazonci looked at those pigs, he said: "What are these things? They are rats brought by these people!" He took them to be omens and ordered the pigs and the dog killed and the people dragged them and threw them in a weed patch.

Before they left, the Spaniards asked the Cazonci for two Indian girls from among his relatives and took them along, lying with them along the road. The Indians who traveled with them called the Spaniards *Tarascue*, which in their language means son-in-law. Later the Spaniards began to apply this name to the Indians, but instead of calling them *Tarascue*, they called them *Tarascos*, which is the name they have now, and the women are called *Tarascas*. They are quite embarrassed by these names, saying that these names come from those first women taken by the Spaniards to Mexico City.

The Cazonci went back to his conference with his old men and the lords, and he said to them: "What shall we do? It appears that these people are coming now." His old men replied: "They are on the way, we must open up a way to escape for we have been seen and found." The Cazonci spoke: "So be it, old men, as the gods wish it. Well, did my father know it and even though

69

the poor fellow were alive what could he say?" The old men said to him: "So it is, Sire, as you say, what could we do when we received the news? Gird yourself, Sire, let us go see what they say for they come again."

Four more Spaniards came and spent two days in the city. They asked the Cazonci for twenty principals and many people and he granted their request. They left with the people to go to Colima and came to a village called Hac-zgran, where they stayed, sending the principals and the people on ahead so that the lords of Colima would come to meet the Spaniards in peace. But the lords of Colima sacrificed all of them and not one returned. Uneasy about their return trip and about waiting for the messengers, the Spaniards went back to the city of Mechuacán where they stayed two days and then journeyed to Mexico City.

25. RUMORS OF THE SPANIARDS AND WAR

News of the arrival of the Spaniards at Tagimaroa [Taximaroa] came to the Cazonci's ears and each day messengers reported that there were two hundred Spaniards. This was about the time of the feast of Cohora Cosquaro [Caheri Conscuaro] on the seventeenth of July, which is in the rainy season of this land. Their captain was a man by the name of Cristóbal de Olí [Olid]. Knowing about their arrival and that they came to make war, the Cazonci feared that they would kill him and all his people so he called a meeting of the old men and the lords and asked them what should be done. In attendance at this meeting were the following lords: Timas, who falsely called the Cazonci his uncle and who was an important person, others called Ecango, Quezequampare, Taseavaco alias Vizizilci, Cuinieranguazi, Don Pedro, who was a brother of Tashavaco, and other lords. The Cazonci spoke to them and said: "What shall we do? Each one speak your opinion for by whom else are we to be advised, by outsiders?" Their answer was: "You decide it, Sire, for you are the King. What could we say? You alone must decide." The Cazonci acquiesced and issued his orders: "Send runners throughout the Province ordering all the people of war to gather here. Let us die for all the Mexicans are dead and now the Spaniards come for us. What are the Chichimecas and all the people of the Province good for? There is no lack of people. There are the Matalzingas, the Otomis, the Betamas, the Cuitlatecas, the Escomaechas, and the Chichimecas. All these augment the arrows of our God Curicaveri. What are they for if not for this purpose? Let the leader or Lord of every village prepare to suffer. Go and publish it."

The runners went throughout the province and the lords and the priests gathered people. The Cazonci called Don Pedro, whose father had been a priest, and said to him: "Come here, for I hold you to be my brother in whom I must have confidence, for the old people, my relatives, are dead and are on their way; they have gone a long ways and we shall follow them. Let us all die quickly and take our ravages of the common people. Go, gather war people in Tagimaroa [Taximaroa] and other villages." To this, Don Pedro answered: "It shall be, as you say; we shall not fail in anything you order for you have ordered it and we shall heed your words; I shall go, Sire."

Don Pedro, who now is governor, departed with another principal, named Nuzundira, and in a day and a half they arrived at Tagimaroa [Taximaroa], a distance of eighteen leagues from the city of Mechuacán. All the people of Ucareo, Acambaro, Araro, and Tuzantlan gathered together, and they were all in the forest with their bows and arrows. On the road Don Pedro met a principal called Quezecuapara, filled with fear, coming from Tagimaroa [Taximaroa] [where the Spaniards were now located]. Don Pedro greeted him with a welcome which the principal did not immediately answer but soon he asked what Don Pedro was doing. Don Pedro explained: "The Cazonci has sent me to gather the war people from the villages of Tagimaroa [Taximaroa], Ucareo, Acambaro, Araro, and Tuzantlan and other principals have also been sent to gather the war people from throughout the Province." The principal said to him: "Go if you wish, I do not want to say anything but all the people of Tagimaroa are dead, Don Pedro."

71

That afternoon when Don Pedro arrived in the village of Tagimaroa, he found no Tarascos there because they had all fled, and he was taken prisoner by the Spaniards and the Mexicans. The next morning they took him before the Spanish Captain, Cristóbal de Olí [Olid], who called for an interpreter of the language of Mechuacán. The interpreter who came was called Xanaqua, one of the people captured by the Mexicans who knew the languages of both Mexico and his own Mechuacán. Through him Cristóbal de Olí [Olid] asked Don Pedro: "Where are you from?" Don Pedro answered: "The Cazonci sends me." Then Cristóbal de Olí [Olid] asked: "What did he tell you?" and Don Pedro replied: "He called me and said, 'Go to receive the gods [for that is what they call the Spaniards], see if it is true that they are coming; perhaps it is a lie, perhaps they only came as far as the river and then turned back because of the rainy season. Go, see, and report back to me, and if they have come, let them come at once to the city.' This is what he told me." Cristóbal de Olí [Olid] replied: "What you have said is a lie, it is not that way, but you want to kill us and you have all gathered together to make war on us. Let them come quickly if they are going to kill us or perhaps I shall kill them with my people from Mexico." Don Pedro answered: "It is not that way for if it were I should tell you." Cristóbal de Olí [Olid]: "All right, if it is as you say, go back to the City and let the Cazonci come with a gift and receive me at a place called Quangaceo which is near Matalcingo. Let him bring the richest blankets, the kind called *Cazangari*, *Curice*, *Zizupa*, *Echerea Tancata*, and other light blankets, chickens, eggs, and fish, the kind called *Zuecepu*, *Acumarami*, *Vrapeti*, *Thira*, and *Patos*. Bring it all to that place, do not fail to comply and heed my words." As a warning, the Spaniards hanged two Indians from Mexico City because they had burned some wooden fences in the temples of Tagimaroa. Then Cristóbal de Olí [Olid] said to him: "Tell the Cazonci not to be afraid, that we shall do him no harm," and Don Pedro agreed to tell the Cazonci.

The Spaniards went to hear Mass and Don Pedro was with

them. The Indians also went and saw the priest with the chalice uttering the words of the ceremony and they said to themselves that he must be a medicine man like theirs who looks in the water and reads the future. They also thought that in this way the Spaniards would know that they wanted to make war on them, and they began to fear.

Mass over, Christóbal de Olí [Olid] called five Mexicans and five Otomis and told them to go with Don Pedro to Mechuacán. The interpreter who came with the Spaniards, called Xanaqua, said to Don Pedro as he departed: "Go, Sire, at an auspicious time and tell the Cazonci not to make war, that the Spaniards are very generous and do no harm, that the blankets, corn, gold, and silver he has should be hidden away, for the Spaniards will take it all as soon as they see it. This is the way the Mexicans did, they hid everything." Don Pedro spoke: "What you have told me is enough, you have been very generous in what you have said and I shall repeat your words to the Cazonci." He left with the Mexicans and the Otomis and they went as far as a place called Vasmao, some three leagues before Matalcingo and he said to them: "You stay here while I go ahead." Don Pedro hoped to keep the Mexicans and Otomis from seeing the war people and quickly going ahead he found eight thousand men of war under a Captain Xamando in a village called Yndeparapec. Don Pedro spoke to them, saying: "Separate and go away from here for the Spaniards are not angry but happy and the Cazonci is to receive them at a place called Quangaceo." Then the Captain asked: "Well, why did Quezeguempare, who came ahead, throw fear into us and tell us that they had killed everybody in Tagimaroa?" Don Pedro answered him: "I don't know, he refused to talk to me when I met him." The Captain with these people was called Tahavaco, alias Huizizilzi, and was an older brother of Don Pedro to whom he said: "Hurry, brother, the Cazonci is getting impatient for he is very anxious to have the news that you may bring him. At dawn I am going to the city with the people."

73

26. FEAR AND SUICIDE

At length Don Pedro arrived at the city of Mechuacán and found all the war people and all the servants of the Cazonci on the brink of going with him to drown themselves in the lake. (See Plate 18.) He had been persuaded by some of the principals who wanted to eliminate him and take over the seigniory. Don Pedro appeared before the Cazonci who said to him: "What news do you bring, how are the Spaniards?" Don Pedro explained: "They are not angry and they come peacefully," and he repeated the Captain's request that he should go to receive them. He described how the Spaniards were armed and the several kinds of blankets and fish that were to be delivered to them.

At this point, Timas, who had sought to eliminate the Cazonci, interrupted, "What did you say, snivelly boy? You must have said something to the Spaniards. Away with you sir, we are ready to drown ourselves. Were your Grandfathers and your forebears perchance slaves of someone that you want to be a slave?" Turning to the Cazonci, Timas said: "Let Huizizilzi and Don Pedro, who brings this news, remain to face the Spaniards." Don Pedro answered, saying: "What could I say to them? That interpreter called Xanqua [Xanaqua] is from our own city. As I left the Spaniards, he told me what we should do and said that we should not make war against the Spaniards." Then Timas said to the Cazonci: "Sire, have copper brought and we shall put it on our backs and let us drown ourselves in the lake. That way we shall reach the Inferno quickly and catch up with the dead ones." Don Pedro spoke to those who were saying this to the Cazonci: "What are you saying? Why do you want to drown yourselves?" Then Don Pedro said to the Cazonci: "Before you drown yourselves, go up on the mountain, receive the Spaniards and let them kill us first, then you may drown yourselves in the lake afterwards. Sire, take heed, these people are lying, they want to kill you; they are all fleeing with their blankets and jewels. If it were true that they wanted to die, why would they carry off their treasures as in flight? Sire, do not believe them." Then the Cazonci answered: "You have spoken well."

Timas and the others who were trying to induce the Cazonci to drown himself got drunk and sang in preparation for drowning themselves. Don Pedro also placed a lot of copper on his back and told them: "I do it not to die. Let us go now; let us all drown ourselves, as those principals said to the Cazonci, 'Sire, drown yourself so that you will not go begging; are you perchance a choreboy and of low birth? Were your forebears perchance slaves? Kill yourself as we shall; you are no better than we and we shall follow you and go with you.' " The Cazonci continued: "That is the truth, Uncles, wait a little." He bedecked himself, put some gold bells on his legs, turquoise around his neck, and green feathers on his head. The principals did likewise and said to him: "Bring out the plumages that used to belong to your Grandfather and let us put them on for awhile for we know not who is to be the King and the one to wear them." The Cazonci ordered the plumages brought out, also the golden bracelets and the round shields of gold. The principals took them and they all danced. Don Pedro was very sorrowful and was asking himself: "Why do they take away the Cazonci's jewels? Why do these people want them? Why do they not go ahead and drown themselves and die? How they deceive him—lie to him—plot to betray him and—want to kill him! How did they know what I learned from the Spaniards? I, the one who went to them, I heard it clearly. They are not coming in an angry mood. I saw the Lords from Mexico who are coming with them; if these were slaves why would they be wearing turquoise collars around their necks, rich blankets and green plumages as they do? How is it the Spaniards do not harm them? What are these people talking about?"

The women who were in the Cazonci's house asked Don Pedro about the news. His answer was: "Ladies, I brought very good news that the Spaniards are neither annoyed nor angry. I do not know what these principals are talking about." The women were frightened and wrung their hands and wept. "We are sorry that you did not bring him this good news earlier," they said. Don Pedro was very worried because he was alone, for his brother Huizizilzi had not yet come.

The Cazonci was in one of the rooms of his house while the principals were calling him and demanding: "Sire, come on, come on out." The Cazonci had had a small door made secretly in a wall of his house which faced on the road. At night he had all the fires put out and slipped out this door with all his women, went quietly up the nearby mountain and escaped from the hands of the principals. Drunk as they were, the principals followed him, wearing their ornaments with their bells tinkling, along the road. The Cazonci fled to a village called Vrapán some eight or nine leagues from the city. When the principals learned about it they followed, and when they caught up, he spoke to them: "Welcome, Uncles, what brings you this way?" They answered as if they had been with his party: "Sire, we came asking for you. Where are we going? Are we going far?" The Cazonci answered: "Let us stay here and see what news there is and what the Spaniards will do when they come. Huizizilzi and his brother, Aniniarangari, are over there already; let us wait and see what news they bring us; let us see whether they have been mistreated."

When the Spaniards arrived at the city, all the chiefs and lords who remained were disconsolate upon learning that the Cazonci had fled. They asked: "How did he leave? He had no compassion for us. Whom are we to serve and favor if not him? Those who took him away did great wrong."

Ten Mexicans sent by Cristóbal de Olí [Olid] arrived from the city and when they saw how sad the people were they asked the principals the cause. They answered: "Our Master the Cazonci drowned in the lake." The Mexicans replied: "What shall we do? Let us return quickly for this is an important matter. They returned and reported the information to Cristóbal de Olí [Olid], telling him that the Cazonci was drowned, to which Olid replied: "It is well, we have done well for we must take that city."

Before the Spaniards arrived, the people of Mechuacán sacrificed eight hundred of the slaves held in prison so that they could not escape and join the Spaniards. Dressed in their war outfits, Huizizilzi and his brother, Don Pedro, and all the chiefs and lords of the province took the war people and went out to receive the Spaniards at a place called Apupato, about a half league from the city on the road to Mexico City. There they drew the line against the Spaniards and told them not to cross it, asked them to explain their coming and asked them whether or not they came to kill. The Captain answered: "We do not want to kill you. Come quickly and join us, or is it you who want to make war against us?" They replied that they did not, and then Captain Cristóbal de Olí [Olid] told them to leave their bows and arrows and join him. Then all the lords and chiefs dropped their bows and arrows and, accompanied by some archers, they went over to the Spaniards. They were well received and embraced, and everybody went back to the patios of the large temples where the Spaniards practiced some combat tactics in the large patio, firing some shots which caused the Indians to fall prostrate with fear. The Spaniards then went to the houses of the Cazonci which they examined, after which they returned to the patio of the five large temples.

The Spaniards took up quarters in the temples and in the houses of the chief priests, called *Pirimu*, which were ten yards wide. The steps and the entrances to the temples were covered with blood from the sacrifice that had been made, and many bodies of the sacrificed were still there. The Spaniards examined them to see whether they had beards and then went into the temples and rolled the sacrificial stones down the steps along with a god called Curitacaheri who was the messenger of the gods. When the people saw this they wondered why the gods did not become angry and curse the newcomers. In their fear they brought great quantities of food for the Spaniards and as there were no women left in the city, for they had all fled to Pázcuaro [Pátzquaro] and other villages, the lords and old men did the grinding and made bread for the white men.

The Spaniards stayed in the city six moons [these people counted twenty days as a moon] with their army and accompany-

77

ing people from Mexico City. All were furnished food, bread, chickens, eggs, and fish, of which there is plenty in the lake. Four days after they arrived they began to ask about the idols, and the lords told them that there were none. Then they asked for the dress ornaments and the Indians delivered many plumages, round shields, and masks, and the Spaniards burned everything in the patio. Then they began to ask for gold, and many Spaniards went into the houses of the Cazonci to search for the metal.

27. PLUNDERING THE GOLD

From his ancestors the Cazonci had inherited great quantities of gold, silver, jewels, round shields, bracelets, halfmoons, liprings, and earrings which he kept for his feasts and expeditions. He inquired of the guards who kept the records what quantity there might be and they said, and others since have said, that in his house the Cazonci had forty chests, twenty filled with gold and twenty of silver, which were called *chuperi* and were dedicated to the feasts of their gods. There must have been a large amount. He likewise had large quantities of his own in a house in another place called Yehecheniremba. On an island called Apupato there were another ten chests of fine silver in round shields, 200 shields in each chest; miters for the captives they sacrificed and 1600 green plumages of the kind used by Curicaveri; a like amount for the Goddess Xaratanga and another for her son Manovapa. There were forty jackets of rich feathers and forty of parrot feathers. These had been placed there by this Cazonci's great-grandparents. Likewise, in another house there were ten chests of round shields, 200 in each chest, of not quite such fine silver placed there by the father of the deceased Cazonci, called Zuangua. There were 4,700 green plumages, five jackets of those rich feathers, called *chatani*, and five of parrot feathers. On another island called Xanecho there were eight chests of round silver shields and fine silver miters, called *angoruti*, 100 shields and silver miters each in their own chest, and 400 of something like round loaves called *curinda*. This silver, dedicated to the moon, had also been placed there by his father.

On another island called Pecandan there were four chests of fine silver, 100 round shields in each chest, and twenty round shields of fine gold that were divided among those chests, five in each one. The guards were there and the guardianship of this treasure passed from father to son by succession. They also made seedbeds and offered them to that silver. They had their major treasurer over all of them. On that same island of Apupato the Cazonci had still another silver treasure.

The story goes on to tell that as the Spaniards entered the Cazonci's houses where the forty chests were, twenty of gold and twenty of silver in round shields, they began to steal from the chests. The thieves must have been young men, for they hid the loot under their capes. The Cazonci's women saw them steal this treasure and followed them as they left the Cazonci's house, beating them with heavy canes. Although the Spaniards had their swords, they dared not harm the women, instead they protected their heads with their hands and some lost their loot in flight, others got away with it. The principals were around and the women began to insult them, asking why they wore the lip-rings of valiant men, saying they were useless at defending the gold and silver that was being carried off by the thieves, and shamed them. Still, in the belief that they were gods, the principals told the women not to harm them for what those gods were carrying off belonged to them.

When Cristóbal de Olí [Olid] learned about the chests of gold and silver, he had them brought out and taken to the houses of the chief priests where he was lodged. The Spaniards opened them and began to choose the finest for themselves, putting aside those which were not quite so good. They cut each shield in two with their swords, put them in some blankets and made two hundred loads with them. Then Captain Cristóbal de Olí [Olid] ordered Don Pedro to take those loads of gold and silver to the governor, the Marquis del Valle [Hernan Cortés], in Mexico

City. He ordered them to go in groups of twenty Indians and remain within sight of each other along the road. Small flags were placed on their loads, and the *Tamemes* were told to keep in sight of each other along the road by watching the flags.

Don Pedro, and the Spaniard who accompanied him with those loads, met the Marquis at a Mexican village called Cuyacán, where Don Pedro was presented to the Marquis. The Spaniards counted the loads and then the Marquis asked Don Pedro where the Cazonci had gone. Don Pedro answered that he had been in such a hurry to receive the Marquis that he drowned in a lake. The Marquis then asked, "Since he is dead, who will be the Master, does he not have some heirs?" To this Don Pedro replied negatively. Then the Marquis asked what had become of Huizi-zilzi and how he was related to the Cazonci. Don Pedro answered that there was no relationship and that "he and I are brothers by the same Mother." Then the Marquis declared: "Your brother will be the Master." He gave Don Pedro some turquoise neck-laces and said: "I had these for the Cazonci, but since he has drowned, throw them in the lake at the place where he drowned so that he may take them with him." After ordering food for Don Pedro, the Marquis told him to go to Mexico City and see how it had been destroyed.

Some principals took him to Mexico City for he had never been there in all his life, neither had his ancestors for many generations. The lords came out to receive him with flowers and rich blankets, and they spoke to Don Pedro and the principals who were with him, saying: "Welcome Chichimecas from Mechuacán, we are glad that we meet again. We do not know the gods who have conquered us. Look at this city of Mexico, named by our God Zinziviquo, and see how desolate it is; they have put women's skirts on us. How is it that they have not stopped you? You who were appointed by the gods have also been conquered. Let it be as the gods have willed it. Be strong in your hearts. We who are many have come to this end. I do not know what our ancestors learned and saw; it must have been very little. We, being many, have experienced this." Then Don Pedro replied to them:

"Well, gentlemen, you have consoled me with what you have said; at last you have seen us. We would not see and visit with each other if they had not treated us this way. Let us be brothers for many years for it has pleased the gods that we be alive and escape from their hands. Let us serve them and make seedbeds for them for we know not what people will come, but let us obey them. Let there be an end to this and let us go back to the Marquis in Cuyacán for we have seen Mexico City."

They gave each other rich blankets and jewels, and Don Pedro and his people returned to Cuyacán where the Marquis sent a welcoming committee to receive them. Letters had come from the city of Mechuacán which claimed that the Cazonci had been found, and the Marquis sent for Don Pedro and accused him: "Come here, why did you tell me that the Cazonci had drowned? They say he is hidden in the mountain, that two principals became afraid and disclosed his whereabouts." Don Pedro responded: "Perhaps it is true as they say, maybe he got out of the lake somewhere, on some small island, and fled when we could not see him." And he began to weep for fear they would kill him. Whereupon the Marquis said: "Do not weep, go back to your country; tomorrow I shall give you a letter and in three days you shall go." The following day Don Pedro was given a letter, much jerky, and many turquoises for himself, and the Marquis gave him this message: "Tell the Cazonci to come to see me, not to be afraid, and to come to his houses in Mechuacán, that the Spaniards will not harm him." Whereupon Don Pedro took his leave, went to Mechuacán and met with the lords and chiefs to tell them how he had made out and what the Marquis said, and they were very pleased.

Huizizilzi, accompanied by two Spaniards, went for the Cazonci. He went on ahead of them to meet with the Cazonci in Uruapán and to prepare him: "Sire, let us go to the city, for two Spaniards have come for you and I hurried ahead to tell you. Do not be afraid, take heart." To this the Cazonci replied: "Let us go for I do not know where I am nor why I was brought here by those who have treated me with such rancor, for they are not my relatives. As I was leaving those principals told me that they had wanted to kill me. What shall we do?" He told the principals he was going over to Mechuacán but they decided to stay where they were.

Huizizilzi and the Cazonci met the two Spaniards who embraced him and said to him: "Do not be afraid for no one will harm you as we have come for you." The Cazonci replied that he was ready to go. After a long trip they arrived at Pázcuaro [Pátzquaro], where they were welcomed by Don Pedro who greeted him warmly. The Cazonci said to him: "You also are very welcome, brother, how did you get along where you went?" To this Don Pedro answered: "I got along very well and there is no danger. All the Spaniards are happy and the Captain said you should go to Mexico City to see him." The Cazonci agreed: "Well, let us go then, for they brought me this far."

They arrived at the city and guards were assigned to the Cazonci so that he might not disappear again, and they asked him for gold. He called his principals and asked them where they had taken the store of gold. They explained that it had all been taken to Mexico City. Wondering where to find more, the Cazonci said, "Let us show them that which is on Pecandan and Huranden islands." He sent some principals to show it to the Spaniards and they went by night, tied up all that gold in skirts and made forty loads out of it consisting of round shields and miters, and took it all by night to Mexico City. Then Cristóbal de Olí [Olid] asked the Cazonci: "Why do you give so little? Bring us more for you have much gold. What do you want it for?" At this the Cazonci questioned his principals: "Why do they want this gold? These gods must eat it, that could be the only reason they want so much." He ordered them to show the Spaniards more gold and silver which was on Apupato Island. They made sixty loads with it and with an added ten chests from the island of Utuyo they made, in all, three hundred loads of gold and silver. Then the Cazonci asked, "What shall we do now that they have taken it all away from us?" He told the Spaniards that there was no more and explained that: "What was here was not ours but yours who are

82

gods and you are taking it because it is yours." Then Cristóbal de Olí [Olid] agreed: "That is fine, perhaps you speak the truth saying you have no more, but you are to go to Mexico City with these loads." The Cazonci cheerfully accepted: "It is a pleasure, Sires, I shall go." He left for Mexico with all the lords, principals, and chiefs of the province, and they wept along the road. The Cazonci said to Don Pedro and to his brother Huizizilzi: "Maybe you did not tell me the truth when you told me the Spaniards were happy in Mexico City. I managed to escape from the hands of those principals who were trying to kill me and now you want to kill me in Mexico City and you have lied to me." This accusation they denied: "Sire, we have not lied to you, we told you the truth. Wait until you see how happy they will be over your arrival before you accuse us of lying. You shall see that we have told the truth."

The Cazonci went to Cuyacán to meet the Marquis, who received him warmly and was quite pleased that he had come, urged him not to worry and assigned some houses for him to stay in while he was in Cuyacán. The Marquis then called together all the lords of Mexico and told them that the Master of Mechuacán had arrived, that they should be happy, that they should frequently invite him to dinner, and that they should love each other very much. The Marquis also suggested that the Cazonci visit one of Montezuma's sons who was imprisoned for sacrificing many Spaniards and had, as the Cazonci saw, not only been imprisoned but had had his feet burned because of his crime. The Spaniards warned the Cazonci, saying, "Now you have seen the penalty for what he did, be careful lest you meet the same fate.

He spent four days there, and the Mexicans invited him to many fiestas so that the Cazonci was quite happy, and he said: "The Spaniards certainly are generous, I did not believe it." The principals reminded him: "Now, Sire, you have seen that we did not lie to you. We shall not leave you alone. We shall attend to all the orders of the Spaniards and the Nahuatls. Eat and enjoy yourself and do not worry, let us see what they will say and order us to do."

The Marquis called him and said: "Go to your country, I now consider you my brother. Have your people take these anchors. Do no harm to the Spaniards who are in your seigniory for they will not kill you. Give them food and do not require tribute of the villages for I must commend them to the Spaniards." To this the Cazonci agreed, saying that now that he had met the Marquis he would come to visit him many times.

The Cazonci departed with his principals and went joyfully and happily along the road to Mechuacán. When he arrived the Spaniards did him no harm and the Captain told him to enjoy his house and to rest. No one entered his house because the Captain had issued orders that no one should go in except the principals.

At about the time of the feast on the fourteenth of November[6] of this year, the Cazonci sent Don Pedro and 1,600 men with two Spaniards to take the anchors to Zacatula. Along the road they told Don Pedro that he should bedeck himself because he would be seen by the lords of Zacatula. He put many turquoise collars around his neck, delivered the anchors, and returned to Mechuacán with a great quantity of cacao which the Spaniards gave him for Cristóbal de Olí [Olid].

As soon as Don Pedro arrived, the Cazonci called him and said to him: "Now, what shall we do with those presumptuous principals who tried to kill me and from whose hands I barely escaped? They shall not escape from mine. Go and kill them for you are a valiant man." Don Pedro said: "Let it be as you command," and departed taking forty men with him, each one with his club. He passed the lake at dawn and the principal, called Timas, had fled to Capaquaro, stationing spies along the roads. He knew that the Cazonci wanted to have him killed and was awaiting whoever was coming to kill him. Don Pedro and his men arrived and found him seated with turquoise collars around his neck, some gold earrings in his ears, gold bells on his legs, and a clover-leaf wreath on his head, and he was drunk. Don Pedro had a letter in his hand and when the principal saw him, he

---

[6] According to Caso, this is the feast of Caheri Uapanscuaro. See Alfonso Caso, "The Calendar of the Tarascans," *American Antiquity*, Vol. IX (July, 1943), 11–28.

asked: "Where are you going?" Don Pedro answered: "We are going to Colima for we are being sent there by the Spaniards," and he went up close to him and said, "The Cazonci has sentenced you to death," and the principal wanted to know why, what had he done? Don Pedro replied that he did not know, only that he had been sent. Then the principal, called Timas, pleaded: "Why have you come? Are you a brave man? Let us fight it out. What shall we fight with? Bows and arrows or with clubs? You are a very brave man. Where were you in time of danger in the battles where enemies were fighting enemies? Did you kill anyone there? What have you come for? You are quite welcome for my nephew the Cazonci commands it; so be it. I came near killing him myself. Be gone all of you for you are not to kill me. I shall hang myself tomorrow or some other day for you who come to kill me are most miserly and covetous." To all this Don Pedro responded: "Why do you accuse me of stealing? You are the one who robbed the Cazonci of his brothers and killed the Lords. Why are you ashamed to die?"

Timas, the principal, went into his house and told the news to his women. They burned a great deal of fiber and some of his adornments to take with him. He also killed one of the women to take with him and then went back to Don Pedro and the people who had come to kill him. He began to give them drink, and Don Pedro took the wine and threw it on the ground, whereupon the principal asked him why he spilled it and what was wrong with it. Then Don Pedro scolded him: "Did I perchance come to visit only to drink with you? I am hungry, not thirsty." The principal retorted: "Who does not know that you are a brave man and that you conquered Zacatula." Don Pedro answered: "You are being sarcastic with what you say about my conquering Zacatula. Did not the Spaniards conquer it?" At this point Don Pedro seized him and ordered his people to kill him. They beat him about the neck with their clubs and crushed his head. They dragged him through the village before he was dead. His women did not know about his death for they thought the sentence would be executed later. All who had been with him fled in fear.

Some of the Indians who accompanied Don Pedro entered Timas' house and began to take blankets from the women. It was their custom when they killed someone to steal everything in his house. Don Pedro admonished them not to do it and ordered them to return the blankets. They objected, saying that it was the custom but he ordered them returned. The women began to weep for the dead principal, saying: "Oh, Sire, wait for us for we want to go with you." Don Pedro consoled them, saying: "Do not weep or mourn; stay here for we came to kill only him. Stay here with your children and be not afraid."

They buried Timas and his personal effects at a place called Capaquaro, after which Don Pedro returned to the city. He was sent out again to liquidate the other principals who had tried to kill the Cazonci and all their personal effects were confiscated.

The Spaniards set out to conquer Colima, even using women to transport their equipment. They succeeded without losing a single Spaniard but many of the war people from the village, under their Captain Huizizilzi, died in the battle. The Indians from Mechuacán took their gods, dressed in the customary fashion, to the war and at the appropriate time, without objections from either the Spaniards or Huizizilzi, sacrificed many of the Indians of Colima. Later, joined by Cristóbal de Olí [Olid] and reinforcements, they went on to Las Higueras where de Olí [Olid] died.[7] Shortly after this the Spanish made their census and gave assignments to the tribes.

After the census was taken, the Cazonci went to Mexico City, and the Marquis asked whether he or Don Pedro had any children; to this question he replied no, but that there were principals who did have, and the Marquis then ordered the children of the principals brought to Mexico City to be taught the Christian doctrine in San Francisco. At the time of the feast of Mazcoto, on the seventh of June, fifteen boys, encouraged by the Cazonci to learn, were sent there for a year.

---

[7] Our priest-interpreter apparently was not too well informed on current events. Olid was beheaded by the order of Gil González and Francisco de las Casas in the market place of Naco (Honduras).

Not long afterward, a chapter of the Padres de San Francisco was established in Guaxacinco and an old priest named Fr. Mindechues, along with other priests, were sent to be guardians to the city of Mechuacán. The Indians were quite pleased with Fr. Mindechues. The first religious house had been established in Mechuacán some twelve years earlier, at which time they began to preach to the people and to try to stop their drunken sprees, but the Indians were very stubborn and the religious almost gave them up as hopeless on several occasions. Later, more religious came from San Francisco and established themselves in Ucario and Cinapaquaro, and from there they went about setting up houses. As the good Lord knows, results were produced in these people, notwithstanding their stubbornness. They gave up their drunkenness, their idolatry and pagan ceremonies, and they were all baptized. They improve slowly each day and will continue to get better with the help of our Lord.

28. THE INDIANS' IMPRESSIONS OF THE SPANIARDS

When the Indians first saw the Spaniards, they marveled at such strange people who did not eat the same kind of food or get drunk as the Indians did. They called the Spanish Tucupacha, which means gods, and Teparacha, which means big men and is also used to mean gods, and Acacecha, meaning people who wear caps and hats. As time passed they began to call them Christians and to believe that they had come from heaven. They were sure that the Spaniards' clothes were the skins of men such as the Indians themselves used on feast occasions. Some called the horses deer, others *tuycen*, which were something like horses which the Indians made from pigweed bread for use in the feast of *Cuingo* and to which they fastened manes of false hair. The Indians who first saw the horses told the Cazonci that the horses talked, that when the Spaniards were on horseback they told the horses where they were to go as they pulled on the reins. They also said that Mother Cueravaperi had given them the wheat, seeds, and wine

87

they brought when they came to the land. When they saw the religious so poorly dressed, wearing their crowns and not wanting either gold or silver, they were astonished. Since the priests had no women, the Indians thought they were priests of a god who had come to the land and called them Curitiecha as they did their own priests who wore fiber wreaths on their heads and some false temples. They were amazed that the priests did not dress as the other Spaniards, and they said how fortunate are these who want nothing.

As time went by some of their priests and witches made the Indians believe that the religious were dead men, that the habits they wore were shrouds, that, in their houses at night they shed their forms, become skeletons, go to the Inferno where they have their women, and return by morning. This tale lasted a long time, until they began to understand more. The witches also said that the Spaniards did not die, that they were immortal, that the baptismal water which was sprinkled on their heads was blood, and that the Spaniards split open the heads of their children. For these reasons they dared not baptize their children for they did not want them to die. The Indians called the crosses Holy Mary, because they did not know the doctrine and they thought the crosses were gods like those they had.

When they were told that they were to go to heaven, they did not believe it, saying that they had never seen anyone go. They would not believe anything the religious told them nor did they trust them. They said the Spaniards were all as one and they were sure that the Monks had been born with their habits on and had never been children. These beliefs also were long lived and even now they still do not believe that the Monks had mothers. When the religious said mass, the Indians thought that they could see the present and the future by looking in the holy water. They did not trust those witches [Catholic priests] and would not tell the truth in confession for fear they would be killed. Should an Indian go to confession, all the others would spy on him to see how he did it, and the more so if it were a woman. Afterward they wanted to know what the priest had asked and said, and they told everyone all about it.

The Castilian women were called *Cuchahecha* which means ladies and goddesses. They thought that the letters which they were sent to deliver could talk so they dared not lie at any time. They marveled at every new thing they saw, for they are greatly interested in novelties. They called horseshoes "coats of mail" and "iron shoes" for horses. In Taxcala [Tlaxcala] they brought rations of chickens for the horses as well as for the Spaniards. They were astonished to hear what the priests preached to them and called them witches who knew everything they did at home, or they knew it because somebody told on them, or because they had confessed to them.

29. THE IMPRISONMENT OF THE CAZONCI

After the Spaniards came to this province the Cazonci ruled the city of Mechuacán a few more years, and the lords of the tribes still remembered that he was their Master and served him secretly. The Marquis sent a well-to-do man named Caycido to the city to take charge of the Indians. He brought with him an interpreter, a good Spanish translator they say, who mistreated the Indians. While the Cazonci was away in Pázcuaro [Pátzquaro] the principals got drunk, took their bows and arrows, and killed the interpreter. The officers of Justice learned about it later and sent the Bachelor[8] Ortega from Mexico City to administer justice. The principals who had been accomplices in the death of the youthful interpreter were sentenced to death by clubbing.

When the religious came from San Francisco, the Cazonci was baptized and given the name Don Francisco. He then gave two sons to be educated by the religious.

In Xicalán, a village of Uruapán, the Spaniards mistreated the Indians and they killed another Spaniard. The Bachelor

---

[8] Bachiller. This does not refer to a single man but to what could be called a high school graduate. Baccalaureate degree.

Ortega enslaved many of them and the village was almost entirely depopulated. More Spaniards were killed in other villages. The Spaniards said it was by order of the Cazonci, but he denied any connection with the deaths and said they should kill the Indians who were responsible.

For these reasons and because the Indians of the villages still served him, the Spaniards became angry with the Cazonci and complained that he issued orders to kill the Spaniards, that he would dance dressed in the skins of the Spaniards, that he robbed the villages, that he had sent war people against the Spaniards, and that he had called up the warriors from a village called Cuynao, which he kept at hand to kill the Spaniards. At this time Nuño de Guzmán came from Panunto [Panuco] to be President, and soon afterward the Cazonci died and was buried. The new governor of the province was Don Pedro, who saw all this happen and described it later.

Before Nuño de Guzmán came to Mexico as president, however, the Marquis sent Andrés de Tapia to the Cazonci with the information that another Master, who was to be governor, was coming to the land and that his headquarters would be in Mexico City. This was to be made known to the Cazonci, along with instructions that if he were asked for gold and silver he should not deliver it to Guzmán but send all of his treasure to the Marquis. He was not to hide or keep any, and if Nuño de Guzmán should ask for it, he should tell him that it all went to the Marquis for shipment to the Emperor.

After hearing this the Cazonci agreed and said that there was a little gold and silver left over from what they had taken and told him to take it. "Why do we want it? It belongs to the Emperor." Twice they brought gold and silver in quantity which Tapia took to the Marquis.

Nuño de Guzmán arrived in Mexico City and immediately sent for the Cazonci. Godoy,[9] now the chief constable in this city,

---

[9] This was Antonio de Godoy, a former muleteer sent to Michoacán by Nuño Beltrán de Guzmán and the *Audiencia* as a *justicia* or chief official of the civil government.

arrested the Cazonci, Don Pedro, and another lord called Tareca de Xenoanto, from the village of Oliber, saying that he was an important principal and a relative of the Cazonci. Many others were also arrested. Godoy took them all to the village of Amixco telling them not to worry, that they were being called by President Nuño de Guzmán. The Cazonci was agreeable, refused to be worried and insisted that the Spanish had information for him. Godoy encouraged them with the thought that they would soon return and that Guzmán would be quite pleased with the Cazonci's visit.

They arrived in Mexico City and Nuño de Guzmán was quite pleased with the Cazonci and Don Pedro, and he extended a welcome to them, explaining that he had called them and that they would talk the next day; in the meantime they were to enjoy themselves. The next morning Nuño de Guzmán sent for them and when they came before him, he asked: "How is it that you come empty-handed? What have you brought me? What do you mean? Did you not know that I had come?" To this they replied: "Sire, we brought nothing because we left in a hurry." Then Nuño de Guzmán asked: "Who among you will return to Mechuacán? Have you heard of a village called Tehuculuacan and another called Avatlan populated only by women?" They replied that they had not heard of it, and Nuño de Guzmán asked if their ancestors had not told them about it, but they said no, they had been told nothing. Nuño de Guzmán then issued instructions: "We must go to that land. Make many cotton jackets, many arrows and round shields, twenty bows with their copper tips, many sandals, and war coats. Commend it all to one among you to superintend the work." The Cazonci said to him: "Let my brother go." Nuño de Guzmán agreed and told the Cazonci: "You stay here and wait for me; we shall go together, for I have to go to war. Send for the gold you have there in Mechuacán." The Cazonci objected to this: "Sire, I have no gold now, Tapia brought it all." Nuño de Guzmán asked why he gave it to him, and the Cazonci said: "Because they asked us for it as you do now." Nuño de Guzmán wondered why he believed Tapia. The

THE CHRONICLES OF MICHOACÁN

Cazonci explained: "Don Pedro will go too and see about looking for any gold that may have remained and bring it to you."
Nuño de Guzmán answered: "Meanwhile, you are to stay here
and a Christian will stay and guard you. Have no worry, why
should you not be at home here as much as in your own house?"
The Cazonci objected: "It would be better if I went somewhere
else to stay." And Guzmán countered: "I do not want you to; you
are better off here in my house. If you want to go somewhere, take
a walk along that terrace." To this the Cazonci replied: "All
right. Let it be as you say." A Spaniard locked him in a room,
and Don Pedro was sent on his way: "Go, brother, back to our
land. This is very important, he does not want to deal with us
gently and slowly. Let us look for some gold which we may give
him. While there, ask who has gold and send it here so we may
give it to him." Then the Cazonci added: "When you get there,
talk about it among yourselves." In saying goodby to the Cazonci,
Don Pedro said: "Sire, peace be with you, take courage, as it is
for us to suffer and that we be treated this way." The Cazonci
agreed: "So shall it be, may providence go with you."

Don Pedro went to Mechuacán and reported what was happening to the principals, and everyone began to weep. They
searched for gold and silver and brought in six hundred round
gold shields and as many more of silver.

One of Guzmán's interpreters, called Pilar, kept threatening
the Cazonci because he was not bringing the gold fast enough
and demanding, when it arrived, that it should be shown to him
first. When all that gold and silver arrived in Mexico City, they
showed it to Pilar first. Making certain that Guzmán did not
know about it, he took two hundred of those round shields, one
hundred gold ones, and one hundred of silver and said to the principals: "I shall speak in behalf of the Cazonci, have no fear."
They showed the rest of the gold to Nuño de Guzmán who asked:
"Why do you bring so little? You are holding back, send for
more." It was night when they delivered the gold to Guzmán,
and he told them to put it in his room.

No principal was allowed to see the Cazonci, and only Abalos was there with him as a Nahuatl interpreter, and the Cazonci never went out. The Spanish jailer on guard would ask the Cazonci for gold, and he agreed to give it to him in exchange for his freedom. Each time that he was to get out he would give the jailer two cupfuls of gold and two of silver, but the Cazonci never got farther than the door to speak to his principals when the guard would make him go back in. The Cazonci sent again for gold and silver and said to the principals: "Go again to my brother Don Pedro and ask him what I must do for I am not a man to be held in this fashion. Tell him to bring more gold."

The messengers went to Mechuacán and reported the Cazonci's predicament, and the principals said: "What shall we do? Where would we have it? Let us look for it everywhere," and they searched and found four hundred round shields of gold and as many of silver. They took it to Mexico City and showed it to the interpreter, Pilar, according to his instructions. He took exactly one hundred round shields of gold and the same number of silver. Then the principals said to him: "Sire, what shall we do? Since you take all of this, why do you not speak in our behalf? We could take our Master back to his house where he ought to go, tell it to Nuño de Guzmán." The interpreter agreed to do so with assurances for their safety.

They showed the rest of the gold and silver to Nuño de Guzmán, who asked the Cazonci why he furnished so little and whether he was not ashamed to present such a small quantity to the President. The Cazonci objected that he did not know where there was any more. Guzmán needled him, saying he was not much of a Master if he did not supply larger quantities and added the threat that if it was not brought, he would be treated as he deserved for he was a villain and harassed the Christians. "Knowing how I have treated you, why do you want the gold? Bring it all, for the Christians are angry with you and say that you steal tribute from and rob the villages. They want to kill you because of the trouble you cause them. I do not believe them. Why do you not believe what I tell you, do you want to die?" The Cazonci rejoined: "I am pleased to die." And Guzmán took him up: "All

93

right. Put him back inside there for he wants to die and let him not get out. Are you perchance laughing at what I tell you? Why? I have not mistreated you." They put the Cazonci back in the room where he had been and he began to weep, saying: "What shall we do? Go again to my brother Don Pedro; let him request the gold that is in Uruapa, which my Grandfather offered to the gods; also that which is at Zacapu, and in the villages of Naranjan, Cumachen, and Vanique, because that is mine and I am not taking it away from the chiefs. Maybe the chiefs of the villages will not sympathize with my misery and will refuse to give it, knowing that they say that I rob the villages for the Spaniards and they have complained to Guzmán."

The messengers arrived in Mechuacán and went through these villages and delivered the Cazonci's message to the chiefs who said: "Why should we not really give it to him for whatever is here is his," and they brought it all to Mechuacán: two hundred round shields of gold, two hundred of silver, some gold lunettes, earrings and bracelets, and they took it all to Mexico City. Again, the interpreter, Pilar, as was his custom, secretly took out a hundred of those jewels, including gold bracelets, lunettes and earrings without Guzmán's knowledge. The rest was taken to Guzmán, who threw it on the floor and stamped it peevishly. It was night when the delivery was made. The Cazonci was a prisoner in Mexico City for nine moons, each moon being twenty days by the Indian reckoning.

30. THE CONQUEST OF XALIXCO

Messengers arrived in the city, saying that Nuño de Guzmán was coming with soldiers to conquer Xalixco [Jalisco]. Before he left, the Indians saw a large comet in the sky which they took to be an augury of impending calamity.

Guzmán arrived in Mechuacán with all his people, and the four hundred cotton jackets he had ordered were ready with four hundred bows and arrows with metal tips[10] and many others

10 These figures of supplies "ordered" do not agree with other figures given in

made of copper. The Indians had also gathered four thousand loads of corn and countless chickens.

Guzmán and his men received the lords who were escorting the Cazonci, and Guzmán said to him: "Now you have come to your house where you want to be. Shall we stay together in my lodgings or do you want to go to your house?" The Cazonci replied: "I should like to go to my house for a while and see my children." Guzmán objected: "Why would you go there? You are not in your land and these houses are not yours. Let your children and your wife come here, for no Spaniard will molest you. They will cover a bed with a canopy for you and you shall stay here." To this the Cazonci answered: "So be it. Who am I to gainsay your word; it shall be as you wish." Then the Cazonci issued instructions to his servants: "Go tell the old men and my women that they will not see me again, that the old men shall console the women, that I am not well in the chest, that I think I am about to die, that they should look after my children and not abandon them; tell them how I am here and to make ready to furnish food for the Spaniards so that they will not blame me if something is amiss, and that the principals are in charge of the people for whatever need may arise."

The following day they took the cotton jackets and all the things he had ordered to Guzmán. He was angry and asked: "Why do you bring so few?" And the Cazonci reminded him: "You have taken them all to Aninao." Guzmán retorted: "And is that why you bring so few?" He drew his sword and struck Don Pedro several broadside blows across the shoulders and then placed the Cazonci and Don Pedro in chains. He then ordered the Cazonci to take Don Pedro's houses and sent the interpreters, Pilar and Godoy, to frighten them into telling about the treasure they had, and why they had delivered it by night. They began to question him: "Is it true that 8,000 men went to make war on

the *Relación* or with other sources that discuss the subject. The instructions given earlier in the *Relación* (p. 91) state ". . . many arrows and round shields, twenty bows with their copper tips . . . ." It is not clear whether this is an exaggeration on the part of the priest-interpreter or his informant.

Aninao and that they took with them the war jackets and arms? Tell the truth. What is that country like? You can tell us the truth for we are not going there." Don Pedro and the Cazonci answered saying: "We do not know about it." Then the Spaniards asked them: "How is it that you and those of Aninao are not friends and you do not get along with them?" They replied that they did not know that country.

At this point the Spaniards asked the Cazonci: "How is it that one of your rank finds himself in this situation? Are you not ashamed of your condition? When will you show Guzmán the treasure you have? He is very angry and he has prepared a brazier full of coals" (making signs indicating the burning of the feet). The Cazonci replied: "Where should I obtain more gold?" The Spaniards rejoined: "Since you want to die . . . ." and they began to torture them and they hung them up. There was also one of the Nahuatl lords called Juan de Ortega, and they began to torture him in his private parts with a slender branch.

Father Fray Martin, who was the religious guardian in this city, learned what was happening from some boys who reported it to him. He took a crucifix and went to the house where the Spaniards were torturing Don Pedro and the Cazonci. The priest asked why they were being treated in this fashion and the Spaniards replied: "They will not tell us the road we have asked them about." The priest turned and asked Don Pedro and the Cazonci: "Do you know the country?" They replied: "We do not know and how can we tell what we do not know?" The priest turned back to them: "Why do you treat them this way since they do not know the road?" Their answer was: "We are doing them no harm." After admonishing them, the priest returned to the monastery, and the Spaniards spoke to the Cazonci and Don Pedro: "Let us go where Nuño de Guzmán is." They were carried bodily to Guzmán's lodgings while Abalos and Don Alonso were being arrested.

Guzmán was very angry and said: "Stupid, who told the priest? I cannot take you to war even though the priest be on your trail." Guzmán wanted to depart and asked the Cazonci for eight thousand men, saying: "Send orders to all the villages; if you do not produce as many as I say, you shall pay." The Cazonci replied: "Sire, it is you who should send the orders to all the villages for they are yours." And Guzmán answered: "You are the one who must send orders—are you not the Master?" Then the Cazonci sent his principals to all the villages. And Guzmán added, "Have the gold brought from the villages." The Cazonci explained: "They will refuse to bring it even if I send for it, so why should I send for it?" Then Guzmán asked: "If they should not have any gold, you yourself shall give the chiefs a beating so they will bring me some."

Eight thousand men were gathered from the villages, counted and presented to Guzmán, who accepted them as sufficient in number. He ordered that they take care to prevent any from escaping for their duty was only to accompany him to his destination and return. He was to depart three days later. The Spaniards began to divide the eight thousand men who had been supplied among themselves, each one trying to get the most without counting them, and in the confusion many ran away. The lords were made prisoners and the Cazonci, in chains, was carried in a hammock.

All the Spaniards departed, going to one of the rivers of the Chichimecas, twelve leagues from the city, where they made camp on a river bank. By this time the Cazonci had become discolored; he would not eat anything, and his face had turned nearly black. The principals showed him their loads to prove that they had brought them all and that they had not left any of the *Tamemes* along the way. He indicated his approval and said: "Take good care of them." They took them to the lodgings of Nuño de Guzmán's manager. The Spanish also put the Nahuatls in chains and handcuffed Abalos for two days.

Several Spaniards took the Cazonci aside, apart from the rest, to a weed patch on the river bank and began to talk and question him: "Show us the skins of Christians that you have. If you do not have them brought here we will have to kill you. If you have them brought here, you shall go to your house and you shall be

Master as indeed you are. You shall also tell us the truth, whether eight thousand men went to Aninao and took the war jackets, bows, and arrows. And, is it true that you have made pits there for the horses to fall into?" The Cazonci answered, saying that none of that was true, and the Spaniards told him again to tell the truth. They tied his hands, poured water in his nose, and began questioning him about gold, and they asked him: "Is it true that you have a large idol made of gold?" To which he replied that he did not and they asked again: "Do you mean to tell us you have no more gold?" To which the Cazonci replied: "I shall ask to see if there is any more." The Spaniards said that wherever the gold was they would go and get it. The Cazonci then explained: "I do not know but there may be a little in Pázcuaro [Pátzquaro]." The Indians of Pázcuaro [Pátzquaro] delivered four hundred lunettes and round shields made of gold and eighty small golden tongs to the Cazonci. He told them not to give Guzmán more than two hundred of them and ordered the Indians to take the rest back. Guzmán became very angry when he saw such a small delivery.

The Spanish also tortured Don Pedro, who bore the marks of the cords on his arms until his death, and they also tortured Don Alonso and Abalos, demanding the golden idol and jewels. These men steadfastly maintained that they knew nothing about gold or a golden idol, but the Spaniards lied to them, saying: "The Cazonci has told the truth about everything and three days from now he will return to his house. If you, too, tell the truth you also shall go to your houses. Tell us how much gold the Cazonci has." In answer, they explained: "We have not seen it ourselves nor do we know anything about this matter." The Spaniards insisted: "They say he has a great amount of gold." And they replied: "Perhaps he does indeed, we have never seen him with it." The Spaniards were adamant: "Of course he has gold and he has told you not to tell about it." But they denied ever having seen it. Guzmán, the constables, and a hunchbacked Nahuatl interpreter left off questioning these two and ordered the old men and the old priests brought in. Guzmán asked them about the gold and they answered: "We are old men, what can we say? How can we know anything about this? We are as nothing and useless." They were questioned no further but Guzmán then issued the sentence that the Cazonci be tied to the tail of a horse, dragged alive, and burned.

They tied him on a mat hitched to the tail of a horse which a Spaniard was riding, preceded by a crier who shouted as he went: "People, look! This stupid fool tried to kill us. He has been tried and this sentence was handed down against him: that he be dragged alive. Look at him, see the example. Look, you low people for you are all stupid." After he had been dragged for a time, they untied him from the mat, for he still had life in him, and they secured him to a post. The Spaniards commanded him to tell whether he had accomplices in this foul deed and how many, saying that he alone was to die. The Cazonci replied: "What do I have to tell you? I know nothing." They garroted and strangled him until he was dead.

The Spaniards then piled wood around his body and burned it, and Guzmán had his servants gather up the ashes and throw them in the river. The fear inspired in his people by his frightful death made them flee. A few of his servants still had some of his ashes and buried them in two places, in Pázcuaro [Pátzquaro] and somewhere else. With those that were buried in Pázcuaro [Pátzquaro], they also interred a round gold shield, lip-rings, earrings, all the fingernails and hair that had been clipped since he was a child, his war coats, and little baby shirts, because this is the custom among them. It is also said that somewhere else they buried some of those ashes and that they killed a woman to be buried with him. The location of this burial spot is unknown.

After the death of the Cazonci, they put the people in chains because they were trying to run away. Don Pedro barely escaped being sentenced to death also, but it was said that the accountant Albornoz wrote a letter to Nuño de Guzmán, admonishing him that Mechuacán would be lost if he killed Don Pedro.

Guzmán departed from Xalixco, taking the army, and went to the village of Aninao, where it was said that the Cazonci had held the eight thousand men. They examined the site of the village and took a turn around it. Guzmán and the Spaniards agreed that it was true that the Cazonci had gathered war people here. They arrested the lords, put them in chains, and took away from all the *Tameme* people their bows and arrows and kept them. Early in the morning all the people of Aninao fled, and not a soul was to be found in the village. Guzmán spoke to the lords of Mechuacán: "Why will you not tell the truth? Why did you send a message telling them to make their escape? Find the bravest men among you and go look for the Master of the village." But they objected, saying: "Where are we to go for we know not the land." Guzmán told them: "Go, you know each other."

Twenty principals departed, going to the village to which all the people of Aninao had fled. But the people of Aninao had all been sacrificed there, and the principals returned to report this news to Guzmán, who departed immediately for the village with his army. Upon seeing the bodies of those who had been sacrificed, he destroyed the entire village. He was now convinced that the Cazonci had not stationed war people there, nor did the Spaniards find the pits [to trap the horses] which they had been told about.

Guzmán went on with his army to another village called Acuycio and then continued conquering village after village. Later he found a Nahuatl, who spoke the language of Mechuacán, and became concerned that the presence of the man meant that the war people were assembled. Guzmán immediately had Don Pedro, who as a prisoner was traveling at the rear of the column, brought to him. Don Pedro found out from the Nahuatl that there were no war people. Guzmán took Don Pedro with him to Xalixco and held him prisoner there along with Don Alonso and other principals. Brother Jacobo de Testera and Brother Francisco de Bolonia, religious from San Francisco, visited the land of Xalixco and begged Guzmán to permit the lords to return to Mechuacán. Subsequently they returned and Don Pedro became governor of the city.

31. CONCERNING THE GENERAL ADMINISTRATION OF JUSTICE[11]

There was a feast called Yzquataconscuaro[12] which means Feast of the Arrows. The day after the feast court was held to try offenders who had been rebellious or disobedient, and all were imprisoned in a large jail with a jailer appointed to guard them. There were those who four times had failed to bring wood for the fires when the Cazonci had issued a general order throughout the province to gather wood. There were also enemy spies, those who had not gone to war and those who had returned without leave, wrongdoers, doctors who had let someone die, bad women, sorcerers, vagabonds, those who had neglected the Cazonci's seed-beds, the produce of which was destined for the wars, those who damaged the maguey, and victims of diseases of the genital organs. All these were residents of the city and of all the other villages. Included also were disobedient slaves who refused to serve their Masters and the slaves who were not sacrificed in the feasts. All were imprisoned in one big jail and the prisoners were called *vazcata*. If they had committed four offenses they were sacrificed. Offenders were brought to justice every day, but on this particular day they held one general court session.

Each day for twenty days before the feast, court was held and justice meted out until the twenty days had passed. The husband who caught his wife with another man would slit the ears of both as a public sign that they were taken in adultery. He also

[11] Nicolas León, as noted in the Foreword (p. VII), maintains that the original *Relación* is lost and that the Escorial manuscript C–IV–5 is a copy. The physical makeup as well as textual relationships throughout C–IV–5 and the Peter Force copy give evidence to support León. Note, for example, the opening sentence on page one of this translation, "it has been told, *in the first part*, . . ." (italics ours). It is quite obvious that either something is missing or the "chapter" entitled "Concerning their government" is out of place, or both. At this point the manuscript is broken, and someone—we do not know whether it was the original writer or the one who made the copy—labeled all material from this "chapter" to the end of the volume as Part II. Since we have no Part I, we have, for consistency, deleted the heading Part II from the manuscript.

[12] Caso, in his "Calendar of the Tarascans," pp. 16, 18–20, 24, 28, has an interesting analysis of this feast, concluding that it was the feast of Uazcuata Conscuaro and that it came on June 27.

took away their blankets and then he appeared in court to state his complaint, showing the blankets to the person in charge of administering justice. This evidence was held to be sufficient proof of guilt.

If the defendant were a sorcerer, evidence would consist of an account of those whom he had bewitched or killed. If he had killed someone, a relative cut a finger off the hand of the dead person and took it, wrapped in cotton, to substantiate his complaint. If the offender had pulled up somebody's green corn, some of the corn stalks were brought in as evidence. The Cazonci's sorcerers were supposed to be able to see coming and past events in a saucer of water or in a mirror. Thus, if in this fashion they saw thieves fleeing, the sorcerer's statement was valid evidence and the thieves were brought with all the others to court, where justice was administered by the chief priest as the representative of the Cazonci.

When this day of justice arrived, the chief priest, called Petamiti, would dress appropriately and according to custom. He would put on a shirt called *ucatatataze quequenezza*, hang some miniature golden tweezers around his neck, place a wreath of fiber and plumage on his head in a womanlike braid of hair, a gourd set with turquoise on his back, and a staff or spear on his shoulder. Dressed in this fashion, the chief priest would go to the Cazonci's patio with many people from the city and the villages of the province. He would be accompanied by the governor representing the Cazonci and would take his seat on the small chair which they use. All those who were appointed by the Cazonci, his majordomos, who were in charge of the seedbeds or corn, beans, peppers and other seeds, the captain-general of war, which position was sometimes filled by his governor called Angatacuri, the chiefs, and all those who wanted to make complaints were also present. All the delinquents were brought to the patio, some with their hands tied behind them, some with canes tied to their necks. There was a very large number of people in the patio with their clubs and the jailer was also present. The chief priest, called Petamiti, sat on his low chair listening to the cases of the accused from morning until midday. He would consider whether the accusation brought against each prisoner was true and if he found him guilty of only two or three past offenses, he pardoned him and turned him over to his relatives, but if it was the fourth time, he condemned him to death. In this fashion he heard cases during the twenty days until the day of the feast when he and another priest held a general court and administered justice. If something of great importance came up it was remitted to the Cazonci with their report.

When the day of the feast arrived and all the offenders were gathered in the patio with all the chiefs and principals the chief priest would stand up. Taking his staff or spear he would tell the people the entire history of their ancestors, how they came to the province and the wars they fought in the service of their gods. The narration lasted until nightfall and neither he nor any of those who were in the patio either ate or drank. This history is here recounted in two chapters with the translation from their language of some of the most appropriate statements. The chief priest knew this history and sent other lesser priests throughout the province to tell it in the villages, and the chiefs felt obligated to give blankets to these visiting priests. When the chief priest had finished recounting the history, justice was administered to all the remaining offenders. (See Plate 19.)

32. THE HISTORY OF THE CHICHIMECAS

The chief priest related the following story. You of the lineage of the God Curicaveri who have come here and who call yourselves Eneani and Cacapuhereti, and the kings called Vanacace, all of you who have this family name have gathered here as one. Our god, Tiripenie, Curicaveri wants to complain of you to his own discredit. He began his seigniory when he arrived at the mountain near the village of Zacapo Lacanendan, and after spending some time there, the lords called Zizambanacha learned of his arrival. They were lords in a village called Naranjan near this city. [It should be understood that the narrator always attributed the wars and accomplishment of deeds to his God Curicaveri telling no more about the lords. Most of the time he names the lords who spoke and acted but does not name the people nor the places where they established their centers and living quarters.] What may be deducted from his history is that the ancestors of the Cazonci, in the end, came to conquer this land and were Masters of it. They extended their seigniory and conquered the province which was first inhabited by Mexican people, *Quatatos*, who spoke the same language, for it seems that other tribes had been here earlier. Each village had its chief, its people, and its own gods. As they conquered the territory, they made it all into a kingdom at the time of the great-grand-father of the next-to-last Cazonci who was Master of Mechuacán, as will be told elsewhere.

The history is as follows: The lord of the village of Naranjan, called Ziranzirancamaro, knew that Hireticátame had arrived at the above mentioned mountain and that he had brought Curi-caveri, his god in Virinquarampejo, to the village, Hireticátame ordered the lord of Naranjan to gather wood for Curicaveri's fireplaces. All day and through the night the priests put incense in the braziers or stone basins, performed the war ceremony, and went to the mountain to perform ceremonies before the gods.

Talking to his people, the lord of the village said: "Mark you that Curicaveri was engendered on high with great power and is to conquer the land. Here we have a sister for the god, take her to him and give her not to Hireticátame, but to Curicaveri and to him we will say what we said to Hireticátame. She shall make blankets for Curicaveri to keep him warm, and corn soup, and food to be offered to Curicaveri and to Hireticátame. She shall bring in wood from the mountain for the fireplaces, she shall carry his sash, his mat which he puts under his back, and the ax with which he cuts wood, because she will always be with the gods of the mountains called *Angamucuracha*. She shall make hunting arrows and take his bow when he returns from the hunt. After she has made blankets and offerings for Curicaveri, she shall prepare meals and make blankets for her husband, Tica-

tame, so that he may sleep beside Curicaveri, and they will protect him against the cold. After making the offerings she shall
prepare food for him so that he shall have the strength to reach
the gods of the mountains called *Angamucuracha.* This I shall
tell to Lord Hireticátame because Curicaveri is to conquer the
land."

The messengers went their way and took the woman to
Ticatame who asked them: "For what purpose do you come,
brothers?" They replied to him: "Your brothers, called Zizan-
banecha, send us to bring you this woman who is their sister."
They told him everything that had been said, and he answered:
"All this that my brothers say is very good, you are welcome."
They brought the woman forward and he spoke to them. "My
brothers talk very generously, as is shown by the gift of this
woman whom you have brought and what you have come to tell
me. What you say is not for me but for Curicaveri who is here
and to whom you have said all this. For him she is to make
blankets and offerings. Afterward she shall make them for me to
place at his side and ward off the cold; and food so that I may
have the strength to go to the gods of the mountains called Angamucuracha, as you say. Be seated and food shall be served."
While they were eating, the woman was sent to her room, and
after having eaten, the messengers asked to be excused, saying:
"Sire, we have finished eating, give us leave for we want to return." Ticatame answered, asking them to wait for the blankets
that were to be brought out, and he took leave of them. As they
departed there was one thing he wanted to tell them: "Tell your
Masters, as they already know, that as I and my people go into
the mountains to gather wood for the temples and I make arrows,
I go to the fields to give food to the Sun and to the celestial gods
and those of the Four Quarters of the world; also to Mother
Cueravaperi with the deer which we shoot. I make the salve to
the gods with wine after which we drink in his name. It happens
sometimes that we shoot deer late in the afternoon and we follow them, but when night comes, we leave off and tie up high on
the trees some little markers so as not to lose the trail. Be careful

that you do not take the deer that I have shot because I do not take them for myself, rather in order to give food to the gods. All of you get together and advise one another of this that I tell you. Be sure not to carry them off because this would cause grudges between us and we would quarrel. Do not go near them, but when you come upon one of these wounded deer cover them with branches. Well and good if you eat the meat and make salve to the gods, but do not carry off the skins. Now go in peace."

Time passed and Tiricatame [Ticatame], who lived in the mountain with that woman, had a son called Sicuirancha. Ticatame went hunting one day and shot a deer on the mountain which is called Urinquarapejo, but his aim was bad and the deer was only wounded. He followed it and when night came, he tied some plants together as a marker and returned home. He spent that night in vigil in the houses of the chief priests, and the next morning he dressed to continue the search for his wounded deer. He followed the tracks but did not find it for it had gone into a *quierequaro* seedbed to die, a place near Zacapo. It was the time of the feast of Vapamquaro, the twenty-fifth of October, and women came to gather ears of corn for the feast. They came upon the dead deer in the seedbed. When they saw it, they went back to their house and called others, telling them that a dead deer was in the seedbed. It was reported to the chief, called Zimzamban, and his entire household turned out to seize the deer and take it into his house.

As Hireticátame [Ticatame] was following the track of the deer, he saw some birds, like vultures, hovering on the wing around the place where his deer had been. Then he came upon the bloody spot where the deer had fallen and exclaimed: "Woe is me for they have taken my deer; here it fell, from here they carried it off." He followed the signs, which indicated where they had taken the deer, and suddenly he came upon them butchering it. They did not know how to butcher, for they were cutting the skin into pieces, and approaching them he asked: "What have you done, brothers-in-law? Why have you taken my deer for I warned you not to touch the deer that my people and I have shot.

I would not care should you eat the meat which was not much; but I am concerned about the skin for you have ruined it so that it is no longer a skin nor will it serve to make blankets. We soften the skin and make blankets to wrap around our God Curicaveri."

The other men answered: "What do you mean, sir? We have our bows and arrows and take them with us to kill deer." Hireti-cátame [Ticatame] rejoined: "That is beside the point. Here are my arrows which I made." He went to the deer, pulled an arrow out of its body and said, "Look at this arrow which was in the body, I made it." On hearing this the others became angry, shoved him and knocked him to the ground. Ticatame [Hireti-cátame], like the eagle Vacusecha, was angered, pulled an arrow from his quiver, raised his bow and shot at one of them, a brother-in-law, striking his back. After shooting at another, he returned home where his wife greeted him and welcomed him: "Welcome, Sire, father of Sicuirancha," and he returned her greeting, then said to her: "Take your personal effects and go home to your brothers and sisters, but leave my son Sicuirancha for I must take him with me. I want to move to a place called Zichaxuquero and I shall take Curicaveri there. Go to your house." His wife objected and said: "What are you saying, Sire? Why must I go?" Ticatame explained: "You must go because I have shot your brothers," and she demanded: "What are you saying? Why did you shoot them? What did they do to you?" He retorted: "What would they do to me? All they did was take my deer when I had warned them not to touch any deer I had shot. Go up into the granary and get Curicaveri for I want to take him with me." His wife objected: "Sire, I do not want to go to my brothers and sisters until my son Sicuirancha becomes a man lest he shoot me and mine; I must go with you." Ticatame agreed, saying: "You are right, come, let us go," and getting out the ark housing Curicaveri he bundled him up, put him on his back, his wife took their son on her back, and in this manner they departed. They went down the mountain, and coming to a place called Queregro, his wife said to him: "Sire, you have Curicaveri to favor and help you, but what shall become of me? In my house there is a god called

Vazoriquare. Will you wait here a little, while I go up toward the mountain and at least get one of my god's blankets to put in the chest and have to keep?" Ticatame was agreeable and said: "Be it as you say because the god you mention is very generous and gives food to men." The woman departed, went up a ridge and came to the place where the god was. She not only took a blanket, as she had said, but also she took the idol wrapped in the blanket and brought it back where Ticatame was. He welcomed her back and said: "You are welcome, mother of Sicuirancha. Did you bring back the blanket you went for?" She returned his greeting and said: "Yes, I also brought the God Vazoriquare." Ticatame answered: "It is good, he is very handsome, let them be together here, he and Curicaveri," and he put him in the little chest with Curicaveri and thus they remained together. They arrived at their destination, a place called Zichaxuquero, where they made their houses and a temple which today is tumbled down.

33. THE DEATH OF TICATAME

A few days after Sicuirancha, son of Ticatame, had come of age, his father went to Zichaxuquero, a place some three leagues from the city of Mechuacán. His brothers-in-law, remembering the injury received at his hands, took a gold neckband and some green feathers to Oresta, lord of Cumachen, for him to put on their god called Turesupeme. They asked for help against Ticatame and there formed a squadron by joining with the people from Cumachen. At dawn they were all concealed beside a watering place which is not far from the village. They placed a declaration-of-war sign, a timber completely covered with feathers, by the water so that Ticatame's men would see it and come out to fight. Very early in the morning, the wife of Ticatame went for a pitcher of water. The men in ambush, who were her brothers, greeted her in her own language. They asked her: "Are you perchance the mother of Sicuirancha?" She replied: "I am, who are you that you ask?" And they explained: "We are your brothers. What has become of Ticatame your husband?" She answered that he was at home and wanted to know why they asked. They replied: "That is good. We came to match ourselves with him because he shot our brothers." When the woman heard that she began to weep loudly, threw away the pitcher, and ran back into her house weeping. Whereupon Ticatame inquired: "What has happened to you, mother of Sicuirancha, why do you weep thus?" She explained that her brothers, called Zizambaniecha, and people from Cumachen had come. Ticatame asked what they had come for and she said: "They say they came to match themselves with you because you shot their brothers," to which he replied: "Very well, let them come. I have four kinds of arrows and they shall have a taste of them, especially those that have black, white, red, and yellow flints called *hurespondi*. I, likewise, shall sample the sticks that they fight with to see what they taste like."

His brothers-in-law surrounded Ticatame's house, and he quickly brought out a chest in which he had all kinds of arrows. As they all tried to come through the door at once, they jammed it while Ticatame shot two arrows at a time, killing one while the other arrow would pass through its mark to strike another. He shot many and killed the wounded, but noon came and his arrows gave out so that he had nothing to shoot with. He took his quiver off his shoulder and clubbed them with it, but they all charged at once, speared him with their sticks, and dragged him out of his house dead. They set fire to his house and it burned, for the smoke prevented anyone from entering. They carried off Curicaveri and went their way.

Sicuirancha, Ticatame's son, was not there for he had gone hunting on the mountain. When Ticatame's wife saw the fire, she began to shout and ran around among the dead, finally coming upon her husband who was lying in the entrance, dark green from the wounds caused by the poisoned sticks. Then came his son, Sicuirancha, and he said: "Oh, Mother, who has done this?" And his mother replied: "Who would have done this but your Uncle and your Grandfather; they are the ones who did it." "Woe is me," said Sicuirancha, "and what has become of our God Curicaveri? Have they carried him off?" She agreed that they must have carried him off. "Very well," he said, "I want to go over there too, and let them kill me. Whom do I have here?"

He set out following their tracks, shouting as he went. Curicaveri brought diseases upon those who were carrying him off, such as diarrhea, intoxication, pneumonia, and crippling illnesses, in the manner in which he customarily avenges his injuries. Attacked by these diseases they all fell to the ground and were intoxicated when Sicuirancha came upon them. Curicaveri was in an ark at the foot of an oak, and when Sicuirancha saw the ark, he thought they had taken the god out. He opened it, found Curicaveri still there and took him out. They had carried off the ropelike fetters with which the sacrificial prisoners were tied. They had also taken from the ark a gold ring which with the ropelike fetters had been given to the god in heaven by his parents, and they had carried them all off. Sicuirancha thought: "Let them take them, what good will they do? Who can they feed with them? They will bring them back someday."

He returned Curicaveri to his house. Then he went with all his people to Vayameo, a place near Santa Fe, the one near Mechuacán, where he was Master. Sicuirancha built a temple as well as houses for the chief priests; he also built fireplaces and ordered wood brought for them. Sicuirancha directed Curicaveri's wars, died, and was buried at the foot of the temple. He left a son called Pavacume who was Master in Vayameo, and Pavacume begot Vapeani who became Master after the death of his father, Pavacume. He in turn had a son called Curatame who was Master over the same region. His people went hunting at the places called Pumeo, Viricarini, Pechatato, and at Hiramicu, going as far as a mountain called Paceo. Their hunting took them to other places called Hizipazicuyo, Changüello, and even as far as another place called Coringuaro. All these places are a matter of about a league from the city, or perhaps a little more, and they all returned to gather at the village called Vayameo where their temples were located. They said to each other, "That is all good land where we have been hunting; that is where we ought to have our houses." Those who went on the other side of the mountain said that it too was all good land. Curatame died and was buried at the foot of the temple and was followed by four Masters in Vayameo: Sicuirancha, Curatame, Pavacume, and Vapeani.

34. DIVISION BY OMEN

The last Master died and left two sons who were called, one by his father's name, Vapeani, and the other, Pavacume. At this time Xaratanga had her temple as well as her priests in Mechuacán. It was the custom of a lord called Tariyaran to go to Atamataho for wood, a place near Santa Fe, while the priests, called Vatarecha, occasionally made an offering of this wood to Xaratanga. Thus, those who brought wood from one direction would meet those who brought it from the other. On one occasion the Master who served Xaratanga and her priests drank too much on her feast day, and he began to appropriate the grains that Xaratanga had brought to the land, namely red, green, and yellow chilies. They made a wreath of all these kinds of chili as Xaratanga's priest was accustomed to wearing. Likewise they appropriated black and red beans and strung them, alternating the colors, and put them on their wrists. They said these were Xaratanga's grains that her priest was accustomed to wearing. His sisters, Pacimbane and Zucurabe, also appropriated some of the grains, both red and varicolored grains of corn, strung them around their wrists and said they were more of Xaratanga's beads. They did the same with other kinds of corn, such as white and mixed; they strung it and hung it around their necks, saying they were Xaratanga's necklaces. Since this displeased the goddess, she caused the wine to make them sick for they vomited it and, returning almost to normalcy, they got up. Turning to their sisters, they said: "What shall we do? The wine did not affect us but we feel very ill. Go if you will, and catch some little fish to eat and cure our hangover." Since they had no net to fish with they took a basket, and one woman carried it along the bank while the others looked for the fish. But they could catch no fish because Xaratanga, who was such a great goddess, had already concealed them.

After having fished for a long time they came upon a large snake in a place called Uncuzepu; they caught it and took it home in great rejoicing. Xaratanga's priests, Vatarecha, Cuahuen, and his younger brother Camejan, and sisters Pacinvave and Zucurave, greeted them and said: "Welcome back, sisters, have you brought even a few little fish?" To this the women replied: "Sires, we have caught nothing, but we do not know what we have here." The answer was: "It is fish too and good to eat. Singe it on the fire to get the skin off, and make some porridge. Cut this fish in pieces, put it in the porridge and set it on the fire. It will cure the hangover." After brewing that concoction, they sat down in their house to eat the snake cooked in corn.

After the sun went down, they began to scrape and scratch themselves for they were slowly turning into snakes. When it was nearly midnight and believing they had turned into a snake's tail, they began to weep. They had already turned the greenish black color of snakes. They were all in this condition and early in the morning they went out and entered the lake, one after another, to go straight to Vayameo, near Santa Fe. They swam, stirring up foam and making waves, toward the tribe of Chichimecas called Hiyoca, and shouted to them. The Chichimecas turned about and went to a hill in the city called Tariacuri. The swimmers climbed out at this point. The place where they landed is called Quahueyucha Zequaro from the name of those who turned into snakes and thus disappeared. Seeing this, the Chichimecas, called Vacusecha, held it to be an omen.

A lord called Udecavecare, because of the omen, departed with his god and his people and established himself in a place called Coringuaro Achurin. Another lord called Ypinchuani also left that evil place, took his god Tiripenie Xugapeti, and established himself at a place called Pechataro. Lord Turepupanquaran endured it awhile and finally took his god called Tiripenie to a place called Ylamucuo. Still another lord, called

Mahicuri, moved his god called Tiripeme Caheri to a place called Pareo. This left the two brothers Vapeani and Pavacume, who took Curicaveri along the bank of the lake on the Santa Fe side, put him on a crag there beside the lake called Capacureo, then to another place called Patamagua Caraho. All the gods mentioned here were brothers of Curicaveri, all of whom now were separated, as has been described, and Curicaveri was left alone.

Later Vapeani and Pavacume took Curicaveri to another place called Vazeo Zaravacuyo and set him on the side of the mountain. Then, removing him from there, he was taken to another place called Xenquaran, thence to another called Honcheguero, and there he stayed awhile.

In a like manner, what had happened was held to be an omen by the priests of Xaratanga, called Cuyupuri and Hoatamanaquere, and they took their goddess to one side of the mountain called Taziacaherio, where the snakes had disappeared. From there they took her to Sipixo beside the lake and built her temples, a bath, and a ball court, and she remained there some years. Removing her later, they took her to Urichu, thence to Viramangarun, and later to Vacapu, where presently stands San Tangen, and then to Taziara, Acuezizan, and finally to Harocotin. Since they had Curicaveri, the lords of the Chichimecas went hunting at a place called Aranaran, at Nacaraho, and at Hechuer, which is near Pázcuaro and at another place called Charimangueo. They climbed Viriziquaro and went over to Xarami, Thivapu, and Atupen, a mountain from which they saw the island of Xaraquero in the lake.

35. THE LONG-LOST RELATIVES

When the priests of Xaratanga saw the island, which is also called by the name of Varucaten Hacicurun, there was a great temple on it. Not far away was another island called Pacandan. As they went down the mountain they noticed a man from the first island in a canoe. [Those who live on the island are called *Huren de Tiechan*.] The man in the canoe was fishing with a hook and they wondered what he was catching. The lords suggested they go along the shore of the lake to get as near as possible, and as all agreed they went down the mountain to a place called Varichu-hopataruyo. From there they went along the shore of the lake. The trees made the going most difficult because it was a thick forest and they had to bend branches to get through because there was no road. On arriving on the shore near the fisherman, they called to him and asked what he was doing. (See Plate 20.) He answered with the word *Henditare*, which means that he is a lord. [The people of this lake speak the same language as the Chichimecas, but many of their words are corrupt or are moun- tain terms, which explains the fisherman's answer.] They re- peated the question and he explained that he was fishing. They asked him to come to the bank, for he was at a distance out on the lake. He refused, saying that they were Chichimecas and would shoot him. They urged him to come, insisting that they had no reason to shoot him. He asked them not to order him to come, but they insisted, saying that they needed to talk with him. This time the fisherman agreed, saying it would be a pleasure, that he was on his way, and he brought his canoe to the bank and landed. One of the lords, called Vapeani, who was a brave man, jumped into the canoe and saw that it was full of many kinds of fish, and he asked the islander what they were. The fisherman replied: "What you have in your hand is called *hacumaran*, this kind is *vurapeti*, that one *cuerepu*, that other one *thiron*, and that one *charoel*; there are many kinds of fish in this lake and I fish for all of them. At night I fish with a net and by day with a hook." Vapeani asked about the flavor of the fish to which the fisherman replied: "If we had fire and the fish were broiled you would have no need to ask." To this Vapeani answered: "What are you say- ing, fisherman, look for some wood for we Chichimecas always have fire—hand over the wood." Striking fire with an instrument, they soon had a good blaze going on the bank with the flames and the smoke rising. The fisherman sweated over the broiling of the fish, and as he broiled it he would give it to each one. They ate gingerly at first, then greedily, saying that it certainly had a good flavor.

As the Chichimecas were accustomed to eating all manner of game, each one carried a little net, made of small rings, which was full of rabbits, *chinequen*, quail, doves, and many other kinds of fowl. They took out a rabbit, put it on the fire, and after it was broiled, cut it up, served it, and said to the fisherman: "Eat some of this and see how it tastes for this is what we eat." When the fisherman had taken a mouthful, the Chichimecas asked the islander what it tasted like. He replied: "Sir, this is real food, it is not like bread, but much better! This fish is good food, but it has a strong odor and fills one up quickly. Your rabbit does not have the odor and is true food." The agreeable Chichimecas went on to explain: "You speak the truth, this is what we go hunting for. One day we make arrows and the next we get our recreation by hunting in the country. We do not take the game for ourselves, but the deer we take we give as food to the sun and to the gods who are celestial engenderers, and to the Four Quarters of the world. We eat the leftovers after we have made the salve to the gods. Now you give us information, Islander." The fisherman objected that there was nothing to tell so they asked: "What do you call the temple on that island?" He replied that it was called Varutaten Hacicurin, also Xaraquero. They thought that was fine and asked about the names of the gods worshipped here. The fisherman obliged: "Sire, the principal god is called Hacuizecapeme, his sister is named Purupe Cuxareti, also worshipped are Caroen, Nurite, Xarenivarichu, Uquare, Tangachurani, and a long list of others." They asked in surprise: "Are those their names?" and the fisherman replied that they were. Then Vapeani said: "They were our Grandfathers. As we came this way we thought we had no relatives here; now we have found some. We are all of one blood and we were born together. What is the name of your Master?" The fisherman said he was Caricaten. Then they asked him about the name of the other island. The fisherman supplied the information: "Tiripitihonto, and it has two other names, Vanquipen Hazizurin and Pacandan." They then asked about the names of the gods worshipped on that island. The fisherman named them: "Chupitiripeme, another called Unazihicecha and his sister Camavaperi, and many others." They asked about the name of the Master and the fisherman said it was Zuangua. Then the Chichimecas exclaimed: "They too are our Grandfathers of the road! How strange! We have come upon relatives! What wonders! We are all relatives by blood!" The fisherman agreed that his people were their relatives, so the Chichimecas asked his name and he said he was called Curiparaxan. Whereupon they inquired whether he had daughters and he denied it. At this the Chichimecas contradicted him: "What are you saying? You do have, why do you say no?" He explained: "I have not begotten any children for I am old and so is my wife," but the Chichimecas insisted: "What do you mean, Islander, you do have children. We are not asking for the reason that you are thinking, for we do not want women for the future; we ask because Curicaveri will conquer this land, and you for your part will stand with one foot on the land and one on the water. We likewise shall stand the same way and we shall become one people." The fisherman relented: "You are right, gentlemen; I do have a daughter who is still small and not to be seen because she is small and ugly." They rejected the objection: "It does not make any difference whether she is small; go bring her to us. We shall climb the mountain and tomorrow we shall hunt; the next day we shall meet here and talk. Let no one know about this except you and your wife; you will talk about it with each other." They took their leave and the fisherman rowed his canoe across the lake. The Chichimecas went up the mountain and the following day went hunting as they had planned, and the next day returned to their houses.

Early in the morning the fisherman took his daughter across the lake in the canoe and waited for the Chichimecas who were late in coming for they were footsore. The sun was very high and the fisherman was sitting on the bank fearing that they would not return, and he said to his daughter: "It seems the Chichimecas have deceived us. But let us wait a little longer and then we shall row away in our boat." The Chichimecas, coming down the mountain, looked out over the lake and said: "Why is not the fisherman coming? He ought to have appeared on the lake some time ago and be coming, let us go down to the shore." When they arrived, the fisherman and his daughter were sitting on the bank, and the Chichimecas greeted him, saying: "Well, Islanders, how are you?" He replied: "I was frightened and distressed, thinking you Chichimecas had deceived me." They explained: "We hunted longer than we thought. Is this the daughter you mentioned?" He replied: "Yes Sir, this is she, look how small she is." They explained to him that it did not matter for she would grow up. They said: "We want her right now; we shall talk about the future later. Go, cross the lake again, and report to whoever should know about it among those priests called Vatarecha. Remember, they will call you when they learn about it and they will say to you: 'Come here, brother, you have turned a woman over to the Chichimecas,' and you shall say to them, 'Sire, not I; why should I take her to them alive? By night I fish with a net sitting in the stern, and I take my daughter in the canoe to row. By day I fish for some small fish with a hook and I keep the girl in the canoe, for being small, she would not be seen. Unfortunately, she had to urinate so I went to a place called Varichachopotaco, and when we came to the shore, I told her to go ahead and she jumped from the canoe. The Chichimecas were concealed there in ambush and she was seized and carried off. I tried to take her away from them, but as they are Chichimecas, they began to shoot at me. I was afraid and had to abandon her. How was I to know that they are holding her as a slave? I thought she was already sacrificed and dead, but it seems that they are keeping her as a slave.' Tell them this and no more. Go, do not answer anything nor tell them that you gave her to us." After giving Curiparaxan (the fisherman) these instructions, they departed.

36. THE MASTERS FOLLOW SUIT TO
THEIR UNDOING

Days passed by, and the Chichimecas took Curicaveri and went to live at a place called Tarimichundiro, a district in Pázcuaro. There the girl grew up and Pavacume, the younger brother, married her, and the girl from the lake became pregnant. She gave birth to a son who was called Tariacuri and who later became Master. When the lords of the lake learned of it, they called Curiparaxan and said to him: "Look here, brother, we have been told that you turned a woman over to the Chichimecas." But he denied it: "It was not I, Sires. Why should I turn her over? I fish by night with a net and I used to put my daughter in the canoe to row. By day I fished with a hook while she rowed. We came to a place called Varicha Hopotucoyo [Varichachopotaco], and she said, 'Daddy, I want to urinate.' I told her to go ahead and went up to the bank. She jumped out and went a little ways and it seems that the Chichimecas were in ambush there and seized her. I tried to take her away from them, but since they are Chichimecas, they began to shoot at me and I was afraid and returned home. They carried her off and I thought she was dead. How would I know they were keeping her captive? But that does seem to be the truth, also that they still have her." The lords answered in a lighter tone: "What do you mean, brother? We do not ask for the reasons that you think. Tell us about it if you will, because each one of us has a daughter and we want to bring the Chichimecas to the island and marry the daughters off to them. One of their lords could be the sacrificer here on the shore in our temple. Another could be the priest in Cuacari Xangatien, where he would perform the sacrifices. This would place them in each quarter to do the sacrificing. Since you are accustomed to talking with them, go and see what they say." They departed, and Curiparancha [Curiparaxan] went over the lake, fishing with a pole as he went.

He found the Chichimecas at Tarimichundiro and told them what the lords of the lake had said, and that they should go over to the Island. They were agreeable and said they would go. All the Chichimecas gathered and went to a place called Zurumbo on the bank of the lake. The lords, leaving the others behind, went over in a canoe to be received warmly by the Islanders. After eating, the Islanders called a barber and had the Chichimecas' long hair cut, making some round, bare spots like temples on the crown of their heads. They gave them each a wreath of fiber and a string of tiny golden tweezers to wear around their necks. Pavacume became the sacrificer and Vapeani stayed in Quacaci Xangatien [Cuacari Xangatien] a few days.

All this became known to those lords who had gone off on their own because of the omen of the snakes. They had come a matter of a league and a half from Pázcuaro before Vapeani and Pavacume brought their people to Pázcuaro. They sent some messengers to the lake people with these instructions: "Go see our brothers, the Islanders, and ask them why they have accepted the Chichimecas on the island? They have no need of them. Why did they take them in? Or of what advantage are they, for they hunt on the mountain all day, and all are turned vagabonds with their long bows in their hands? Since those Islanders are not discreet they will have children who will be one quarter Islander and another quarter Chichimeca. Are they not sensible enough to reason this out? They will lose their gods, and they are not small. Then, too, how does it happen that the Chichimecas are not sorrowful, for Curicaveri is a small god who was engendered on high? Go and tell them to cast them out of their houses, and make them go back across the lake. It is not for envy nor any other purpose that we say this. Let them not fail to hear what we all say. The words of the people of Coringuaro will be understood."

When the embassy arrived and the message was delivered to the Master of Xaraquaro, called Caricaten, it was not believed. After some days other messengers were sent from Coringuaro with these instructions: "Ask them why the people of the lake do not believe what we tell them. Why did they give the Chichimecas those women? What need of them did they have? What good are the Chichimecas? All day long they wander about the mountains hunting. If the Islanders lived here in Coringuaro they would have very good corn fields, pigweed seeds, and much chili. They could bring fish here which could be offered to our God Uren de Cuavecara. And they in turn could take ears of corn, pigweed seeds, kidney beans, and chili to offer to their God Acuiecatapeme. What need do they have of the Chichimecas for those things? Tell them to cast the Chichimecas out of their houses and take away their wide belts, lip-rings, ear-loops and braids. Throw them out roughly and send them away. The Islanders must believe what we say to them."

Hearing this second embassy, the Islanders finally believed and took away the Chichimecas' lip-rings, ear-loops, and wide belts and roughly cast them out of the houses, driving them across the lake. They were slobbering because their lip-rings had been torn away. All those people who had been living near the lake went back to their first settlement called Tarimichundiro, a district of Pázcuaro, and there they rested.

37. THE FOUNDING OF THE TEMPLES AND THE WAR WITH CORINGUARO

After they had established themselves in a district of Pázcuaro called Tarimichundiro, they built their temples on top of some very high rocks on a site called Petazecua. The temples were built there because their legends say that the God of the Inferno sends them those sites for the temples of the principal gods. Then moving on upstream, they came to a place that was reported to be the site of the gods called Zacapuhamucutin Pázcuaro, a place they had wanted to see. Although there was no road because of the dense forest of oak trees and dense thicket, they continued upstream, coming out at the spring [in the Bishop's patio], which is formed by water coming from Cuirisquataro, a place higher up on the hill where the big bell is located.

They descended to the house which is now in the hands of Don Pedro, governor of the city of Mechuacán, and down to a place which later was called Carop or Pázcuaro [Pátzquaro]. They went about looking at the bodies of water there, and when they had seen them all, they said, "This is, without a doubt, Pázcuaro. Let us go see the sites we have found for the temples," and they went to the place where the cathedral was to be, and there they found the previously mentioned high rocks called Petrozequa [Petazecus], which means temple site. Nearby there was a high place which they climbed, and on reaching the top, they found some stones standing as if to be sculptured into idols. This caused them to say: "It certainly is here. Here these gods say that they are the gods of the Chichimecas, and this site is called Pázcuaro. Look, there are four of these gods, this stone is the one to be called Zeritacherengue, and this one, the older brother, Vacusecha, this one Tingarata, and this one Miecua Ageva." Now they went to another place where there were more large stones, and they recognized it as the place their gods had spoken of and they said: "Let us clear this place." Thus they counted the oaks and the trees there, saying that they had found the place their gods had singled out for them.

Their ancestors had held this place in great veneration and they claimed that it was the seat of their God Curicaveri. The former Cazonci used to say that here and nowhere else was the door to heaven through which their gods came and went. They always brought their offerings here even though the seat of government was moved to different places. Afterward, by hand and using dirt, they built a patio putting up stone walls on some sides to level and smooth it. In this patio they made three temples, three fireplaces, and three houses for the chief priests.

Days came and went and the people of Coringuaro said: "Remember how close we came to killing the Chichimecas and they, being Chichimecas, will never forget the injury. They do not know how to forget. Go and take this message; say to them: "Bring an offering of wood for the gods against us and let the priest cast the scents on the fire; let the sacrificer bring fragrances for the prayer to the gods against us. We too shall bring wood and the priest and the sacrificer will cast the incense on the fire. The third day we shall meet and we shall all play behind the mountain and we shall learn how we are looked upon from on high by the celestial gods, the Sun, and the gods of the Four Quarters of the world." This you shall say to the Chichimecas, for this is what their gods are accustomed to saying to the lords, for it is their business to go about destroying villages, and they are happy when they anticipate a fight."

The procedures they specified—for some to bring wood and others with the priests to cast incense on the fire—had always been their custom before they went to war. They performed these ceremonies so that their gods might favor and help them in their battles. At this time the lords name those against whom they are to be helped. The messengers found the lords of the Chichimecas and told them: "Your brother Chaushori [Chanhori] says for you to bring wood for the temples against them, and for the priests to cast the incense, and that they will do likewise." When they heard this, the lords of the Chichimecas agreed, saying that the next day they would go with their bows and arrows. The messengers returned and reported the answer.

The Chichimecas did not have many adornments for war, and it is not known where they found eagle feathers to make some plumages for their backs. They used white chicken feathers to make a flag, and as agreed, on the third day they all went to a place called Ataquao. The people from Coringuaro also went to the same place, and both groups came together at midday. The battle began with some throwing rocks, others using clods, and the lords of the Chichimecas shot arrows because it was the common people who threw rocks and clods. They lost face when they suffered head injuries, and when it had happened, they would wipe the blood away with their hands so that it would not fall on the ground, and they would sprinkle it with their fingers towards the heavens for the purpose of giving food to the gods. The two brothers, Pavacume and Vapeani, lords of the Chichimecas, were shot and wounded and were taken back to their houses in Tarimichundiro, while the people from Coringuaro returned to their village.

38. THE LORDS OF CORINGUARO SENT AN OLD WOMAN TO SPY ON THE LORDS OF THE CHICHIMECAS

It was held to be wrong for those who had been shot or otherwise wounded to sleep in their house because of the danger that it constituted. So the wounded went with the lords to the House of the Eagle. Inside the house the wounded would lie for three days on beds which were raised above the ground by cane supports. At the entrance they would place smoking canes which were brought from the fireplaces by relays who collided with each other as they entered with the canes or went back to get more.

The lords of Coringuaro wanted to send someone to inquire about the lords of the Chichimecas, for they had been treated very badly when they were shot, and since they were Chichimecas, they would not forget. The question was, who would go to find out whether or not they might die? Someone asked: "Is there a need for someone to go? There is Curazapi's wife, who is from Sinchangato, and she says they are her nephews. She could go into their houses and talk with them. Let us send her." They sent for her, gave her some food and said to her: "What will we do, aunt? We are in trouble for we shot the Chichimecas. We met them in a clearing called Ataqueo, and there we played behind the mountain and shot the two brothers. We do not know whether we wounded them fatally or not. Why do you not go find out how they are?" She agreed, saying: "I will be happy to do so, sirs, certainly I shall go." They instructed her to return with the answer and gave her two blankets for herself and two others to give to the brothers as if they were her own. "Note carefully what they say when you leave, for the words you speak are to be your own and let them not think that they are ours." She replied: "Sires, I shall go, have no care and do not be downcast about this, for whether they are well or dead I shall find out, I shall speak to them." She departed and arrived about nightfall at the place where they had their house in Sichangato [Sinchan-

123

gato], and she had with her the two blankets which they had given her. It was winter, a time of rains. It is not known how she got through, but she arrived at midnight at the House of the Eagle.

The Islanders were on one side of the house, and the Chichimecas on the other, keeping watch together, for they had come from the lake to see them. The old woman came striding through the dewy weeds and entered the house. Shaking off the dew, she passed by the guards and bent over Vapeani who was not asleep. He asked: "Who are you?" She replied: "It is I, your aunt, the wife of Curazapi." He asked her what she was doing, and she answered: "Oh, Sir, I have just learned about it from him who had to tell me for mercy's sake, and as I understand it, you met in the clearing and you both were shot, you and your brother, then I said I want to go visit the poor fellows for they were shot. If the poor fellows are dead, I will put these two blankets in the fire to burn in their name, or if by good fortune they are alive and have sight, I shall cover them with these blankets which I got in spite of my poverty in exchange for a little corn. This is why I come, Sire, and what I am doing; all in all, I came to ask how you are." To all this Vapeani replied: "Listen to what this woman is doing here. What does she mean?" He called to his brother and told him: "This is a bad woman who comes from the Coringuaro village with this story. Get away from here, you who talk and awaken these Lords." The old woman replied: "Sire, let these blankets stay here and you lie on them." Vapeani replied angrily: "Listen to what she says. Why should they stay here? Take them back with you, you deceitful woman. Where could we use them or appear in them?" And the old woman went out of the house and departed.

Since the Islanders were not asleep, they awakened their people, saying: "Get up for these Chichimecas are two-faced and talk two ways at once. Some of them have come from Coringuaro so that early in the morning they will shoot us and destroy our village." They all got up quickly and angrily took the lords out of the house. The Islanders left, crossed the lake again, and went to their houses.

39. THE CORINGUAROS AMBUSH THE CHICHIMECA LORDS

Days came and went and the Coringuaros said: "We came near killing them, and as they are Chichimecas, they will not forget the injury. Go to the Islanders and tell them to send messengers who, speaking as if it were their idea, will say: 'Your fathers-in-law send us to you because your women, who are among us, will not eat and are starving to death for love of you. Since they do not quarrel, it seems that they love each other well and are good couples. They have never committed a wrong and, even if they get drunk, they do not jeer at each other. Now we are greatly concerned and worried for their sake. Go to our brothers, Lords, and ask them why they do not cross the lake and come and get them, for nowhere is it customary for women to die far from their villages.' This you shall tell them, and we shall ambush the Chichimecas on the shore of the lake for they will not fail to come because they are not discreet, and in this way we shall kill them. You shall say further to the Islanders that if they will bring their fish here to Coringuaro, they may take back corn to their islands in the lake."

The messengers went to the Islanders, who replied that they would be happy to co-operate. The Islanders brought along a gift of fish, crossed the lake and landed where Vapeani and Pavacume were sitting making arrows. Vapeani and Pavacume greeted them and asked them why they came. They replied: "Sires, your fathers-in-law and your parents sent us, saying: 'Go to our sons-in-law and tell them that our daughters cause us great concern, and we are worried about them. They weep all day and one would think that their husbands quarrel with them, but they do not, rather they have been good couples. Even when they drink wine the husbands do not seize their wives by the hair, and they treat each other well. Why do you not come for them, for it is not the custom for women to die far from home? This is why we come, Sires.' " Vapeani turned to his brother: "Brother, without question, we must go," and Pavacume agreed that they should. They decorated themselves, putting on their paint, the customary rawhide wreaths on their heads, their quivers on their backs, war jackets, deer hooves, and took their bows and arrows in hand. As they took to the road, the priests of the temple, called Chupi-tani, Mizivan, and Tecaqua, spoke to them, asking where they were going. They replied: "Messengers came from the lake and told us to come for our women." The priests were alarmed, saying: "What are you saying, Children, it would be better not to go for those are not the words of the lake people but of the people of Coringuaro. Look, if you go we shall be in trouble. If you want to go somewhere to enjoy yourselves, go somewhere else, not there." But they insisted that they must go. The old men then gave their advice: "Well, go sons, and each one of you take a young man who is fleet of foot and let him go along the road ahead, and you follow behind at a distance so you will not be taken by surprise somewhere." They said they would do so and, in time, they came upon a place called Cazapahacarucu, where the runners, going ahead of them, were ambushed by the people of Coringuaro. Alarmed, Vapeani and Pavacume stopped, and Vapeani said to his brother: "It is true, the words were those of the people of Coringuaro, let us go back." And they returned home.

Days went by, and the lords of Coringuaro agreed among themselves that they had done many wrong things to the Chi-chimecas which the Chichimeca lords would never forget. They sent word to their brothers, the Islanders, and asked them to take this message to the Chichimecas: "Our daughters give us great concern and worry because their love for you will not let them eat and they are starving to death. They go up in the high part of the temple called Puruaten and do nothing but weep all day long while watching the smoke rising from the Chichimeca camp. Always they look in the direction of the Chichimeca camp and they never want to eat. Do not think there is danger anywhere as the last time when we tried to shoot you. We did not know that the people of Coringuaro had set up an ambush and we also got caught there. Tell the Chichimecas not to come here to the island, that we shall take the women out to meet them at a place called Xanoato Huacacio. We shall take them there and they may take them back if they will, else the women are going to live far away. We shall tell them that we are put out with the lords of the Island of Pacandan and the way they treat us for we put our nets along the shore to catch fish and they break them and smash our canoes and oars. Who are they to do this, being so few on an island? Tell the Chichimecas that some morning we shall meet the Coringuaros and destroy them for the trouble they cause us, and we need the help of the Chichimecas because they are brave men. We tell them this because we have confidence in their bows and arrows. Go tell them this. They will not fail to come for they are not discreet." This is what they told the Islanders and the Islanders responded, saying they would take the message.

A gift was made up of fish which the Islanders delivered, placing it in front of Vapeani and Pavacume who, as they all sat down, asked what brought them there. The Islanders explained: "Sires, our fathers-in-law sent us," and they recounted the entire message so that Vapeani said to his brother: "We must go, brother, without question, for they say that they are to tell us why the villages are to be destroyed. This is a serious matter and we must both go."

They armed themselves and the priests, Chupitani, Mizivan, and Tecaqua, asked them where they were going. Their answer was: "Messengers came from the island in the lake and said that our women will be brought out to a place near here called Tanoate Hucacio [Xanoato Huacacio]. They are to bring them and we are to go there to get them." At this the priests warned: "Children, we should greatly prefer that you not go for those are not the words of the Islanders but of the Lords of Coringuaro." But they insisted: "No, Grandfathers, they want to talk with us for they say that we must destroy Pacandan Island." The priests said: "May it prove to turn out that way; children, let each one take two good young men who are fleet of foot to go in advance, examining all parts of the road so that you will not endanger yourselves. Let us not think that this is a game, and let us not be mocked. Go along the road watchfully." When they departed, they sent the runners ahead. But the Coringuaros had arranged themselves in three ambushes, and they let the runners and spies go by. Unaware of the ambush, Vapeani and Pavacume came along behind them and went as far as the third ambush where Vapeani was shot and killed. The younger brother, Pavacume, was very swift and began to run toward his people, but they caught him while he was climbing a mountain called Zacapuhacuzua, near Pázcuaro, where the Nuguatatis live, and there they shot him.

The two were brought together, and when the priests, their relatives, learned about it, they took a necklace of gold called *cazaretaqua* and some plumages and went to the place where the Islanders were gathered around the two dead lords, Vapeani and Pavacume, punching them with oars. The old men arrived and chided them: "Well, children, you have fought according to the rancor and ill will that you felt, you have seized and despoiled them." In answer they explained: "Grandfather, we did not kill them for they were already dead when we landed; it seems that the people from Coringuaro were already here in ambush and killed them." The priests objected to this: "Children, why do you say that? It is enough that you shot them, we beg you to give them to us. Take these plumages to wear during your feasts and this golden necklace to wear around your neck." The Islanders asked: "Why should we wear those plumages? Did we perchance kill them ourselves? We had no reason to kill them. Take your Lords, for we took them from the Coringuaros who were carrying them off to their villages." "Why do you say this?" asked the priests, "Why do you not take the plumages? Take them to wear during your feasts." The Islanders finally agreed and took them home. The priests took the bodies to Pázcuaro to the place where their temples were built on top of the site called Petazequa, and where they were burned. They played trumpets and gathered up the ashes, placing them in some jars which they decorated with two marks of gold, turquoise necklaces, and dressing them well, placed green plumages on top of the forms, and buried them with trumpets blowing.

40. THE TRAINING OF A MASTER

Upon their death the two Masters, Vapeani and Pavacume, left three sons, one called Tariacuri, son of Pavacume, whom he had by the daughter of the fisherman, and the two others, Cetaco and Aramen, sons of Vapeani by another woman, who were older than Tariacuri, who was still of tender age when their father died. Tariacuri was small and the priests Chupitan, Nurivan, and Tetaco, who were brothers, devoted themselves to educating him, saying: "Lord Tariacuri, you are now of age,[13] gather wood for the temples, give wood for food to Curicaveri because the Islanders of the lake have made you an orphan for they killed your father, your mother, your uncle on your mother's side, and your servants, because you were on the island of Xaraquero when you were born. Gather wood for the temples. Remember this wrong in order to avenge it upon the uncles of your mother. Remember that if you do not, there is a temple on the island in the lake where they perform sacrifices, and there they will apply the sword to sacrifice you. Remember, too, the other island called Pacandan where they also make sacrifices and there, too, they destroy. Then there is Coringuaro, where they make sacrifices, and they would kill you there as they would in Cumachen, Zacapua, and in Zizaban, which is Naranjan; there is where they killed your Grandfather and Grandmother. In Zichaxuquero they killed another of your Grandfathers called Ticatame, remember that there too is a temple and they make sacrifices in all these places.

---

[13] The meaning here must be that he was now the ruler with Chupitan, Nurivan, and Tetaco, acting somewhat in the position of regents. The *Relación* makes it quite clear that he was still very young but custom and tradition have made him the ruler. Chupitan, Nurivan, and Tetaco served and were his constant companions for the rest of his life.

"They may kill you if you do not become what you ought to be and do not listen to what we tell you. Fortunate is he who is to become King, or is it that you who are to be King are not a Lord but one of lowly estate and of the lower class? Who is to bring great quantities of wood for Curicaveri's temples? You who are to be King, are you a poor, miserable wretch? Your head will then be raised upon a long pole after killing you if you are not the one who ought to have wood brought to burn in the temples as food for the celestial gods, the gods of the Four Quarters of the World, and of the Inferno. Satiate with wood all the existing gods, remembering that Curicaveri is very generous, for he makes houses for his people, he makes families and women to be in the houses, and old men who build fires. He causes the possession of jewels and slaves, both male and female, and causes golden earrings to be placed in the ears, golden bracelets on the wrists, turquoise necklaces around the neck, and green plumages on the head. Gather wood for the temples, sacrifice your ears because fortunate is he who is to become King."

Having said this, they seized him by the ears, saying: "Sire, Lord Tariacuri, as you are not yet of age, remember to avenge the dishonors, fail not to hear us, Lord Tariacuri; woe be unto you if you do not, for you will stretch your neck to watch others eat and you will probably go about in a tattered blanket if you heed not what we tell you. Remember that we are old; would that we were Masters of the people, but only one is to be Master. Fortunate are you, Lord Tariacuri; listen to what we say," and the old men never ceased in their counsel, for they were worthy men and faithful in the service of the temples. For this reason they dedicated themselves entirely to educating him day and night and their voices never tired.

By this time his cousins, the sons of Vapeani, one called Cetaco, the older, and the younger, Aramen, were grown men, and there were days when they would go about getting drunk and running around with women. They always took Tariacuri with them and because he was so young and small they carried him on their shoulders. When they learned of this, the old men admonished them. "Look, Lord Cetaco and Lord Aramen, you drink wine and you run around with women; take your people and go to a place called Vacanambaro, and there you may drink wine to your heart's content; you may run around with women and there will be no one there to say anything to you or to do you any wrong. Go and leave off setting a bad example for him who is to be Master so that he may not become accustomed to your ways. First let him gather wood for the temples."

"So be it," they answered, "just as you say, Grandfathers," and they departed. So the priests had Tariacuri alone, and all day and all night they did nothing but teach and advise him. The old men worked so hard at what they would say that he listened to them and he began to gather wood and branches for the temples and he would take it to the patios of the temples.

One day Tariacuri, having a house in Tarimichundiro, a district of Pázcuaro, went to Pázcuaro. He gathered wood for the temples called Ziripemeo and Aquaracohato, and took wood to another place called Gongoan, adding his wood and branches to the existing supply, placing on top an arrow which was the sign of war. He took wood to the other side too, to a place called Huriquamacurio, and again he placed an arrow on top of the wood. In this manner he went about placing arrows on the boundaries of his enemies. He also took wood to another place called Vanita, to Chacario, to another place called Zacapo Hacurnay, and to Axangua Hurepangayo and to Camembaro. In this manner he went about marking the boundaries and placing arrows wherever he put wood and branches. In the same way he took wood to another place called Xaramutu, and thus he came to the edge of the lake near a place called Atario on the boundary of the Islanders. The Islanders were living in a place called Tupuxanchuen without fear of anything around the entire shore. They had put their nets out to dry on some poles near the shore and had placed their fish there to dry also. Here Tariacuri built a large fire which made so much smoke that the people, seeing the fire and the smoke, fled in a mad rush to save themselves. They left behind their grinding stones, their water jugs and pitchers, the fish that were spread upon the ground, their blankets, and jumped into the lake raising high waves, but no one was drowned. The children cried, everybody shouted, merely because of the smoke and everything was abandoned.

He went as far as Zirumbo and built a fire there too, making great smoke as he did in another place called Chutio. In each one of these places the Islanders fled shouting, and jumped into the lake, merely because of the smoke, for no one was driving them away. They too left some adornments and a great many fish spread along the shore. From here Tariacuri went to a hill called Xanoato Huacacio, and here again he made a great smoke, causing the entire population to flee, not only these but also those from Parceo and they made a great splash when they jumped into the lake. The people of Charaben and Xaramutaro did likewise, and Tariacuri built his fires with great smoke at Haramutaro, at a place called Cuiris Tucupachao, and thus frightened all the Islanders into the lake in great droves. From the last place he saw the islands of Xaraquero and Cuyumeo, whose people, including the children, began to shout and run. The women took their babies on their backs and they ran off in all directions, for in their fear no one knew where to go. In this fashion he surrounded all the people of the islands, for there was no place where they could get to the shore, even to farm, much less to get wood.

41. THE CONSPIRACY AGAINST TARIACURI

After a few days Caricaten, Master of Xaraquero island asked, "What shall we do? Tariacuri has surrounded the island. Where shall we go to get wood for the island? We are getting hungry. What shall we do? Where shall we go to make our seedbeds? Let something be done here on this island for we are surrounded on all sides. We used to make seedbeds over on the shore. Let us send messengers to Zurumban, our brother, and see whether he will help us." (See Plate 21.) So he called the priests and said to them: "Go to Zurumban, for he is a Master, take this fish, and tell him who the Chichimecas are, how many of them there are, and ask whether he will go with us to destroy them. We are many more than they for there are not many Chichimecas, but they get together in the forest and do these things to us."

The priests called on Zurumban, who was always drunk and never ceased drinking. He had a wreath of fiber on his head, for he was one of Xaratanga's priests, and some miniature golden pincers around his neck. The old men, Canagecua and Uxuriqua, approached him and he asked them what they wanted. Their answer was: "Sire, you see here this fish sent to you by your older brother Caricaten, who told us to bring this fish to his brother Zurumban and tell him that Tariacuri has him surrounded on this island and he cannot get out. He has nothing to burn. He has no place to make seedbeds for we are besieged on the island. What does Zurumban, the Master of the village, think of all this? He is a native of this place and not from Tariaran, where he lives. He is an Islander and is of the lineage of Haparicha; Vinturo-patin is his god, also a native of Aparicha, who left the island because of a famine sent by Mother Cueravaperi and because it did not rain for a year. Over yonder they made their seedbeds so that they could eat. Zurumban was seized there and so became their slave. Because he gathered wood for the temples of the Goddess Xaratanga, they favored him and he became the principal priest, and the God of the Inferno heard him. A mole came out on top of the earth in the middle of the road where he was bringing wood in Unguani. That mole stood up in the middle of the road and then and there ordered him to be Master and told him that he should accept Xaratanga as the goddess and that is the way it is now. Who is Tariacuri that we should not get together in a single morning and destroy him?"

Zurumban laughed heartily at the embassy of the Islanders. His answer to the messengers was: "What can you poor people say or do, for Tariacuri knows the celestial gods very well, as well as Mother Cueravaperi, and the Gods of the Four Quarters of the world and the God of the Inferno. He is well known to all of them. How can you do him any harm since it was your women who gave birth to him? Since they gave birth to him, why did you not drown him then, when you could have thrown him in the lake? Now you can do him no harm for the gods know him well. Sit down and eat and I will speed you on your way." When they had finished eating, they begged to take their leave. Zurumban replied: "God speed you and you may expect the priest Naca. I shall send him tomorrow and I shall be there; war people will be called together, for if it is true that there are very few Chichimecas we shall all get together and destroy them. Tell this to our brother Caricaten."

The following day Zurumban called Naca and ordered him to gather the war people. They collected some short shirts called *Ucata Tararenauequa* and some fiber wreaths and gave them all to Naca to take with him. Zurumban gave him instructions: "Take a message to Coringuaro and you will go to the island of Xaraquero. The people of Coringuaro will come there, and so will the Islanders; we shall go another way, and in this fashion we shall kill the Chichimecas."

Naca departed along a road by which there was a village called Siraneni and the Master there was called Quaracuri. As Naca passed by his door, Quaracuri said: "Welcome, brother; come eat for you were passing my house and you must be hungry; welcome, Sir, you must eat." Food was brought out for both Naca and Quaracuri. They ate, then washed their hands, and Naca said he must get ready to go. Quaracuri asked him where he was going, saying: "For I who am old, am I not to know about it?" Naca replied: "Why should you not know? You shall indeed know—I am going to the lake to call the people of Coringuaro: I am going to gather the war people for we are to destroy Tariacuri." Cuaricuri [Quaracuri] answered: "That seems right, sir; I shall know it when you go." Naca asked him: "Well, brother, will you go with me and bring your war people?" Cuaricuri [Quaracuri] answered: "Of course, sir, it is only a short distance to the place you describe, and I shall gather the spoils of whatever I make them leave though they be only grinding stones or some of their adornments." To this Naca agreed, saying: "So it shall be, brother, for our gods will make them leave many things." Quaracuri wished

134

Naca a good journey, saying: "You came to my house and I am ashamed of the food I have given you." And Naca left.

42. TARIACURI RECEIVES A WARNING

After Naca left to gather the war people, Cuariacuri [Quaracuri] called a priest and said to him: "Go to our son Tariacuri and tell him that Naca has been going around saying that he is going to the lake to gather up war people and that he is to call up the people of Coringuaro. Tell him that Naca will stay at the lake gathering war people, and that they say that they are to destroy our son Tariacuri. Tell Tariacuri to remember this and be forewarned so that he may not be taken by surprise. To be warned is to have three-quarters of the battle won. Let him be prepared. This is what you must tell him."

When the messenger arrived, he found Tariacuri seated at the business of making arrows. Tariacuri went to meet the priest with bow and arrows in hand and greeted him. Then the priest spoke: "Your father Quaracuri sends me and says: 'Go to our son Tariacuri and tell him that Naca says that he is going to the island to gather war people, and from there he is going to call the war people of Coringuaro and that together they are going to destroy you, that you should be prepared and forewarned'; this is what he said."

Tariacuri asked: "Is it true that Naca is gone to the lake?" And the priest answered affirmatively. Then Tariacuri spoke, saying: "That is all very well; you are welcome; you are not to return to your house soon, but go to the lake. First you shall go to a place called Virichu where you will find my aunt, the wife of Perapaqua. She has canoes and she will take you across the lake to the place called Cuyumeo. There you will land with the canoe and go to the inns and see whether they are drinking wine. Eventually Naca will have to come out to urinate, and you shall go up to him and ask him what is going on and what he is doing there. And you shall tell him, 'Sire, your brother Quaracuri sends me, saying, go to my brother, Naca, and tell him that I was very much ashamed when I gave him so little to eat. Ask him which day and how long from now he will return because I am expecting him and want to give him food on his return. I shall make pigweed bread and maguey wine so that he may drink when he returns for travelers get hot and are thirsty. This you shall say to him in order to learn when he is coming. You shall reply to him according to his statements and tell him also that his brother wants to know which way he is coming because there are two ways, the way he came by Ciriquaretero along an arroyo near there which is a roundabout way, and the road beside the lake by a mountain called Xanoato Huacacio, which comes by Curimizundiro and ends at Apanguco, where begins the way to Varichu Hucario and goes to another place called Hiriquaro and on to Tarevacuquaro. This is nearer than the way he came. If he is to come this way, I shall await him here.' This is what you shall tell Naca on behalf of Quaracuri." The priest's pleasant answer was: "I agree, Sire, I shall go." Tariacuri told him to come back the same way and report whatever he should learn and that he could go home after they had talked.

The priest left and went to Hurichu [Virichu] as Tariacuri had told him and found Perapaco's [Perapaqua] wife, who took him across the lake to Cuyumeo, an island in the lake, where he found Naca, who had been drinking for quite some time. He came out of the house to urinate and there were many people with him. Naca, dressed in a short, broad shirt and feather braid, was surprised on seeing the priest and wanted to know what he was doing there. The priest answered: "Your brother Quaracuri sends me." Naca squatted to urinate and asked: "What does my brother say?" The priest answered, saying: "Sire, he says he is ashamed of the poor reception he gave you for no one told him you were coming. He wants to know when you will return for he wants to know what day to be ready for you so he can prepare a good meal of pigweed bread and maguey wine that you may drink upon your return because it is hot and travelers get thirsty." Naca replied: "Today messengers went to Coringuaro; they will return tomorrow, and I shall be busy all day tomorrow

gathering the war people. The following day I shall return."
Then the priest said: "Your brother, the Master, asks which way
you are coming because there are two ways: the long way by
Ziricuaretero and the short way by Xanoato Huacacio and Curimizundiro." Naca answered: "That is true—I came the long way,
for whom are we afraid of? We are not always at war. Tell him I
shall land at Xanoato Huacacio at a place called Pangue Hacunqueo [Panga Hacuqueo] and I shall go that way. Let him come
along that road and I shall go there to eat; that is my answer."

The priest departed, crossed the lake again in his canoe and
was welcomed back by Tariacuri. The priest greeted him and
recounted all that Naca had said. Tariacuri accepted this, saying:
"What Naca says is quite true. Why should we be afraid that we
should always be at war since we are not; go home and tell our
Father to expect him, to get wine out for him." The priest departed, and Tariacuri explained to his brothers, Cetaco and
Aramen, that Naca had gone to the lake to gather war people,
that he had called the war people of Coringuaro and that he was
to spend all the next day on the island gathering war people who
were to destroy the Chichimecas. He told them that the Islanders
had asked for help from Zurumban of Tariaran, and their
cousins had agreed to co-operate. Then Tariacuri asked them
what they thought about it, and told them to speak up. Whereupon they replied: "What can we say Sire, if you order us to do
so we shall say what we think and we shall help you." "So it is,"
said Tariacuri, "give me that bag." From it he took a knife used
for the sacrifice of ears and said to them: "Take this knife; with
it I fed the Fire God who makes fire in the midst of chief priests'
houses; take also these deer skin wreaths." The brothers replied
that they would be happy to take them. Tariacuri continued:
"Tomorrow, early in the morning, begin making arrows and let
the quivers have four compartments. Put many arrows in them.
About midday take your leave and go to Panga Hacuqueo. Go up
the hillside and put wood there and do not go to sleep. Keep
watch all night until dawn, keeping the fire going. When daylight comes, let two of you climb the mountain called Haracinda.

Lie down on the ground there and watch the lake to see if anyone is coming and how many canoes there are. You are valiant
men, let one of your spies go down and advise the other so that
you may be informed. Let one of you wait for Naca at the landing, and as soon as you know that he has disembarked, begin
sacrificing your ears making deep gashes. Then scatter the blood
on some weeds along the way, also make deer tracks, and take
him the way you made the deer tracks. Continue sprinkling the
weeds and all of you keep going around as if looking for a
wounded deer. Lead him off a ways from the road toward the
mountain where you shall take him prisoner, for we did not begin the war, but rather others began it against us. That was what
the gods ordered Curicaveri, that he should not start the war but
that someone else was to start and that he should be forewarned
to defend himself. God speed you, brothers."

They departed, arriving at Vacanavaro, where they spent the
entire day making arrows. Then they left, taking the trail to
Panqua Hacunqueo [Panga Hacuqueo], which took them to the
top of a little hill. There they kept watch all night, and at day-
break two spies climbed Mount Haracinda, where they lay down
on the ground to keep watch over the lake. Soon they saw five
canoes coming, and as they were about to land, one of the spies
went down and notified those in ambush that Naca had landed.
Quaracuri went to meet him and took food to him. Naca welcomed him and asked what time he had left. He explained that
he had left the night before, "and I brought along the food and
the wine for you." They all ate and drank, and Naca took his
leave, saying: "I've had enough now, brother; I want to be on
my way. I want to take these two jugs of wine for, when the day
gets hot, I shall be thirsty," and he asked to be excused. To this
Quaracuri said: "You have come as we agreed, may God speed
you."

As Naca left, the spy went ahead and informed another who
in turn notified the people, saying: "He is coming, behold there
he comes now." Then the people in the ambush began to gash
their ears and scatter the blood upon the weeds and upon the

138

false hoofprints so that Naca might think that it was the blood of a wounded deer. All were painted, and each had his quiver on his shoulder and deer hoofs tied to his legs.

Naca came up to the people and greeted them; they in turn asked: "But you, brother, where did you go?" His explanation was: "Brother, I went to the lake to buy some fish and I am on my way home." To this the Chichimecas replied: "May God speed you, brother," whereupon Naca, in turn, asked what they were doing there. They explained by saying, "Yesterday we made arrows and this morning we climbed this mountain for recreation. We found a deer but our marksmanship was poor; you can see for yourself that he went this way; here you see its tracks," and Naca asked: "Brother, I met with you today. Will you not give me a piece of the deer with which to make an offering to the gods?" The Chichimecas answered: "You will not make the offering, but you shall take a quarter of it on your shoulder." Naca answered: "That is the way it should be, brothers. Which way is it going?" Their response was, "Where should he go, brother? This deer is very smart, else why is he not here?" Then Naca asked: "Brothers, are you going to catch him?" And they answered: "Why not, for we shall not rest until we have run down the wounded animal, caught it and killed it." At this point Naca took his leave, wishing them a successful hunt and started on his way.

As they saw him leaving, Aramen, who was a very brave man, said to his brother, Cetaco: "Look, brother, he is getting away, what shall we do?" He took an arrow out of his quiver and shot Naca in the back with it. (See Plate 22.) Then he went straight to him, threw his arms around Naca's neck, and they all seized him. At this juncture, Naca said: "Easy, brothers, easy, for you are hurting me; for a certainty you must be Chichimecas, no one else dares to deceive so." The only answer the Chichimecas gave was: "Listen to what this fellow says; go tell it to Tariacuri." So they took him to Tariacuri, who welcomed them and asked what was going on. Cetaco and Aramen answered: "Sire, we have caught him," and Tariacuri queried: "Well, what does he say?"

To this they responded by repeating Naca's words: "Easy, easy, for you are hurting me, you must be Chichimecas for no one else would be so deceptive." Then Tariacuri commanded: "Because he said that, take him to the temple and sacrifice him."

43 . TARIACURI'S VENGEANCE

After they had sacrificed the priest called Naca, Tariacuri ordered him cooked (see Plate 23), then called his servants and gave them these orders: "Take his thighs to Zurumban, who sent him to gather the war people, so that he may make an offering to the gods; take the abdomen and the ribs to the Islanders for their offering, and take the two arms to Coringuaro for theirs. Tell our Priest Quaracuri to use a basket for the legs and thighs and to cover them with berries. Tell him that I will send two old priests to deliver the meat, and so that they will not realize what they are doing, he should tell them not to stop drinking wine. The old men will call upon Zurumban with the meat and he will ask what it is and why they come. They will answer and say that it is meat, whereupon he will ask where this man was caught. They shall answer: 'He was one of Tariacuri's slaves who had intercourse with one of his wives, so Tariacuri had him sacrificed. He sent a quarter to your brother Quaracuri so that he might hold a wake and make an offering with him. Your brother thought the meat was something to be shared and that he should not eat it all. He told us to take it to his brother Zurumban because he drinks wine, and this would help to sober him; and Quaracuri would eat the shin bones.' " This was all according to custom, for when sacrificing anyone, these people would always divide the sacrificed one among the houses of the chief priests, and they would make the offering to the gods and eat the meat.

Tariacuri gave further instructions to the messenger, saying: "Tell Quaracuri to station a fast runner outside Zurumban's village. Quaracuri should order the two old men who were to deliver the meat to watch Zurumban eat it and then leave immediately. They should meet the runner and tell him that Zurumban had eaten the meat. The runner should then go as fast as he could, throwing water on his face so that he would appear to be sweating, and suddenly enter Zurumban's house. Zurumban will ask him why he is sweating. Then the runner will say: 'Sire, your brother Quaracuri told me to run as fast as I could and if you have not already eaten the meat to tell you not to eat it, for it was not one of Tariacuri's slaves; he is the one whom we sent to gather the war people; that if you have not eaten him, do not do so under any circumstance because he is the priest Naca.' " Tariacuri told all this to the messengers whom he was sending to Quaracuri so that it would appear that Quaracuri was sending them.

The meat was delivered by those two old men sent by Tariacuri, and the runner remained hidden quite a while as the old men went ahead and greeted Zurumban and told him the entire message sent by Tariacuri. Zurumban called the women of his household and told them to come quickly and heat the meat. As they heated it, they cut it up and put it on gourd plates. All the principals and the ladies gathered in the patio and they brought the meat out and placed it before Zurumban. They set some out for themselves and brought some to the old men who had brought it, and everyone ate. After eating, the old men begged to be excused for they wanted to take their leave. Zurumban called one of his majordomos called Vyana and another called Cuta and told them to get some blankets for these old men. They brought short shirts and some blankets for each one and for their wives and blankets for Quaracuri, their Master, and Zurumban said: "Take these to my brother Quaracuri, your Master." He wished them a good trip and said: "You have seen how I ate the meat; tell it to my brother."

After they left and had traveled a ways, the runner met them and the messengers said to him: "Go quickly, sir, for Zurumban has already eaten the meat." Then the runner threw water on his face, pretending that he was sweating from running and dashed into Zurumban's house, who wanted to know what it was all about. The runner answered, saying: "Sire, your brother Quaracuri sent me, saying to run as fast as I could, for if you have not already eaten the meat, do not do so, for it was not Tariacuri's slave, but the one we sent to gather the war people, the priest Naca, and for you not to eat it under any circumstances." When he heard this, Zurumban asked: "What is this man saying? Arrest him, capture him." And all the priests and everyone who was in the patio got up as one, and Zurumban repeated his orders to take the fool. But the runner quickly slipped through the patio door and disappeared into the forest. Many pursued him but he was so fast that they could not catch up with him, and he climbed a very high ridge. Zurumban stayed in the patio vomiting, and his women put their hands in their mouths trying to vomit the meat, but they could not because it was already settled in their stomachs and intestines. Zurumban was very much ashamed over the trick that Tariacuri played on him.

44. ZURUMBAN HAS HIS DAY

Zurumban was so shocked by the deception that he exclaimed bitterly over the treatment accorded him by Tariacuri, saying that those were not the words of Quaracuri. He called a servant and told him to gather war people and go to Vacanavaro, "for there are people there who are Chichimecas and that seed plot is not Tariacuri's, but is mine; knock down their granaries and raze their houses, take the breeches off Cetaco and Aramen, the brothers of Tariacuri, and take away their lip-rings, for they did what they have done out of arrogance. For what they have done to us and for insulting us, cast them out roughly, stone them, take the skirts and petticoats off the women and dishonor them, throwing dirt on them afterward."

Vyana took the war people and left; they tore down the granaries, razed the houses, took the breeches and lip-rings off, took all of their goods and drove them out roughly toward Pázcuaro; they dishonored the women according to orders, despoiling all of them and, since they were women, they seized their children and gathered them together to cover up their dishonor, one called

Hiripan and another called Tangaxoan. In this manner they were cast out of the village. (See Plate 24.)

When he learned of this and thinking that they were on his trail, Tariacuri and all his people arose and left their homes as they were, leaving their meals, not even finishing their porridge, tamales and other foods; everything was left in the weeds. Dogs, parrots, chickens, all went into the weed patches, and they went to a place called Hurique Macuritiro, then on to Evarizan Vivio. Tariacuri arrived at Zinzuariquaro and settled at the foot of an oak.

His cousins, Cetaco and Aramen, sent messengers to Tariacuri to tell him that he and they had been sentenced to death. The messengers departed but they found no one in the village and returned to inform Cetaco and Aramen that there was no one there, the entire place was deserted, and Tariacuri's whereabouts unknown. They were angry and said to them: "What do you messengers say? Do you think we dare not kill? Where has he gone? Why did you not follow his trail? Be gone before dawn." They went back to search for him and followed his trail through the weeds. They found him at a place called Hervario Zinzuariquaro, lying at the foot of an oak and surrounded by his women, while the rest of the Chichimecas were scattered among the weeds. When the messengers arrived, Tariacuri said: "Welcome, brothers; it is my fault you have had all this trouble finding me, because I ordered my cousins to come to a place called Yengoan and all of you too, and you will eat there. Go and tell them to come, for there I have a store of shirts so that your women may dress themselves."

When the messengers returned and reported Tariacuri's words, the brothers said: "This is what the King says, that we may take that corn and eat it for it belongs to no one but Curicaveri and not to him; and if we do not take it, where else would we get so much? The blankets that he claims are not his but rather Curicaveri's. Where else could we find another of equal quantity? Why should we not beget children? And here are Hiripan and Tangaxoan, our sons; perhaps they will be mistreated because of

143

our request, but let us go to Quaracuri who ordered this," and so they all departed.

These people had a custom which obligated them or their children to become slaves if they accepted, even as gifts, corn or blankets destined for war from the granaries of the gods. Cetaco went to live with his people on the mountain, and Aramen, his younger brother, who was a most valiant man, established himself at Hiracio, and he and his people settled at the foot of a slope.

Tariacuri returned to Pázcuaro and set up a great market in Parco, a nearby village. To this market there frequently came the wife of Caricaten, Master of the Island of Xaraquaro. Also Aramen, who was very handsome, would come to the same market dressed in his best finery according to the customs of the time. He stationed himself beside the market and Caricaten's wife, since women are incontinent, sent for him and they slept together. She crossed the lake many times to see him, and Aramen would come down to the market where they would meet, and no one saw them for the lords were in the habit of drinking. The women who gathered there became jealous of one another and the other women said to this lady: "You surely are artful; they say you are Caricaten's wife, but see how discreet you are: do you love or think about him who is your husband? They say that the Chichimeca Aramen sleeps with you and that you cross the lake many times to meet him." It was nighttime and Caricaten overheard them. The next morning he called all his women together and began to question them. "Is it true what you say?" And his women answered: "Yes, sir; it is true that Aramen sleeps with her." He began to curse Aramen, saying: "How that stupid fool has dishonored me." Since they could not be alone on the mountain at this time, he sent some old men accompanied by others and gave them the following instructions: "Old men, take this fish to Aramen and ask how he is. When he sees you, he will welcome you and you will place before him this fish; take him and kill him." They took their leave and went to Aramen's house where they found him bathing. He had on a blanket and was seated, drying himself. When he saw them, he extended a welcome to the Islanders, and they returned his greeting, saying: "Your brother Caricaten sends us saying, 'Take this fish to my brother Aramen to eat with his boiled corn.'" He thanked them, asked them to remain seated there and said that food would be brought to them, and they ate. After eating, they begged to be excused for they wanted to go, saying they had finished eating. Aramen asked them to wait, saying he would look for some blankets and some shirts which they could take with them, and he went out.

The lords customarily have their bows and arrows at the door and the Islanders took the bow and arrows, aimed and shot him in the back. When Aramen felt himself wounded, he quickly jumped over a wall and fled into the mountain, where he lay down at the foot of an oak and died. The Islanders took his sisters, bound them and threw them into the lake at the island of Xaraquaro. When they returned, Caricaten greeted them and asked: "Did you kill him?" They answered that they had only shot him and did not know where he went, and that they had brought all his sisters. Caricaten became angry with them, insulted them and said: "Who told you to bring his sisters? Take them to Puruaten's temple and sacrifice them; then throw the stupid bad women in the lake."

When Tariacuri learned about it, he was very grieved and called together his counselors called Chupitani, Tecaquien [Tecaque], and Nurivan and said: "You shall go to Coringuaro, to old man Chanhori, and take this rich plumage to him for he makes adornments with these feathers for his God Huren de Quevecara. He has 800 plumes and 1,200 parrot feathers for his God Huren de Quevecara and other colored ones numbering 1,200 and 1,400 from other birds. You shall say to old man Chanhori that I beg him to grant passage for me and my people across his land in order to go to Mahiquisi, Master of Condembaro, who they say is a very brave man and whose help I need. I ask only that he allow me safe conduct to go to Condembaro."

The messengers departed and came to the Master of Coringuaro. He greeted and welcomed the Chichimecas and they greeted him in turn. They placed the plumage before him, saying that their Master sent them, and they told him Tariacuri's message, to which the Master of Coringuaro replied: "What is this that our son Tariacuri says about which way he is to go to the Lord of Condembaro? This man is so brave that he is crazy. Mahiquisi twists blankets and strikes travelers in the face with them, and if he becomes angry, he sacrifices them. He has a kettle-drum made of a man's thigh and he plays this toy with a man's arm. He drinks wine from a man's skull and in this manner he has gone crazy and is an evil man. To what end should Tariacuri go to him? Let him come here with his people to one of my vil-lages called Tupataro, and he may bring his God Curicaveri. He and his people may drink at the spring called Xaripitio; this is my answer."

With this the messengers returned but Tariacuri had already departed for Coringuaro. They caught up with him on the way and he was glad to see them. They recounted all that was said by the Master of Coringuaro. Tariacuri considered the matter, looked ahead and said: "What does he say about the corn that Chanhori told us to take, and the beans? How can we have chil-dren if they are to ask us for it afterward? Where would we get it? And what he claims, is it his own? Or does it not belong to his god, Huren de Quevecara? When we die they will require it of our children. Look, let us stay here, be this place whatever it may be," and he established himself behind a range called Hoatapejo, and there they built temples, houses for the chief priests, fire-places, and houses for themselves.

45. TARIACURI'S ILL-FATED MARRIAGE

Days came and went and the Master of Coringuaro called his sons together for a consultation: "Let us see what your opinion is; tell me for I want to hear it. You know that Tariacuri has Curicaveri who is a great god. Would it not be good for you to take your sister to him?" And the sons answered: "You have spoken well, Sire; what could we say? Your opinion suffices for it is good." Since they agreed to give her to Tariacuri for wife, he called some old men and said to them: "Take my daughter to Tariacuri on my behalf." And he told them what they were to say. Then he called his daughter and advised her: "Do not go away from your husband, but stay beside him at all times. No matter how he may treat you, say nothing to him and it will please the gods to have a son by him and in this manner we could take Curicaveri away from him. Curicaveri is a very great god, for he and Huren de Quevecara, our god, were begotten together."

The old men took the lady to Tariacuri who, upon seeing them, extended a welcome. At this time Tariacuri was at a place called Zimbani making arrows. (See Plate 25.) The old men greeted him and said: "Your father, Chanhori, sends us to bring his daughter to Tariacuri so that she may take his bow and arrows when he comes in from the hunt and take his ax and the mat from his back when he comes in from gathering wood all day. She will make blankets for Curicaveri, and afterward for Tariacuri, so that he shall have the strength to go to the gods in the mountains: for these reasons we bring this Lady." To all this Tariacuri responded: "You bring her at a good time and what you have told me has not been said to me but to Curicaveri, our god. Be seated and food shall be brought to you!" They were served and asked to be excused, but Tariacuri asked them to wait: "I shall find some blankets and some shirts which you shall wear upon your return. Tell our father that I accept her."

The messengers returned and the woman went into Tariacuri's house and not long afterward she became pregnant. She frequently went to Coringuaro without permission where her friends kept getting her drunk in the houses of the chief priests. (See Plate 26.) The last time she went she did not return, and when Tariacuri came in to bring wood for the temples, there was only an aunt to prepare food for him. He ate and ordered that his aunt be called and asked what had become of the woman from Coringuaro. "Has she gone home never to return again?" The aunt replied that she had not returned and had not even sent a messenger. Then Tariacuri asked his aunt whether it would be a good idea for her to go get the woman. The aunt answered: "All right, Sire, but if I go, what shall I say? I shall be happy to go; why should I not? But if I go, her father will not let me have her. Would it not be better, Sire, if you would go? You could be back in the afternoon." To this Tariacuri replied, saying: "What you say, Aunt, is true; I will go. It is true that we ought to go," and his people all said: "Let us go," and they departed.

They went straight to Zurumban Angatacayo where they caught a deer. Furthermore, all the people carried large bunches of branches and wood. They were traveling in two processions and they arrived in this manner at the village carrying the deer before them. They started a large fire which gave off huge flames and a great deal of smoke beside the ark of the Coringuaro god, Huren de Quavecara. They sacrificed the deer at the foot of the ark, tied it and placed it on its back. All the brothers, relatives and wives of Chanhori, Master of Coringuaro, had been drinking for some time; and Chanhori, his father-in-law, greeted him, welcoming the father of Curatame for that was his grandson's name, that is, the son of Tariacuri. Likewise, Tariacuri greeted his father-in-law who said: "You make me very happy by coming and with the game you bring; you certainly are my son. Dress the deer for we do not know how, and with it we shall cure our drunkenness." Tariacuri quartered and roasted it himself for his father-in-law and gave each one pieces of the roasted deer. At this time his father-in-law said to him: "Son, why did you not bring your wife with you so we could all eat together and converse a little? Why are you so jealous?" Tariacuri answered: "I did not bring her because she has not returned to her house. I came to make an offering of wood to Huren de Quavecara. This was my only reason for coming. After catching the deer, I wanted to enter your house for its sake. We sacrificed it near Curimbaro and for this reason I came here." Then his father-in-law said: "Will you have a drink? I have some good wine," to which Tariacuri replied: "If I drink wine I shall fall upon all of you because you gave me a very bad raiser of children." Tariacuri was very angry and took his bow and arrows and left the house without taking leave. His

148

father-in-law then asked: "Is Tariacuri going back to the same old way at his house?"

It is not known how a brother-in-law of Tariacuri, called Huresqua, knew about this, but he met him on the way. After greeting each other, the cousin asked Tariacuri why he was returning so soon without drinking some wine. Tariacuri answered: "They tried to give me some wine when I first arrived. The first thing they said to me was to ask about your sister whom I have not seen nor can I find her. Why is she not here among you, for it is a long time since she came here and I have come for her now. You all should reprimand her and should not ask me about her for you gave her to Curicaveri when you married her to me." His cousin agreed, saying: "You are right, sir, and perhaps she has indeed come here. I will go back and ask each and every one there, and the old men will take her back to your house."

Tariacuri departed and his brother-in-law went home to his father, Chanhori, and said to him: "You lost my sister to Tariacuri who has come for her because she came home a long time ago." Chanhori called the women of his house and asked them: "Women, have you seen Tariacuri's wife?" and they replied negatively. Then the old Chanhori asked: "Who told her to leave her husband? Go find her." The woman, learning that they were looking for her, voluntarily returned to her house, went into her room and seated herself. The women of the house came to her and told her to get up for her father was calling for her. They took her to him although he was drunk and his entire face was covered with paint. He spoke to her severely: "Look you, where have you been? Your poor weeping husband came for you. It has been a long time since you came back. Who told you to leave him?" She admitted the accusation: "That is the truth, Father; I came back angry for I do not understand what Tariacuri means. I should never have become angry with what he would say to me every day. When he was making arrows he would take one in his hand, show it to me, and say that he was a valorous man and that with these he was going to kill all my brothers and relatives. He asked how can they be brave men? They are trifling. Why do they want to wear lip-rings? Is what they wear a real lip-ring? Is it not rather a stick? They are not strong men, they are women and the clover-leaf wreaths they wear on their heads are only women's ribbons which they put in their hair. Their golden earrings are not made of gold but are ear-bobs for women. Why do they not take them off and put on the masculine kind? And the embroidery they have on their backs is not of brave men but the work of women, and the shirts they wear are nothing but women's blankets and skirts. Why do they wear tiger skins on their wrists? Do they think they are brave men? They would do better to buy strings of beads to put on their wrists. The other insignia of valiant men and the kilts that they wear are not kilts but rather women's skirts and sashes. Their bows are women's looms, their arrows are nothing but shuttles and spindles. Are these the things of brave men? I will kill them and finish them all off; look woman, I will shoot them with these. This is what Tariacuri says to me; not a day goes by that he does not say this, every time he makes arrows. How could I keep from becoming angry when he says the same thing. It is true that I came back out of love for my brothers."

On hearing this fabrication, her father became angry and said: "Mind what you say, for Tariacuri must have said this, for these are not the words of women." He called the old men and told them to take this woman to her husband and they took her back to Tariacuri's house. Along the way they came to a place called Xoropiti and another one called Tarequetzingata. On arriving at each of these places they took notice of her, got her drunk, and committed adultery with her as was their custom.

The next morning Tariacuri returned from gathering wood for the temples and sat down in a portal while food was brought to him. Then the woman came to the door with a gourd plate of fish in her hand. She stopped at the door, crossed herself,[14]

---

[14] Occasionally throughout the *Relación* our priest-interpreter either permits his imagination to take over or there actually was some action taken that he misread. While we have substituted the words "chief priests" throughout the manu-

looked in many times as one who has done some wrong, and kept watch, waiting for an opportunity to enter. She decorated her skirt, tightened it, clasped her hands together, scratched with her fingernail and finally made up her mind to go in. When she entered she put the fish beside Tariacuri and welcomed him, and he in turn welcomed her, whereupon she said: "Oh, Sire, I went to buy some fish." Then she went inside and as she turned her back she stopped at the door. Then Tariacuri called and told her to let his aunt come. The aunt answered and Tariacuri said: "Come, take this fish and cook it all. We who do not eat brothel fish, are we to eat this?" And the woman was at the door listening. Tariacuri spoke again, saying: "Take it and cook it all and leave a little for an offering of fish to Curicaveri, for this woman has done nothing yet except to Curicaveri." His wife entered the house and Tariacuri returned to the mountain for wood for the fireplaces.

46. THE TREACHEROUS WIFE

After spending a few days at a feast in Purecotagüaro,[15] Tariacuri went with his people to perform the sacrifice of the ears, which was customary in these times. He wanted to go somewhere to take his pleasure. From their arks they took out the God Curicaveri and another war god called Pungarecha and put them at the foot of the ark in order that the priests might dress themselves with them, and they put Pungarecha in the patio.

Soon after Tariacuri departed with his people, two men came along behind shouting in a loud voice. Tariacuri called one of the old men who was with him, one called Chupitani, and asked him who those men were. Chupitani said he did not know so Tariacuri sent a committee of old men to meet them. Their

script for the compilers' word "Pope," here we have no idea what action was taken, if any, that could be used. Obviously, the woman would not have "crossed herself" as it was quite some time before the arrival of the Spaniards.

15 Also Purecoracua or Phurecutacuro. According to Caso, the *Relación* is in error in stating that it was February 23. He maintains in his "The Calendar of the Tarascans," p. 15, that the correct date is February 22.

names were Xoropiti and Tareqüesinguata, and they asked the old men whether their brother-in-law was there and they replied in the affirmative. Xoropiti and Tareqüesinguata said that they were on their way to sacrifice their ears in the feast at the mountain called Hoataropejo, whereupon the old men said they wanted to tell it to Tariacuri. They reported back to him about the visitors, saying they came from a village called Yzipamuco and that they were on their way to sacrifice their ears. Tariacuri ordered that Curicaveri and Pungarecha be put back in their arks so that they should not be displeased if something should happen here. He took his bow and arrows and went to meet the visitors. He extended a welcome and asked them where they were going: "We came, brother-in-law, to make a sacrifice in this feast at the mountain called Hoataropejo." Tariacuri made them welcome and said to his people: "We have already made the solemn oath to Curicaveri here. Why is there no wine left over?"

They were going homeward, talking, and when Tariacuri's wife learned about it, she dressed up in her finery and went about greeting the visitors and making them welcome. Food was brought out for them to eat, they were served wine in cups, and Tariacuri washed his hands and served each one wine four times. They invited their brother-in-law and asked him if he was not going to drink. Tariacuri answered: "I will drink later, brothers, because when I drink wine, I become very confused, and if I get drunk, perhaps I shall fall upon all of you here because I am so disconcerted when I drink. You go ahead and drink and I shall pour," and he kept giving them wine. Secretly, he had the axes bound in order to go to the mountain, and they were slipped out of the house. That afternoon he took his leave of them and said: "You are welcome to stay, brothers-in-law, but I want to go for some clover leaves over there by that mountain to make wreaths to protect our heads against the sun." The brothers-in-law asked: "What do you mean, sir, why must you yourself go? Let your servants go," and Tariacuri answered: "My servants do not know the place and I know where it is; I want to go and I will be back soon; in the meantime you keep drinking for there is plenty of wine. I am going now for it is not far." So they wished him good luck and he took his bow and arrows and left the house. He went over by the mountain called Hoatacustio and began to clear and rick the wood that he was to take to the temples and placed the ricks in the order in which they were to be taken. He made a round mound of branches to burn. It was now about midnight and a great flame rose and the burning embers rose high toward the heavens while Tariacuri was lying at the foot of an oak.

After Tariacuri left home, his wife dressed herself up prettily and said to those young men: "Tariacuri is gone and you need have no worry for it is I who live in this house and not Tariacuri. It is his custom to go for wood and he does not drink. I shall pour for you," and she began to do so. After dark, when she would come before them to pour, they began to frolic with her, and they stayed with her that night, being very intimate with her. Since they were all painted up, their paint rubbed off on her face and clothes. In the morning they returned to their village, the woman went back into her house, and Tariacuri was now bringing his wood to the temples. All the people came shouting and Tariacuri was leading them as they took the wood to the fireplaces, unloaded it there, and started a huge fire whose flames shot skyward to great heights with great clouds of smoke.

The two men, Xoropiti and Tareqüesinguata, ran shouting to their village, Zipamucu. Tariacuri went home and found wine spilled and spattered all over his house and the whole place foul with the smell of it. He entered the house at once where his aunt met and greeted him with a warm welcome, whereupon Tariacuri asked: "Where is my wife? Why has the house not been swept?" Her answer was: "Oh, my lord, she is not well; she is in her room there in back where you sleep." Then Tariacuri asked: "What do you mean Aunt, when did she become sick?" His aunt explained that she became ill right after he left home. He asked whether she was very ill. His aunt answered that she had done nothing all night but vomit; maybe she has an illness called "senguero." Tariacuri wanted to go to her immediately, but his aunt said: "I hope you will not go. Eat first while I get her up

153

and bathe her, then you may be with her a little while." But Tariacuri paid no attention and went at once to where she was sleeping. He found a girl sitting beside her and her face was covered with a light blanket. He spoke to the girl, saying: "They say my wife is sick," and she nodded affirmatively. He had his bow in his hand and lifted the blanket from her face with it. Then he saw that she was all covered with paint, her sash in disarray, her breasts covered with paint and wine on her lips. Then Tariacuri said: "Yes, indeed, she surely is sick." He covered her again and went out going straight to the mountain for wood. He refused to eat anything and dared not put his hands on her out of love for her father whose wrath he did not wish to incur, for he was not far away and was more powerful than he.

On the other hand, the adulterers, on the way home, sacrificed their ears making deep gashes and splitting them as was their customary way of punishing those who were taken in adultery. They went home shouting, with blood flowing from their ears. They had a maternal uncle called Zinzuni, Master of Yzipamucu who, upon hearing the shouts, asked: "Who are those people who come shouting and making so much noise?" He ordered one of the old men of his house to go meet them. He did so, extended a welcome and asked them where they had been. They explained that they went to the mountain called Hoataropejo, and there Tariacuri gashed their ears, accusing them of having been caught with his wife, and they were on their way to tell their Uncle Zinzuni. When Zinzuni arrived he asked what the excitement was about. They replied: "Sire, the people you heard are your nephews. They went to the mountain Hoataropejo to sacrifice themselves and Tariacuri gashed their ears because a woman accuses them." The Master of Zipamucu [Yzipamucu] answered angrily, saying: "Look you what you say. Why did they go to the mountain called Hoataropejo to make their sacrifice? They have heard that Tariacuri drinks wine, that he gathers wood all day and all night. He was very generous when he only split their ears. He should have killed them on the spot. Let them go wherever they wish but they may not come here."

154

When they were told this, they went straight to the Master of Coringuaro, called Chanhori, and told him the same story: "Sire, we went to the mountain called Hoataropejo to make our sacrifice and while there, Tariacuri split our ears, accusing us of having relations with our relative, as his wife is not our sister." Then, to make matters worse, they told him what his daughter had said when she ran away, saying that they were all to be killed, for they had planned that story and told her to tell it to her father to stir everybody up. Then they told the Master of Coringuaro: "Tariacuri also says that we are cowards, that he is going to kill us and destroy us all." And they told him everything else that his daughter had fabricated previously and the same way she told it. For this reason the Master of Coringuaro believed it, because he had heard it twice now and he said: "It is true that Tariacuri said this because my poor daughter told it the same way that you have told it; they are all the same words."

47. TARIACURI'S GRIEF AND REMARRIAGE

Tariacuri knew that his wife was ruining him and it grieved him so much that he would not eat. He spent all his time gathering wood for the temples and never went home but went instead to the houses of the chief priests. He would gather wood during twenty days without interruption and then another twenty days. He would eat nothing, was very thin and had lost so much color that he was turning white. He kept tightening his belt as his waist became smaller and smaller, and he could barely stand up. When his aunt saw that he would die if he did not eat, she asked herself: "Am I partly to blame for the cause that makes him want to let himself die of hunger?" She made some porridge and went to meet him, stationing herself at the entrance through the board fence which surrounds the patio of the temples. He could not walk without falling and his men carried him by the arms, one on each side and in this manner they brought him out of the patio. His aunt went to meet him and greeted him with a warm welcome. He asked her: "What is the matter, Aunt?" Her reply was: "Oh, Sire, Islanders have come from the lake and I do not understand what they want. I, being an old woman, what should I say to them, for I do not know what they want to say to you? Sire, would it not be well for you to go to your house to learn what they want?" Tariacuri got up quickly for those people came from the island where he had been born, and he agreed to go with his aunt. When he got there he asked where they were. Her answer was: "They are out there back of the house, I fed them out there. Would it not be well for you to sit down and eat a little so you may have the strength to answer them? There is no telling what message they bring." Tariacuri agreed that it was a good idea. She made some porridge, served it up to him and he ate it quickly. Meanwhile his aunt, clutching her hands in fear, said to herself: "Oh, my, what shall I say; I do not know what to do for it is not true that the Islanders came from the lake. Will he not shoot me dead in this very place? Poor me, what shall I say to him?"

Tariacuri took a jar of water, washed his hands, got up and took his bow and arrows, went out of the portal where he had eaten and called his aunt. When she appeared, he asked where the Islanders were and said he wanted to see them. Then his aunt said: "Oh Sire, poor man; who would come and why should they come? You poor man, you have stopped eating because your wife is a bad woman; she is the kind now who sleeps with men, she for whom you have stopped eating. She is a dolt who wants only to be lustful with men every night, who does not know that you, Tariacuri, have flourished and are famous on this mountain called Hoataropejo, that you are King and your fame reaches the heavens where the gods are, as far as the Inferno and to the Four Quarters of the world. Are you perchance going to give up your name as Tariacuri? For what reason have you stopped eating and drinking? It were better, Sire, that you eat so that you may have the strength to gather wood for the temples, so that you may live many days because you are the Master. Take no thought for that woman because there will be no lack of another to keep you company so that you may be the Master. Perhaps the one you are

156

to have is not born yet. There must be a good one who will help you be the Master. Go to Zurumban, Master of Tariara, you and he shall be Masters." Tariacuri agreed that she was right and told his men that they would go to Zurumban, Master of Tariara, and they departed.

Before they arrived Zurumban learned of their coming and went out to meet them. His face was painted yellow for there was a feast, and he greeted Tariacuri and his people warmly, and taking Tariacuri by the hand, walked to his house talking all the while. On the way they saw a little bird, called *Zenzembo*, hanging from a flower sucking its honey. Seeing it, Zurumban said to Tariacuri, "Oh, what a beautiful little bird; shoot it, Sire, since you are a Chichimeca, shoot it." Tariacuri accepted the challenge: "It is a pleasure, I shall shoot, brother," and he put an arrow in his bow, and when he was ready to shoot, he turned to Zurumban and said: "Watch my shot and go bring the arrow back here." When he released the arrow he hit the mark and said to Zurumban, "I hit the mark, go for it," and Zurumban went through a patch of weeds, found the arrow and the bird. Bringing them in his hand he said to Tariacuri: "You are indeed a Chichimeca for this bird is not easy to shoot for it is so small. How can anyone compete with you? You do not miss a shot and no one can compete with you when it comes to shooting." They continued toward his house talking as they went. And as for the bird, strangely enough, it did not die but was fluttering in his hand as he carried it.

When they arrived at his house he found his women all together, and Zurumban said to them: "Mothers, look: Tariacuri does not miss a shot for you see this little bird which is so small that it cannot be shot. Look how pretty it is." The women handed it about among themselves exclaiming over the marksmanship. Then they served food and everybody ate. After eating, Zurumban said to Tariacuri: "Son, will you not have a cup of what I am drinking?" Tariacuri agreed readily and they served him some wine. Zurumban went into another room and got some yellow coloring material which he brought out to Tariacuri and

157

invited him to put on some of the paint. Tariacuri answered: "What do you mean, brother, how am I to put on that color when I am already painted with this black color, the color of my God Curicaveri, which is this soot. You put it on." The lords had the custom of painting themselves in honor of their God Curicaveri, and it was for this reason that Tariacuri said that he used that color for love of his god. Zurumban would not take no for an answer, insisting that he put the yellow color on and offered to do it for him. He put it on the nostrils and downward and on the nails of his hands and feet, and said that was the way he ought to put it on: "Oh, how handsome you are! and I must put this yellow color all over my body and my face," and Tariacuri told him to go ahead and put it on. Then Zurumban explained: "I put this color on now because I sacrificed some wrongdoers, called *Vazcata*, so that their spirits may go with the offering to Mother Cueravaperi, and they were all yellow."

Zurumban went inside to get two women (they were either his daughters or his wives), had them bathed and dressed, with turquoise earrings, strings of beads around their wrists, and turquoise necklaces. Leading them by the hand he took them to Tariacuri and said to him: "Here you see your mothers, who will take care of you so you will not fall off a cliff when you drink wine because it makes one lose his senses and become confused. In this condition one acts as if he were crazy and this place is precipitous. These women will take care of you and will watch where you go and shall be your handmaids whenever you sleep because you drank wine." Tariacuri said they could stay and both of them were left there. Tariacuri ordered wine for both of them. It being nighttime now for it was already dark, Zurumban said that he was drunk and would go to bed, "so I will not fall over all of you here. You go ahead and sleep." And he spoke to the women: "Place yourselves, daughters, on one side so that Tariacuri will not fall off a crag for there are nothing but cliffs around here and if something should happen to him the blame would fall on us," and to Tariacuri he said, "Go, brother, and sleep well," and Zurumban went into his room.

Tariacuri called the old men, Chupitani, Tequaque, and Nurivan, whom he had brought with him, and gave them the following instructions: "Put some mats in that corner over there and take those Ladies over there to sleep. Cover them for they may want to marry them to someone. Let there be no bewitching noise while bringing them so that there shall be no accord afterward in our disfavor." They took the ladies to the corner where they lay down to sleep and were covered. Then Tariacuri called his old men together and they began to talk and to plan. They did not sleep all night but kept watch so that they might not be taken by surprise.

When dawn broke Tariacuri suggested that they warm themselves at the fireplaces. The lords all had the custom, as explained earlier, of blackening themselves with soot for love of their God Curicaveri, and they held it to be a great honor to go about thus blackened. In order to be most magnificent and so that the black color would stick better, they would put small, wood-torches in the fireplaces and then put them under the shirts which they wore. The heat would make the smoke stick to their bodies, and then they stood out splendidly. This was called *Viriquareni* and for this purpose Tariacuri told the old men to bring those little braziers so that they might use the smoke, and he went out and sat at the entrance to the door to apply it.

Zurumban got up, and when he saw that the girls had already gone out, he asked them: "Did Tariacuri sleep with you? How did you sleep?" Their answer was: "No, Sire, he is crazy and has no sex; after you went to bed, Sire, he called his old men and told them to get some mats for us and they put us in a corner. He said there might be a bewitching noise to argue something unfavorable for him. He and his men held a council and they did not sleep all night. He has gone crazy." Zurumban replied: "It is true, then, that he is a Lord," and he had many pitchers of water brought with two large gourd plates of soap and two large pitch torches which they carried in front for it was not yet daylight. He went to Tariacuri and said to him: "Lord Tariacuri, wake up, wake up, for it is dawn. You ought to bathe a little and we shall drink." Tariacuri's answer was: "Come right on in, I have been awake for quite a while and I am taking the smoke." Zurumban's curiosity made him ask: "All right, what time did you awaken? What do you have on? How do you take that smoke?" Tariacuri explained: "With a large shirt." And Zurumban continued: "Why do you take the smoke with that?" and threw over him a rich blanket, doubled or lined with another one. Tariacuri went into his room, they brought the water in, he bathed, and by that time it was broad daylight. Zurumban came out again bringing a large quantity of wine with him, some of which he ordered poured into the cups, and said: "Sire, I want to give you a little wine to drink." Tariacuri's answer to Zurumban was: "Shall we not go, both of us, to the ark where they guard the gods for I have something to tell you there." Zurumban was agreeable and they went to the place where they guard the Goddess Xaratanga, and Tariacuri spoke in the following manner: "Please hear me, Master Zurumban, you do nothing except to get very badly drunk each day; would it not be well if you were to leave off the wine, gather wood for the temples and have great feasts when you could drink for ten days, since it would be a great feast, and if it were only a small one, you could drink five days? Afterward you would bathe and go into the temples to pray. After that you could take your instruments for the dance; your turtles and kettledrums, and the covenanted wine; the priest called Curiti would make the fragrances, the sacrificer would pray to the gods for captives and you would keep watch at least two nights. Then you would take your Goddess Xaratanga and go to war near the boundaries of your enemies, against Hurechu, Cacagueo, Guacana, and Cuerapan, because there are colored birds there whose feathers you could use to make adornments for your Goddess Xaratanga. There is a river there so that they have two crops each year of a fruit called tomatoes and chili. There are melons, cotton, and cherries which you could bring here to your people so that they would be like others where all these things are grown. Take all your war people there and you shall take some captives. Sometimes when you make your raids your enemies will complain about you and you shall say, it is not I but Tariacuri who comes here by night and surprises your villages and gives me captives for my sacrifices. It is for this reason that I beat my kettledrums, making a feast which you hear. This way your enemies will not blame you but me and they will not make war against you. You see, Zurumban, that I am making you a Lord if you do this, for you are not a Lord but of lowly caste and a beggar, and now I am making you a Lord and you will perform charities."

Upon hearing this Zurumban began to weep loudly and then said: "Oh, Master, son-in-law, you brought these words with you as a King; I shall comply with all that you tell me. Let us go home and you shall eat." They went to his house and were served. After they had eaten, Zurumban called his majordomo, Huyana, and told him to look for some lugs to carry fruit in and prepare loads of blankets for Tariacuri to take. Then he went into a room and dressed two ladies with their best sashes, turquoise necklaces, and blankets. Leading them both by the hand, he took them out where Tariacuri was and said to him: "Go to your house and take these two so that they may carry water for you and be your handmaids." Tariacuri's answer was: "So be it Sire, as you say." They got ready to leave, and Zurumban gave many women servants to his daughters to accompany them. They brought all the bridal apparel and furniture of the ladies, consisting of many mats and women's jewelry. And so it was that Tariacuri departed homeward, taking leave first of his father-in-law, Zurumban. When he arrived home, his aunt came to meet him with a warm welcome. They put away everything that Zurumban had given Tariacuri, which consisted of a great many things. Seeing all this his aunt was overjoyed and said: "You shall see Master Tariacuri that Zurumban is a Lord; look what they have brought and this is nothing compared with what he will send for her with whom you are to be Master." Tariacuri, as was his wont, went to gather wood for the temples, and his first wife, daughter of the Master of Coringuaro, seeing the other women in the house, was dying of jealousy and returned to her village of Coringuaro, never to come back.

48. TARIACURI'S FORMER FATHER-IN-LAW
IS AFFRONTED

It was the feast of Sicuindiro[16] when it was customary to renovate the temples of Curicaveri. Tariacuri took some slaves into the houses of the chief priests to keep watch with them during the vigil of the feast. He stationed himself by the door.

The old man Chanhori, first father-in-law of Tariacuri, was angry because Tariacuri had taken other wives in place of his daughter, and he said: "What arrogance is this on the part of Tariacuri who has so greatly insulted us," and he said to his people: "The land that Tariacuri has is not his," and he called some priests and got some blankets from among the adornments of his god Huren de Quavecara. The priests adorned themselves, took their goddess on their backs and, playing their trumpets, they came to the place where Tariacuri was established with his god Curicaveri, a placed called Hoataropejo, where he had built a temple.

When the Cazonci or other Masters sent these people to live in a different region, it was their custom at the time for those who were moving to take a stone from near their god, or a part of the god, and wherever they settled they would establish the name of the god they had brought from their village. They would tell the same fables and hold the same feasts as in their previous villages.

When the people of Coringuaro arrived, they took the body of Curicaveri, threw it into a corner, and said, "This temple does not belong to Curicaveri but rather to our God Huren de Quavecara," and they plastered it with white and red earth as was their religious custom. Then they took the slaves which had

16 One of the few feasts about which León, Seler, and Caso agree. They all translate it as "flaying" or "where flaying is performed." Caso dates it September 15. See Caso, "The Calendar of the Tarascans," pp. 15, 28.

been captured for Curicaveri and sacrificed them to their own god.

So all the Chichimecas arose and left that place to go to a mountain called Upapohato where they built new temples. Tariacuri called together the old men called Chupitani, Tacaqua, and Nurivan and gave them instructions: "Take a load of very yellow, copper plated axes and present them to Huren de Quavecara, the God of Coringuaro, so that he may use them to make little bells for adornments, and tell old man Chanhori that I beg him to lend or sell me a piece of land where I may put my God Curicaveri. He knows that it is very rocky here."

The old men called on Chanhori and gave him the message, whereupon he replied: "Tell Tariacuri to stay where he is even if it is rocky, for all land is good; corn grows and ears earlier there than here, and the melons and pigweeds do too. Tell him not to go to Cuinuzco nor to Tapamecaracho because I am making a seedbed to provide wine for my God Huren de Quavecara. Tell him this and tell him to drink from the arroyo called Curingüen." The old men brought the message back to Tariacuri who said: "Well, let us stay here since Chanhori is so niggardly and ungrateful," and he stayed there a few days even though he should have moved immediately.

Tariacuri took Curicaveri and all his people to a place called Urexo, and there he caused a temple to be made of sod. Once more the people of Coringuaro wanted to destroy Tariacuri and with their war people they surrounded him. But Curicaveri gave his enemies the diarrhea, drunkenness, and crippled them, and they became senseless; they fell on the ground and would embrace each other and in their confusion they fell by the temple. Some old women would take them into the temple for the men could not, and Curicaveri's priests sacrificed them there. All day long the sacrifice went on and the blood ran down to the foot of the temple and then ran in a stream across the patio. (See Plate 27.) The heads of the sacrificed, placed on poles, made a great shadow.

When it was over, Tariacuri called his old men together and

said to them: "If my wife, the daughter of the Master of Coringuaro, were a man, she would have been a most brave man, for being only a woman she has caused to be killed some of her brothers, uncles and her grandfather, thus giving on this day food for the gods and has appeased their stomachs; my wife has been a brave man." What Tariacuri meant by these words was that his wife had started that war in which his god Curicaveri had confounded his enemies, that she had been the cause, and that if she had been as good a man as she was a woman there would have been more dead men.

Tariacuri arose and went to a place called Querenda Angangueo, leaving his aunt behind. By this time the people of Coringuaro began to ask themselves what Tariacuri had done to them and said that they would never forget this offense. So they sent spies, but they came back saying that he was in very broken country with many waterfalls so that they could not get close enough. They made disguises and camouflaged themselves to look like jackals, lions, owls, and other birds called *purucuzi*. In this manner they approached and listened beside the houses. Among the spies was the son of Zurumban, but he said nothing about this even though he saw Tariacuri and went into his house, because Tariacuri and his father had talked, saying they were friends and they had eaten and gotten drunk together. After drinking he would leave the house and go through the weed patches to learn how the people could approach.

It is not known how Tariacuri's aunt knew about it, but she entered the house and, as soon as Tariacuri saw her, he asked why she came. He was sitting on one side of the door and Zurumban's son, called Zinzuni, on the other side, and each one had his food and his wine next to him. Tariacuri repeated his question, asking her what was the trouble. Then his aunt answered reluctantly: "I have learned that it is said that the people of Coringuaro are to destroy us. They have sent spies disguised as lions and jackals because they have learned about the broken country where we are. They say not to disguise the son of Zurumban, that he enters your house and that you two eat and drink together as one, that he excuses himself to urinate and goes through the weed patches where the spies are to learn how the war people can come." Upon hearing this Tariacuri became angry and reprimanded his aunt, saying: "Listen to what this old woman says. Who would go about spying? This Lord who is eating here with me is called Zinzuni, son of Zurumban; we are here together and you get out of here with your story." His aunt only replied: "So be it, Sire, for you are together and may it do you good." She was angry as she left. On hearing this the son of Zurumban was very embarrassed, and Tariacuri said: "Do not be worried for that old woman did not know what she was saying; it was only a rumor she had heard somewhere." Then the son of Zurumban said: "Sire, how can I not be sorry for what I have just heard. I cannot now be at ease." Tariacuri went out and brought him five servings of fish and said: "Well, Sire, you may go home but do not be worried; take this fish to give to your sons when you get home." The son of Zurumban accepted and went home. Tariacuri followed him with his god Curicaveri and his people.

His father-in-law, Zurumban, learned of his coming and met him on the way where they greeted each other. Zurumban, pretending to be compassionate and to weep for his son-in-law, put saliva on his face and said that he was most welcome, and upon arriving at his house, he said: "Around here there is no wood for you to gather for your temples, which you do all day and all night. You can see there is no forest here. Go to a place called Vacapu where Anachurichenzi is the Master and there you can gather wood for your temples."

So Tariacuri and his people went to the village of Vacapu where he was received by the Master, and he stayed there some days. Then, taking Curicaveri from there, he went to another village called Zurumuharupeo where the Master was called Atapezi, and he, too, received him. He stayed there awhile, then taking Curicaveri, he and his people moved on to a place called Santangel. The Master, called Hapariva, gave him a genuine and warm welcome, built him a temple, houses for the chief priests, and one for himself. There he could gather wood for his temples, and Tariacuri and his people finally established themselves.

49. BLACKMAIL BY BROTHERS-IN-LAW

The people of Coringuaro were no longer ruled by Chanhori because he was too old, and one of his sons, called Uresqua, became the Master. It was a custom among these people that, when the Master of the village became very old, they would elect his son and make him Master before his father died. The son would then govern the village as is now seen in the case of Coringuaro, where being very old, Chanhori, before his death, let his son take over.

Now the people of Coringuaro knew that Tariacuri had established himself, so Uresqua called his old men and sent them to Tariacuri with a message. He said: "Go tell Tariacuri that we know that he made a foray westward and brought back many feathers, long green ones, white ones, parrot feathers, other rich bird feathers of a yellow color—the good kind—turquoise necklaces, precious stones, gold and silver of the best, necklaces of sea shells and many other things. Tell him to bring it all here for our God Huren de Quavecara for those adornments do not belong to his God Curicaveri but to Huren de Quavecara."

The old men called on Tariacuri, who asked them what they came for. They replied: "Sire, your brother sent us to you," and they related their message. Tariacuri agreed: "It is true, that I went where they say and that I brought back everything they mention. Be seated and you shall eat and I shall speed you on your way." They were given food and after having eaten they begged leave to return, but Tariacuri asked them to wait a little. He called for some chests and began to open them. They were full of many kinds of arrows. He took many of them out, wrapped them in a cotton cloth and called the messengers, saying to them: "Take this package to your Master for this is what he asked for." The old men replied: "Sire, he did not tell us to bring back

166

arrows, but long green feathers." Tariacuri retorted: "What are you saying old men? Look you, for this is what they ordered." Their reply was: "No Sire, for we do not know what this is." Tariacuri reiterated his statement: "This is it, for you did not understand correctly." They also repeated their objection: "They did not tell us anything, Sire, except green feathers." Then Tariacuri untied the cloth, began taking the arrows out and said: "Come here and listen to what I say. Look, this arrow painted green is called Tecohecha Xungada and these are the green feathers they ask for." He showed them another and said, "These are the turquoise necklaces they speak of, and this one with the white feathers is the silver they ask for, this one with the yellow feathers is the gold, and these with the red feathers are the red plumes, these are the rich feathers and these flints mounted on them are blankets, and these four-colored flints in white, black, yellow, and red are nutriments: corn, beans, and other seeds. This is what they ask for, take it to them." (See Plate 28.)

The old men accepted the arrows, took them to their masters and gave them Tariacuri's answer. Uresqua, the Master of Coringuaro, laughed long when he heard the answer and said: "Listen to what he says, and call our sister, she who was in his company awhile; perhaps she will know whether these arrows have the names Tariacuri gives them and whether what he says is true." His sister came and they told her Tariacuri's answer to which she countered: "He who says that is a crazy old man for are not these arrows some canes with little rods inside them? And did he not find these rocks around there? And what he calls green feathers, are they not simply feathers from the tails of eagles and falcons which he shot and put on these arrows? All these and what he calls rich feathers are paint and neither gold nor silver. He is talking nonsense in what he says. I never heard him say such things when he was making arrows nor did he give them such names." Her brothers agreed that it must be that way and they took the arrows, broke them all into pieces, threw them on the fire and burned them.

As their father, called Chanhori, was very old, they carried him by the arms to bring him in where his sons were and he said to them: "What have you done? You have already brought these arrows, it would have been better had you not burned them; rather we should have found a hide or a quiver to put them in and offered them to our God Huren de Quavecara for these arrows must have some quality of deity and our god would have been nourished by them a few days. Well, since it is already done, so be it. I who am old have now heard this. Now I am glad that I have not died so I could hear this." His boys replied saying: "Look, why is this timorous old man coming? Why should Tariacuri shoot us? Who will dare to make war against us? We are alone here but there are so many of us that no one dares to come against us."

Messengers from the island of Pacandan crossed the water and went to Tariacuri with this message: "Sire, the Islanders send us to ask that you be good enough to return to your house in Pázcuaro because others are taking possession of your establishment there. They do nothing but quarrel among themselves over the place because the war people from Coringuaro came from one direction, the Islanders from another, and the war people of Tariara from a third. The Islanders want you to return." Tariacuri laughed and asked: "What do the Islanders want of me? Are they not the ones who mistreated me? What help do they want from me? Am I to kill their enemies? Go and make war among yourselves and you tribes destroy each other."

As the people of the islands were fighting each other, the people of Pacandan destroyed the tribe of Islanders called Uren de Tiecha. When they saw they were being defeated, they again sent messengers to Tariacuri telling him how they had fought and asking what they were to do; they told him he should have respect, that he was born on their island and that he should help them and that the Masters are of two opinions. Tariacuri answered: "That is as true as the way you treat me. Go and buy yourselves from each other. Ransome yourselves, and ask for the grinding stones, the pots, all the jewels, and sacrifice the old men and old women to the gods." They ransomed themselves, took the old men and old women and sacrificed them to appease the gods. Then Tariacuri came with his people to the mountain called Arizizinda, Pázcuaro Mountain, and at midnight he began to blow his little whistle on top of the mountain. He imitated the eagles and when the Coringuaro heard the whistling at midnight they all rose up from the settlement at Pázcuaro and returned hurriedly to their village stirring up great clouds of dust. The Islanders dashed into the lake making much foam and the people of Tariara also returned to their village raising great clouds of dust. They all fled and Tariacuri and his people returned to their settlement in Pázcuaro.

50. TARIACURI FINDS HIS LOST MOTHER AND NEPHEWS

As previously indicated, Tariacuri had two nephews, the sons of his brothers, Cetaco and Aramen. The two nephews were called Hiripan and Tangaxoan. There is no further mention of these nephews so that they appear to be dead because they became orphans. They went away with their mother during the persecution of Tariacuri by his enemies.

Now the story goes on to tell that when Tariacuri returned to Pázcuaro, he immediately asked about his nephews, the sons of Cetaco and Aramen. He called together his old men, Chupitan, Tecaqua, and Nurivan and said to them: "Inquire and learn for me the whereabouts of my nephews Hiripan and Tangaxoan." Then he called his son, Curatame, the one whose mother was the woman from Coringuaro, and said to him: "Son, I want you to be married; go to your village of Coringuaro where you were born and where you will find the God Huren de Quavecara. Gather wood for his temples and you shall see that everyone in Coringuaro gets drunk, but do not follow their example, rather since you have seen my life and how I go for wood for the temples and gather wood all day and all night and put incense in the braziers for the gods, you already know all you need. Gather wood for Uren de Quavecara and do not get drunk." After giving him this advice his father sent him, accompanied by others, to Coringuaro. As soon as he was settled, he began drinking, and his father learned about it to his sorrow and disowned him. In the meantime he had not stopped searching for Hiripan and Tangaxoan. Let us leave Tariacuri for the present and follow the fortunes of the two boys.

They accompanied their mother to a place called Pechataro and from there they went on to the following villages: Asivynan, Cheran, Asipiyatio, Amatejo, and finally to Asaveto where there was a market. There were a few Chichimecas there who lived in the mountains and the boys went to see them. They had nothing to eat so the boys went to the market where, although they were the sons of a lord, they went about as orphans and ate what they found on the ground in the market, such as half-chewed roots and carob beans trampled under foot by the people. If people were eating in the market the boys would approach and quietly gather up the crumbs. Those who were eating would sprinkle the crumbs with soup and give them fillips. Their mother and her daughter wandered about elsewhere begging in similar poverty. By chance the wife of one called Ninquaran saw them, stopped to look and said: "Children, you should not eat that stuff under foot nor get yourselves dirty. Where are you boys from?" They replied angrily: "Sister, we do not know where we are from, why do you ask us?" Whereupon she asked their names and they replied: "Sister, we do not know our names, why do you ask us?" She replied: "I was only asking, have you no mother? Does she not tell you your names?" Their answer was: "Yes, sister, we have a mother and she tells us our names." Then she chided them: "Children, do not speak angrily that way for I was only asking." At this point Tangaxoan said: "Yes, sister. My name is Tangaxoan and his name is Hiripan." On hearing this the woman said: "What are you saying, children? You are my nephews, I am the niece of your father, for your father and mine were brothers." They replied: "So it is. One, they say, was called Cetaco and the other Aramen, the ones who begot us." At this juncture she exclaimed: "Oh, Sires, you must come to my house."

170

"Let us be on our way," they urged, "Let us go, sister." "I have a cornfield there," she said, "and the thrushes are eating up my green ears of corn. You shall shuck them and eat green corn canes right there." She gave them a home and they in turn would guard her cornfield, keeping watch for the thrushes and scaring them away.

Eventually a lord of Hetoquaro called Chapa heard about them and sent some old men saying: "Go by the Chichimecas who are said to be at Hucaricuaro, find out whether the boys are with the wife of Ninquaran, and as handsome as they are said to be, and if they have a very pretty sister. Bring them here: one shall be a priest, the other a sacrificer, and their sister shall make offerings for Curicaveri." When the old men arrived, the aunt hid the children. They went back four times and each time the aunt hid the children. Then the aunt said to them: "Go back to your land, sons; take your mother, take some ears of green corn and prepare some food for the road." Food was prepared for them to take along and she said to their mother: "Take your sons again as you brought them for they say that Tariacuri is back in Pázcuaro. I do not want Tariacuri to come and set war signs here and kill them in the war. Take them away and I shall soon follow you."

The mother left with her sons and took them to a place called Sipiaxo, thence to Matoxeo, and from there to still another place called Timban. At this point they asked: "Mother, where are we going?" "Boys," she said, "we must leave here, we shall go to a place called Crongariquaro where there is a brother of mine called Cuyuva who is your uncle." They agreed readily and they all went to Crongariquaro, entered the house of Cuyuva, and said to the lord: "Sir, we will cook the game you catch and we will bring wood from the mountain to burn at home, we will plant your crops and carry your children on our backs if you will let us stay in your house." He told them they were welcome and ordered a room swept clean for them and lodged them in it. But the youths did not comply with everything they had promised. Each day they went to the mountain to gather wood for the temples all day and at night too. They wandered about all the ranges seeking wood all day and did not return at night. Cuyuva lost all hope that they would perform any service for him and asked where his nephews had gone. "They do not fulfill what they promised me; they are crazy for they wander about the mountains like all Chichimecas who do not have houses."

Cuyuva ordered their mother ejected from the house and told her to go wherever she wished. The poor woman had taken up spinning and had ground flour in the service of the Master. They had given her a little corn which she kept in some pots and she had some old shawls. She and her daughter were cast out of the house along with the pots of corn which were spilled over the patio. She gathered it up in some old shawls and set it at the foot of a cherry tree where she also put her small supply of nuts. She embraced her daughter and the two of them wept. The two boys came back, bringing wood for the temples, their backs were raw for the sharp branches had torn their skin and they had their belts pulled very tight because they had eaten nothing and were very hungry. In their hands they carried stones with which they had cut the wood for they had no tools. They entered the house and found their mother and sister's room abandoned whereupon they asked where their mother and sister had gone, but no answer was forthcoming. Tangaxoan came upon one of the girls of the house and began to question her. "Did you see the old woman leave? Where did she go?" The girl answered: "Oh, Sire, you two are most unfortunate. When were you going to make a fire in the house? And when were you going to carry the children on your backs as you promised when you came here? They say you wander about the mountains as the Chichimecas who have no houses. This is what they said to your mother and sister and they threw them out of the house. They are out there, both of them, at the foot of a cherry tree." Tangaxoan said: "So be it, sister, we are leaving," and they went away through some weed patches. Their mother began to weep loudly when she saw them with their raw, bleeding backs and the twigs sticking in them. They had had nothing to protect their backs from the branches, nor did they have cinches, for they had knotted roots together to tie the wood with and the knots stuck in their backs.

The mother embraced them both and began to weep with them. They told her not to weep for she would make the tears come to their eyes. "How could you say that he was our uncle, Mother?" "That is the truth," she said, "but he is a niggardly and ungrateful one." Then the boys asked where they should all go. She said they had another uncle in Hurechu, called Ambava, and that they would go there.

They arrived at the village of Hurechu and there they promised the same as in the house of their other relative: that they would make fires at home and plant the crops. A room was swept clean for them, the mother moved in and they went to the mountain. They continuously brought wood for the temples and their backs were rubbed raw as before. Again they were cast out of the house and told to go where they wished. They found their mother outside the house once more and asked: "What trouble is this, Mother? How is this, did you not say he is our uncle?" "That is true, boys," she said, "but he is a miserly one." The boys replied: "Let us leave this place, where shall we go?" The mother said they should go to another place called Parco where there is another uncle called Zirutame. They went to the house of that uncle, their mother's relative, and promised the same as the other times. On hearing this the relative wept bitterly, embraced them and said: "You are most welcome. Bring wood for the temples? When was it the custom for Lords to go to the mountain for wood? I shall bring wood from the mountain for you, I shall plant your crops, carry your children on my back, be your slave, find axes and cinches so that you may bring wood for the temples."

This one received them in proper form and said to them: "There is our God Curicaveri in Pázcuaro and your brothers the Chichimeca Lords. Go! Carry wood to their temples." They began to bring wood from the mountain and they took it to the temples of Curicaveri at Pázcuaro.

All this time Tariacuri had continued asking about his nephews, Hiripan and Tangaxoan. Now they were bringing wood to the temples in Pázcuaro and placing it by the door. On one occasion, when they brought wood, the priests were asleep and the boys took some small tubes of fumes and went home. The following day and two nights they brought wood to the temples again and on the third night when they brought it the old priests, called Chupitani, Tecaqua, and Nurivan, were not asleep. When they brought the wood at midnight and began to take the fumes as was customary in the houses of the chief priests, the priests said to each other: "Look how handsome those youths are," and Chupitani got up with one of the tubes in his hand, went toward them, and said: "You are welcome, boys." They greeted him and he asked where they came from. They said they were from a place called Parco, and he then asked what their names were. Hiripan replied: "Why do you ask, Grandfather? [That is what they call the priests.] I do not know what our names are." Chupitani went on: "Do not be angry, boys, is there no old woman who can tell you your name?" Tangaxoan answered: "Why does my cousin answer so angrily? Of course, Grandfather, we have a mother. My name is Tangaxoan and my brother's name is Hiripan; my father's name is Aramen and the name of my cousin's father is Cetaco." "What are you saying boys?" asked the old man, "behold, there is your uncle, and he asks for you every day." They answered, "That is the way it must be, Grandfather." Said the old man, "I want to go tell him." They told him to go, then Tangaxoan said to his cousin, "Brother, let us go for they will tell him and they may catch us here," and they departed.

Tariacuri was in the wake house keeping vigil and praying in a corner with some gold earrings in his ears and some red leather footwear on his feet. Chupitani felt his way to the corner and when Tariacuri sensed him he asked, "Who goes there?" Chupitani answered, "Sire, awaken for your nephews, Hiripan and Tangaxoan, have come." "Well, where are they?" asked Tariacuri. "They are sitting there by the door," said Chupitani and

Tariacuri told him to call them, but when he went to do so they had gone, and there was no one at the door. Then Tariacuri asked what was the matter. Chupitani explained that they had gone and there was no one there. Tariacuri became angry and asked, "Why did you let them go? Where do they say they went?" Chupitani replied that they were said to be from Parco. Then Tariacuri said: "Go for them at the break of dawn," and even before dawn they went for them taking blankets. They found the boys, their mother and sister and, taking them by the arms, delivered them to Tariacuri. When he saw them he wept loudly, put his arms around them and said: "Oh, Lords, you are very welcome." Embracing them, he wept with them, they exchanged greetings, and he asked them where they had been. They told him about their travels and the life they had lived, where they went and how they had returned. Tariacuri repeated his welcome and in turn related his troubles and the persecutions of his enemies and his return. Then he said of himself, "What have I, Tariacuri, done that they will not cease persecuting me? My enemies from Coringuaro will persecute me and now my Chichimeca relatives, the ones called Cuezecha, will persecute me as well as others called Simato, Querique, Quacangari, Angazique, and many others of my relatives persecute us because they think we are without favor; let them pursue you and me also. You are welcome, boys, we shall be as one and let us all die together." "This is no time to be sad, Sire," they consoled him, "let come whoever will, we shall be spies in the war." Food was brought and they ate. (See Plate 29.) Then they went to their houses which their uncle had ordered for them some time ago in Yavacuytiro. He also had ordered houses for the chief priests so that they might keep the vigil there, and the boys brought wood for the temples and their uncle Tariacuri advised them.

51. TARIACURI AND CURATAME DISAGREE

When Tariacuri learned that his son Curatame was drunk all the time in Coringuaro, he called his old men and said: "Go get my son Curatame for they say he is following the example set by the people of the village with their drinking and that he never sobers up. Tell him to come to a place called Xaramu, that I have made a temple for him there and a house for the chief priests so that he may have a place to keep the vigil." They succeeded in getting Curatame to meet his father at Xaramu (see Plate 30), and Tariacuri made his son an offer: "Gather wood first for the temples, then you shall come where I am and be Master, and I shall leave this house and go somewhere else."

While Curatame was there he did nothing but drink, and the nurses who raised him got him at odds with his father because the wine tasted good to them and they wanted to continue drinking. They would say to him: "Lord Curatame, Tariacuri says, Curatame is my son. Why did he order you to come to this place? Why did he not send you to another place called Parexaripitio for it is not far from there to wine. The people there are very wealthy and drink wine whenever they want to, because there are magueys there." They continued to say this to him until he believed it. During the afternoon of the feast of Puracotacuaro, Tariacuri arrived to participate. Curatame called his old men and ordered them to tell his father to come to him in the morning for they needed to talk a little. The old men found Tariacuri in the houses of the chief priests, keeping his vigil in a corner. When he saw the old men he asked them what they came for. They replied: "Sire, your son sends us," and they recounted their embassy. The old man replied: "My son is right because he is Master; tell him that I shall go early in the morning, that I shall be there to eat for I have not yet given him any plumages. This is my answer."

When dawn broke they tied together all the plumages they were to take to his son, and Tariacuri said to his women: "Let us go for we shall eat there in my son's house. They say that he calls me." He wore a blanket of duck feathers and a clover-leaf wreath on his head as he departed with the old men going ahead. He took along many plumages for his son, who had gotten up early, begun to drink, and was already drunk and dancing about

176

the house. As Tariacuri approached, his son went out to receive him, stumbling along and dressed as for a feast with bells jingling. He greeted his father extending a welcome to which Tariacuri replied: "May luck be with you, Master." When they arrived at Curatame's house, he got out the drinks and served white maguey wine. Since Tariacuri had not eaten, the wine made him drunk immediately and his son Curatame said to him: "You are welcome, father; let us talk a little." His father replied: "I am glad, son, what do you want to say? Now, you know that we have returned from the persecution; they had all united to persecute me, is this what you want to say? What else are we to talk about?" Then his son seized him by the throat and said: "What is this old man saying?" and threw him against the wall, saying, "Are you the Master? Why do you want to talk? Begone to the lake; go to the lake for you are an Islander," and he struck him again and asked, "Are you a Master just because you are haughty?" At this point Tariacuri became enraged because he was a brave man and said: "Yes, that is the way it is, I am not a Master but an Islander. What makes you a Master? You are from Coringuaro and you are only a part of the God Tangachuron, you are a newcomer; get you hence to your village of Coringuaro. I am not a Master, neither are you; these are the ones who are to be Masters: Hiripan and Tangaxoan, these are the true Masters."

Tariacuri returned to his house, bringing back all the plumages he had taken to give to his son. He did not return to Pázcuaro but went to a suburb called Cutu, where lived a principal called Tariachu who left his house to Tariacuri and replaced Curatame as Master in Pázcuaro. Hiripan and Tangaxoan were always on the mountain gathering wood for the temples.

A year later Curatame captured a lawbreaker and, fifteen days later, went with him into the houses of the chief priests to fast, as was customary. It was the vigil of the feast so that Curatame called his old men and said to them: "Go tell my father Tariacuri to come see my feast, and take the same invitation to my cousins Hiripan and Tangaxoan even though they may come only to look. Tell them I want to break my fast and they may see the match between this lawbreaker and a rascal, who are to fight." The old men delivered the message to Tariacuri and he replied: "Tell him to come out and dance for I will go." The messengers left and Tariacuri called his women to tell them why the messengers came and said: "We are going to the feast. Have you prepared anything yet?" They replied affirmatively and took him to see what they had done. There were fish cooked many ways and many fruits. He called his old men, Chupitani, Tecaqua, and Nurivan, and said to them: "Come here and see which is better, the feast they invited us to or all this we have here, all these foods?" They answered: "Sire, one only gets tired of watching Curatame's feast and gets dust in his eyes. The enjoyment lasts for only a morning. This food here is a far greater thing. Who can make out without eating? All this is like milk which man is raised with. Who wants to go a day and a night without eating or without sleeping? Even a crawling child when given a piece of bread eats it." Tariacuri rejoined: "That is true. Come here, women, and put this food back in the house. We are going to the district called Zacapu Hacarucuyu. There we shall be spies so that our enemies from the lake may not take us by surprise. Meanwhile, he who is Master shall have his feast and give food to the gods while we shall have our feast by spying on the Islanders." Hiripan and Tangaxoan did not go to Curatame's feast either but went to a mountain called Xanoato Hucayo to hold their feast by waiting for their enemies from the island while Curatame was having his feast. "Our uncle will have let him know by now," they said. "He will go to the feast. Why does Curatame want us to see his feast?"

They went away leading all the war people and carrying two flags. Tariacuri had already departed by another road and arrived with his people at the foot of a mountain in the district called Zacapu Hacarucuyu. Tariacuri's old men suggested: "Let us select some spies from among us and station them at intervals as lookouts to see which way the Islanders are coming so we will not be surprised here like boys, for we have women with us." They selected a few to be lookouts and it was now time to eat.

Hiripan and Tangaxoan, who were in their blinds near the place where Tariacuri and his people were taking their ease, said: "Let us raise our God Curicaveri for it is now midday so that we may not be blamed for this." They all got together and put weeds on their heads, then they divided into two wings and traveled two roads to the village. The old men who were on lookout saw them coming and shouted that their enemies were coming and to tell Tariacuri for the sake of the women; that two squadrons were coming bent over and with their heads covered with weeds. The women had no time to hear all the news but fled in all directions toward the village and raised a great cloud of dust in their rush. They made a great noise as they tied together and carried off their jewels and gourd plates that they served in. Hiripan and Tangaxoan saw them from a high point and threw off their weed camouflage. They thought the women were their enemies in ambush because of the cloud of dust and they raised their flags. When the spies saw the flags they shouted: "They are our people; go tell Tariacuri so the women will stop running and not fall and be hurt for it is no one but Hiripan and Tangaxoan." When Tariacuri heard this he burst into laughter and said to his women, "Calm yourselves, Mothers, for it is only my nephews," and laughing loudly he said, "We are not so brave, go and receive my nephews; tell them to hurry." Hiripan and Tangaxoan approached their uncle who greeted them. Their backs were raw and bleeding from the branches in the forest. All their people were not with them and Tariacuri said: "We were seized by great fright, all of us including your mothers; look how brave we are for we thought that you were from the lake." They replied that they had noticed that. Tariacuri turned to his women and asked: "Mothers, was there nothing left over from the food that was lost?" They said there was and he told them to bring it, that his nephews were starving and that they would all eat. They brought food cooked in many different ways, but Tariacuri ate alone. He ordered that his nephews be served and they ate. After eating, he called them and asked: "How is it that there are so few of you, why are there no more?" They explained

179

that they had divided into two parts, whereupon he asked whether they had been advised of Curatame's feast. They answered: "Yes, Sire, they told us about it and we said, let us have our own feast somewhere else while the Master is having his." Tariacuri said: "That is why I came here too, so as not to be at his feast." Then he told them: "Go on over there, it is still morning; you are young and have good eyes and you can enjoy the games. You will be there tomorrow and the next day, then on the fourth day you will come back to where I am, and do not forget to come, boys." They objected: "We ought not to go there—it is no place for us. Many common people go there, they perform their natural functions all over and the whole place has a foul odor. It is all mixed up with bad women. We want to go where you made our temples and the houses for the chief priests. We will climb the mountain and make ricks of wood for the fireplaces and we will spend these days in vigil in the houses of the chief priests." Then Tariacuri asked: "Masters Hiripan and Tangaxoan, do you mean what you say?" They said they did, and Tariacuri told his women to leave them alone for his sons wanted to talk a little while. Then he told Hiripan and Tangaxoan to come closer and asked: "Did you really mean what you said?" They reaffirmed it and Tariacuri said: "Listen, if what you say is not true, you will not live long; mark you well, then, whether it be the truth." Hearing this they stood with bowed heads and wondered.

52. TARIACURI PREPARES HIS NEPHEWS TO BE MASTERS AND FORETELLS A UNITED KINGDOM

Tariacuri said to them: "If you speak the truth when you say you do not want to go to my son's feast, hear me, Masters; there will be three Masters: Hiripan shall be Master over one part, Tangaxoan over another, and my youngest son, Hiqugage, over another." (See Plate 31.) At that time, Hiripan was a sacrificer, and the old man, seizing both of them by the ears, began to tell his nephews the following: "I look for mats on which to throw the symbols of their rule; there will be no more Masters in the villages, they shall all die and their bodies will be thrown into the weed patches. Who, in the service of the gods, do I have to talk with? Look at this lake where the Islanders live, how shall we conquer them? You see how large it is and that they are well established. What shall we do with the Islanders? Listen to what I tell you. Caricaten, the Master of the island, is dead, and his son called Quanta was Master for only a while. For a while the former Master had wood gathered for the temples and then died. He left two sons, called Cuynzurumu and Utume, and their sister, called Zizito. None of these Islanders will be Master. There is Aristaquata but no one will obey him. There is the Master, called Varapame, on the other island of Pacandan, whose father, called Zuangua, has died. Old man Chanhori in Coringuaro is dead and his sons are filling the position as Masters; they are called Cando Huresqua, Sica, Zinacuabi, and Chapa. They are all quarreling over the seigniory, but none of them will be Master. They shall all die in the war for one of them told me something important. Chapa's mother is a slave and for this reason no one will obey him. I said to him, Chapa, why are you not the Master? You should be. Maybe your mother was a slave but your father was a Master. I want to give you a share in my God Curicaveri for whom you may bring wood from the mountain."

In their time these people used to say that he who would be Master would have to enjoy the favor of Curicaveri and that if this favor was not forthcoming he could not be a Master. Hence, the Master always guarded him most carefully as did his sons after him. Since Tariacuri gave him a share in Curicaveri, he established himself in Tetepeo where Curicaveri took many slaves. At times Chapa had as many as two hundred slaves captured in war, thus slowly enlarging his seigniory. From thence he took Curicaveri to a place called Aranguario, and from here on, Curicaveri destroyed everything as far as Tiripitio. When the people of Coringuaro learned about this, they gave him a wife in return for which he shared the slaves he captured in war. Sometimes when he captured a hundred, he brought only forty to Pázcuaro and took the other sixty to Coringuaro. Later he would bring no more than twenty slaves, then five, for he took them all to Coringuaro. Sometimes when he captured a hundred, he would bring no more than one to Pázcuaro and would take all the others to Coringuaro. "I would return his slave to him and say: why are you so haughty? Why do you bring only this slave? Where did you take all the hundred slaves you captured? You capture them but the God Curicaveri, who captures them to favor you, is not here. I gave you an interest in Curicaveri. Take your slave back. You do it only because in Coringuaro they gave you a wife and for this reason you divide the ones you capture." Then Tariacuri threatened: "Sacrifices are made here too, and the blood of the sacrificed never stops running for it is always fresh because we sacrifice continuously."

Since the slave was returned, he was afraid and took Curicaveri to a mountain called Tarecha Hoato where there was a village called Xenguaro. There Curicaveri conquered a goodly piece of land, and then he was taken farther on to a place called Hucariquareo; here too he captured another piece where there are some temples near Vayangareo on the way to Mexico City. From thence he took Curicaveri to Hetoquaro, where land was captured from the Otomis who were living in the vicinity. From this place he went on to establish himself in the village of Hararoty, for Curicaveri favored him.

"By now, boys, I had repented, saying I wished I had not shared Curicaveri thinking that Chapa was to be King, for he is known to all the Gods of the Heavens and of the Four Quarters of the world. Now I feared that he would be King and I repented. Now, boys, Chapa is dead, leaving the following sons: Hucaco, Hozeti, Vacusquazita, Quanirescu, Quata Maripe, and Xaracato. All of these are Masters now and they contend among themselves for the seigniory. They have divided the plumages among themselves and each one holds his own feasts separately. They all do a dance called *Ziziquivaraquan*, another called *Ariven*, and a third called *Chereque*.

"It has always been the custom that the high priest had charge of the wood for the fireplaces of the God of Fire and that he wore the corresponding insignia: a gourd on his back, a spear on his shoulder; he was carried on the backs of the people and it was his duty not to get drunk. But, in Hetoquaro, he left off his insignia, the gourd, the spear, the fiber-wreath that he used on his head, the little pincers around his neck, and he left the houses of the chief priests to mingle among the common people and join in the dance called *Ziziquivaraquan*. The sacrificer, another who also used the insignia of the priest, such as the gourd on the back, also left them all off and joined the people in the *Ziziquivaraquan* dance. Even the priest called Tucime, who was in charge of the serious business of carrying the gods on his back and who was assigned to the temple to blow the trumpets at midnight, descended from the temple, joined the people, and took part in the dance. Likewise, the cloistered women who were in charge of making offerings to the gods, came out and participated in the gaiety. Everybody took part, even to the men joining the women. This was all done there in Hetoquaro and it was not long until the men took the women off and fornicated with them. Not long afterward each one was carrying on her back a child in its cradle. All these things they had done, including deserting the service of the gods, were taken to be auguries. Reeds and weeds appeared in houses, bees built their hives in a single night and by morning their swarms were hanging from the arks, even the little trees began to bear fruit, so much so that the branches were overloaded and bent downward; the magueys, even the little ones, began to shoot up long blades that looked like timbers, the little girls became pregnant while still children and had breasts as large as the women because of the pregnancy, and the children, small as they were, carried children on their backs.

"The older women began to produce knives made of black, white, red, and yellow stone. They also began to build temples everywhere, all fenced about with oak planks. Then they began to get drunk and they were called Black Cloud Mother, White Cloud, Yellow Cloud, and Red Cloud Mother. In their drunkenness they became dispersed as there were no old men in the village who would question their actions and say to them: 'It was never thus in the past. Let us say our prayer in the house of the chief priests and keep the vigil, let us bring wood, too, for the temples. Look at the auguries for they are not good omens.' Everything was lost in Hetoquaro, including the service of the gods. There will be no King there either. It is all a desert because there has been no rain in a year. Since they were our gods, everything was lost through starvation. The Master of Hiraro called Chicuircata, and another called Thiacani took them as slaves. They were chastized by the gods, and I, through them, for the evils they did in Hetoquaro. They imposed starvation so that he who had five children began to sell them, one child for a little corn and two tamales. When he had sold all the children, he would sell his wife for a tamale and, in the end, having nothing else, he would sell himself so they would give him something to eat. This is what was done by a Master called Ticuricaia, and by another called Thiacani of Araro, and for this reason Hetoquaro was deserted.

"In the same manner in the village of Caniqueo, the Master, called Sicuindicuma, died and left his sons called Cocopa and Vacusquacita Zancapa, but not one of them will be the Master, rather all will remain deserted. In the same way, in Cumachen, Hencivan was the Master. He died and left sons called Tangaxonondo and Carata. Neither one of them will be a Master either for they enter the village of Eronguariquaro and make friends of those people. Following the example of the people of the village, they set about getting drunk in a sitting position, for no one could drink that wine which belonged to the god Tares Upeme, the god of Cumachen who was a very great god, for he was thrown out of heaven when the gods were drinking. They cast him to earth for which reason this god was lame and that wine was the only kind he could drink. Also, the kettledrummer called Zizamba and another who was a sacrificer drink it and go about drunk in his house. There will be no Master there in Cumachen either; look for mats, boys, on which to pile the spoils which we shall take away from them in the war—there will be so many spoils, Masters Hiripan and Tangaxoan, that we shall have no place to put them all.

"Look you also at the village of Zacapu where there was a Master called Caracomoco; he is not fit to be a Master for he is of low class and a poor beggar. There was no place where he did not sleep, for he slept on all the mountains for the sake of having some dream. But no revelation or dream came to him so he came to the village of Zacapu and began to gather wood for the temples of Querenda Angapeti. He brought the wood and placed it all over the patio; then he went to the middle of the patio to sleep by the long timber down which the gods descend from the heavens. Later he slept on a seat called *Vonaquaro*, thus each night he approached closer to the temple of Querenda Angapeti and finally reached Sirunda Aran, the messenger of the God Querenda Angapeti. Being thus at the foot of the temple he still had no dreams so he began to climb the steps. He would sleep one step higher each night hoping to have a dream. He was about to reach the top when the Goddess Pevame, wife of Querenda Agapeti, saw him coming and said to Sirunda Aran: 'Come here; do you not see a man climbing up and about to reach the top of the temple here? I do not know what his name is, nor do I know what to call him. What is worse, I do not know where Querenda Angapeti is; go look for him and report this man who is coming to the top of his temple.'

"Sirunda Aran went southward where Querenda Angapeti had a house, women, wine to drink, and dance drums. Not finding him there Sirunda Aran went westward, also in vain, thence north with the same result, and finally to the Inferno. Having failed to find him in all these places where he had houses, he went to Heaven where he holds his great feasts. There he found him all dressed up with a tiger skin on one leg, a turquoise necklace around his neck, a colored fiber wreath on his head, green plumages, and ear-loops in his ears.

"When Querenda Angapeti saw Sirunda Aran coming, he entered his house to lie down and sleep. An old man was at the door as a porter, and Sirunda Aran approached him, greeted the old man and said, 'Open up for me.' The old man retorted: 'What are you saying? I am not to open the door, for Master Querenda Angapeti is sleeping and you may have come to get his women out of the house.' Querenda Angapeti heard from inside and called for Sirunda Aran to come in. When the old man heard Querenda Angapeti speak, he told Sirunda Aran that the Master was up and to come in and let his errand be known. Querenda Angapeti asked his purpose and Sirunda Aran explained: 'Sire, your wife sent me to find you and ask you to be good enough to come at once to your house for a man has climbed up near the entrance to the temple. She does not know who he is nor what he wants.' Querenda Angapeti answered: 'I have already seen him climbing up and he does not know us. His name is Caracomaco. What does he come asking for? To take my adornments which are the insignia of a Master so he shall be as I? Go and tell him that there is a woman in the village of Huruapa who is as poor as he, who goes about selling water and who hires herself out to sell corn by the stone and that he should marry her. Tell him he is not to stay in Zacapu for there shall be no other Master there but I, that no one shall be in my place for I am the Master of Zacapu, but he may be the Master in Quarecuaro, near Zacapu. Tell him his wife is not staying with him but in another village called Quaruno and that she will come every twenty days to her husband so that they may be together as one. Then they shall beget a son but the couple shall not be Master for they will be dead in the weed patches and only the son, alone, shall not be harmed.' "

"Now you see, boys," said Tariacuri, "that Querenda Angapeti ordered the future of the village of Zacapu and for this reason the past Master, called Caracomoco, is dead. His wife, who is old, still lives and they say she fills her husband's place and governs the village where it is not the custom for the women to bring wood for the temples but is the business of the men. There are many principals there with large gold lip-rings whose business it is to gather wood for the temples, which is men's work, as well as to attend to the wars. It is said that the old woman called Quenomen, to make herself feared, has two black bands on her face, a round shield at her side, and a club in her hand. Where is it the custom for old women to wage war? They ought to attend to their children. These auguries appear in Zacapu. Why do they not sacrifice that old woman, quarter her and throw her in the river?

"There will be no Master in Zacapu either, for where is Zurumban, boys, my father-in-law in Tariaran? He had these sons: Cacapu, Aramen the oldest, Vaspe, Terazi, Cariqua, Tupuri, Hivacha, Zinzumi, Hanzivia, Quama, and a daughter, Mavina; they say she is still alive but blind. All his boys turned out bad and disappeared in many directions. My father-in-law, Zurumban, keeps guard over the Goddess Xaratanga, and that girl, his daughter, called Mavina, has a bad reputation. She went to the Trangezu and had a tent or pavilion built there, called *Xupaquata*, and dressed as the Goddess Xaratanga. Using a chamber in the pavilion, she would seat herself on many painted blankets, call in all the handsome youths who passed through the market, and go to bed with them. It was said that she told them that if she were a male she would not sleep with any woman. This is what that woman was doing. Would to god that her brothers would sacrifice her and throw her in the river. For these reasons there will be no Master in Tariaran where Zurumban is.

"Well, look, boys, in the village of Tacambaro where Cavujancha is acting-Master, he is actually an official of the temple, whose duty is to place the offerings for the gods. He was favored by the Goddess Xaratanga which is why he is Master of Tacambaro. Cavujancha has two sons, Tarando and Horohta, and neither of these will be Master.

"Look for mats, boys, on which to place the spoils of war. This that I have been telling you is the way it came about, my sons, Hiripan and Tangaxoan. I have no companion to take charge of the wood for the temples and of the service of the gods. I, Tariacuri, am alone; I alone complain for the villages of Pangacuran, Savinan, Arzan, and Capacuaro . . . there are all those Masters there, and then there are Vanzan, Hutaco, Hozi, Tuinchumba, Ynziquanto, and Hapunduri; every day they have their differences; they quarrel over their boundaries and their fields and they all take up bows and arrows. The gods come down from the heavens to be nourished by the blood from their slaughter. I scolded them and they became angered with me asking what Tariacuri means. Why does he not say it to the lake? When we had differences among ourselves we would kick him and conquer him. Let us agree in order to fix him so he will not say any more to us. These plumages we have and these adornments were not taken from anyone by force but were left to us by our ancestors. That is why we use them in our feasts. This is what they agreed to in the villages which belonged to our people, and for these reasons there will be no more than three Masters and you shall be they. Go, sons, enter into the house of the chief priests for your vigil and prayer."

Hiripan and Tangaxoan agreed without question, went to their houses, and began to bring wood to the temples.

The entire preceding chapter was held in great reverence by the Cazonci, and the priest who knew this story was required to repeat it frequently. He claimed that this chapter is the doctrine of the Masters and that it is advice that Tariacuri had given to all of them.

53. TARIACURI IMPRISONS ZAPIVATAME

Having acquired advance information, Hiripan and Tangaxoan set up an ambush with their people in a place called Xanoato Hucacio, over toward the island of Xaraquaro, for a principal called Zapivatame was coming at dawn in a canoe from the island. Tangaxoan took up his position in his canoe and from there came out very quietly from his ambush to seize the victim. Zapivatame told them to be careful for they would injure him inasmuch as they wanted to shoot him. He asked the whereabouts of Tariacuri. Being angered with him they retorted: "Look what you are saying. Why would Tariacuri come here?

Tariacuri is back there in his house." To this Zapivatame replied: "That is why I ask for I have come to see him." The others answered: "Listen to what this fellow says; go tell Tariacuri, our uncle, what Curicaveri has taken and that he is enough even though he is only one." They went to tell Tariacuri who greeted the messengers, and they told him that his nephews say that Curicaveri had captured only one. Tariacuri accepted this and said that it was enough even though it was only one. Then the messengers said that his nephews say that the captive asks for him. He asked whether they had harmed him and the messenger replied negatively. Then Tariacuri ordered that they go back and tell them to let Zapivatame hasten to him.

When his nephews arrived, Tariacuri went out to receive and greet them. He invited the Islander whom they had captured into his house to eat, and all the people ate too. Tariacuri carried on the consultation within his apartment so that no one knew what they talked about. Later, the captive came out dressed in a white shirt and a blanket which Tariacuri had given him and with his oar on his shoulder. He left Tariacuri's apartment, took leave of Hiripan and Tangaxoan, who were in the patio, wished them good luck and they, in turn, wished him Godspeed.

Then Tangaxoan arose and said to his brother, Hiripan: "Look, brother, that fellow I captured is getting away," whereupon Hiripan replied: "Let him go for inside there he and my uncle must have agreed upon something." "Even if that be the case," said Tangaxoan, "did I not capture him?" Just at this moment Tariacuri called them and said: "Boys, go to your houses and make arrows all day today and tomorrow. In the afternoon you shall show them to me. Let the quivers you put them in be wide, with four compartments, and put many arrows in them for there is no telling what message they will bring from Lake Xaraquaro. They may be coming to gather people against Curicaveri, our god, for they are bringing their gods. They say they want to come put themselves under the protection of our God Curicaveri because they are afraid of a war, or perchance it is witchcraft and they come to gather people to fight."

Hiripan and Tangaxoan went home and they and all their people made arrows for two days. On the afternoon of the following day they came and showed them to Tariacuri, putting them all in the patio. He accepted them, saying they were good and that they were gods. "With each one of these our God Curicaveri will kill; he will not loose two arrows in vain." Then he spoke to the boys: "Hiripan and Tangaxoan, go to Xanoato Hucacio, which is the way the Islanders are supposed to come. Take some spies who may station themselves on top of the mountain to watch the lake and see whether anyone is coming and whether anyone stops them. If they cast high foam with their canoes, it will be a sign to you that the Islanders tell the truth because it is said that the people of other islands will not let them come. If the canoes come calmly you shall leave your blinds and return to the village ahead of them. If they raise a hue and cry leave your ambush and, at the point of disembarkation, let fly a few arrows." His nephews agreed to do it that way.

They departed at nightfall and took up positions behind a small mountain, stationing two spies on top of the mountain who, at midnight, saw that people were coming across the water from the island in their canoes. Others came from behind the island and intercepted them. The prow of each of these last canoes bore images of their gods called Carocuchango, Nuriti, Xarenave, Varichu Uquare, and Tangachurani. As they came they all raised a great cry across the middle of the lake. The Chichimecas arose, shouted and went to the top of the little mountain, near the landing, and let fly a few arrows in the direction of the Islanders. (See Plate 32.) At this, the second group of Islanders left off chasing the first group whom they had stopped, and people from another island called Cuyumeo came a roundabout way with their old men and women, their boys and girls and many others, and all came to join Tariacuri. The latter received them all, welcomed them and fed them. Tariacuri sent them to establish a village at a place called Aterio and there they built their temples, the houses for the chief priests and, all working together, they brought wood for the temples of Curicaveri along with the Chichimecas. They all went together on forays, one of which took them to a place called Tupu Parachuen and others took them to Ycapetio, Ahiracio, Acharan Dauchao, and Axarapen. However, they captured no enemies and returned to Pázcuaro. On their return they did not speak to Tariacuri but went along the lake shore to a place called Varicha Hopatacuyo. They kept going this way, skipping along to other places called Sirumutaro, Hopiquaracha, Apucunda Hacurucu, Hoatatetengue, and to Tirindini and so came close to Coringuaro. They did not go clear to the village but turned back toward Pázcuaro [Pátzquaro] coming to a place called Parazu, from whence they went to another place called Pacahacupaca where they made a great smoke to throw fear into their enemies. Seeing the great smoke, the people of Coringuaro were quite disturbed because it was within their territory. They got into their canoes one morning and began to row in flight, shouting all the while. Hiripan and Tangaxoan, with their people, took up the chase killing many and took many Coringuaro prisoners. They went to a place called Queretapuzicuyo, in Mechuacán, and made great fires and large clouds of smoke there also.

When Tariacuri learned of this he was quite frightened that his nephews had entered so far into enemy territory and called them back. The messengers gathered a lot of wood, roasted many birds, tied together many rabbits, captured deer, gathered ears of corn, and went in search of Hiripan and Tangaxoan who welcomed them. The messengers delivered their message: "Gentlemen, your uncle sent us to tell you that he wanted to talk with you." The nephews departed immediately and when they reached Tariacuri they exchanged greetings and they themselves gave him all the game that had been collected, whereupon Tariacuri said to them: "You have caused me no little concern the way you have gone about making fires and great clouds of smoke. What would happen to us if we got into trouble because of this and you are so few? Mark you that Curicaveri is here and that our enemies are not far from us here in Yzipamucu and Coringuaro. What would become of us if they carried you all off?" Hiripan and Tangaxoan attempted to calm their uncle's fears: "No Sir, Uncle, who is there to carry us off? Everything is calm and we have stationed our spies." At this Tariacuri asked where they had established themselves, and they described the location: "We are very well situated. There are many mountain trees, rabbits abound, deer are plentiful, and there are many beautiful birds. It is a most inviting place to be." This caused Tariacuri to ask: "Well, boys, do you think you are well off there?" They answered affirmatively and added that they would gather wood for the temples. Tariacuri was pleased and said: "May Providence be with you, boys. Keep your spies posted to avoid any uprisings for I am worried about you and very sad." They promised not to worry him, dinner was served and they ate. They were given mats to protect their backs against the wood they were to bring from the mountain, cinches to tie it with and they went back to where they were first.

Time passed and Hiripan and Tangaxoan got very good corn and beans at a place called Naranjan. By night they gathered wood for their temples and the people tilled the land early each day on the bank of the lake. They planted corn and beans there and both grew well, the corn into stalks and the beans into pods. They hunted rabbits, birds, and deer, and they all went to take a gift to Tariacuri which consisted of the first fruits and offerings of what they had harvested.

When he saw them, Tariacuri welcomed them warmly and they returned his greeting. He asked where they had obtained all this, and they explained: "By day we worked the land on the banks of the lake and by night we gathered wood for the fires, we made fields there, and we said to ourselves all this has been produced, let us take this to our Uncle so that he may make an offering to Curicaveri." Tariacuri replied approvingly: "You have done well, boys, and accordingly we shall offer it to Curicaveri and then we shall eat what is left over," and they were served. Then they crossed the lake again to their settlement.

54. INTERRUPTED PENANCE

Hiripan and Tangaxoan frequently crossed the lake to take gifts to their uncle. They also made many fires and great clouds of smoke in their territory, all of which was observed by Curatame, who was the Master in Pázcuaro, and he learned that they had established their settlement there and were appropriating a large territory. He called his old men together and said to them: "Go to my father and ask him what he has to say, for it is his sons, Hiripan and Tangaxoan, who are doing all this; what is the meaning of all this; why do you call them your sons?" The old men delivered Curatame's message and Tariacuri answered: "What have I to do with them? I do not know what they are trying to do." The old men replied: "That is why your son Curatame asks where they want to be Masters, for he already is Master. He asks that you send someone for them because they must be doing it out of hunger. Let Hiripan get out the urinal for him, for he urinates a great deal because of the wine he drinks continually, and let Tangaxoan hold the cup for him whenever he drinks, and that he [Curatame] will give them food if hunger is their trouble—this, Sire, is what your son Curatame says." Tariacuri objected to all this: "I do not want to send anyone nor go tell them; you go and tell them the same thing you told me. How could he say that I should send someone? You can tell them just as well."

Curatame's messengers departed and called upon Hiripan and Tangaxoan who were sweating over the making of arrows. Their ears were thick and swollen because of the blood they had taken from them to make a sacrifice. They greeted Curatame's messengers and asked them why they came. They answered that the boys' older brother had sent them and they delivered the message: "Sirs," he said to us, "go ask my father what he has to say for he begot Hiripan and Tangaxoan, that they are his sons. What is it that he orders them or says when they go so far to make smokes? Where are they to be Masters for he already is the Master? That if you do it because you are hungry, you [Tariacuri] should send for them, that I [Curatame] drink so much wine each day that Hiripan will get the urinal out for me and that Tangaxoan will hold the cup whenever I drink."

When he heard this, Tangaxoan turned purple with rage, stood up and said without further ado: "Listen to what Curatame says, what will we say? We say that we will be Masters. What is he talking about? Is it that he already is Master where we ourselves are to be Masters? And what we are doing here is none of his business; we shall do as we like and he need not concern himself about us. Does he think we are here to make him Master, to give him wine to drink? Let him look for his large cup to get drunk, and if that fails to fill him, let him look for a larger cup and if this still is not enough to satisfy him, let his women lift him up and dunk him in a huge pot of wine and there he shall gorge himself. Let him look for more women and you, who are his servants, go from house to house looking for them and take those who have large thighs and buttocks and stuff his house with them. If it will not hold them all, let them sleep outside in the patio, and his house and his patio shall be jammed with them; and with one hand let him hold them and the cup with the other. Go! And tell him and our uncle Tariacuri too as you go. If what I, Tangaxoan, say is not properly said, it is only said because we are not here to make Curatame Master nor to enlarge his seigniory."

The messengers, on hearing this tirade, were stunned and moved away. They departed and along the way they told everyone all that Tangaxoan had said. Upon hearing about it, Tariacuri was astounded and exclaimed: "You see, you went and got your just deserts and the reasons they gave you explain why they are over there. What can I say to them? You got what you had coming. Go and tell it just that way to my son Curatame."

The messengers departed, delivered the message to Curatame, and when he heard it, he said: "Listen to what those cowards say, and for no reason. You are lucky to get back. And they have stopped gathering wood for the temples."

Hiripan and Tangaxoan crossed the lake again to call on

their uncle. Tariacuri welcomed them while they extended their greetings and placed the game they had brought at his feet. Thereupon Tariacuri set forth a plan: "Lord Hiripan, it would be good for my son Hiqugage to become a sacrificer. Would it not be a good idea for you to take him back across the lake with you?" Hiripan replied: "Whatever you wish, Uncle." So Tariacuri said: "Go to him and find out what he thinks. Perhaps he will go or maybe he will not want to."

Hiripan and Tangaxoan went to Hiqugage's house and, as he saw them coming, he said, "Welcome, Sires," and brought chairs for them and asked, "What is the news, brothers? Have you seen our father? Have you called on him?" They replied: "We have seen him and he says that you are to be a sacrificer." They told him everything that his father had said. Upon hearing this, Hiqugage said: "What my father says is true. For a long time I have been wanting to visit you and I have not yet gone. I know my father does not speak idly so I shall go ahead and you will catch up with me." He had the chest full of arrows bound, and Hiripan and Tangaxoan returned to Tariacuri with the answer. When he saw them coming he asked eagerly, "Well, boys, does he not want to?" They answered, "No, that is not it, Father; he has gone ahead," to which Tariacuri replied: "Well, go boys; let Hiqugage eat weeds and thistles. You three shall be Masters and, like my son, will eat weeds; you shall take him with you now." Hiripan and Tangaxoan crossed the lake again and gathered wood for the temples.

They moved to a place called Pataquen where they stayed in a cave. (See Plate 33.) There again, they and all the people, including the women, gathered branches for the fires. Tangaxoan and Hiripan wanted little to eat so Tangaxoan began to toast dry corn in the hot ashes and that was all they ate. Hiripan had gone to gather weeds and they brought many of those called Hapupata Xaguay. Hiripan would get the roasted corn out of the fire and put it in Hiqugage's hand; Tangaxoan would do the same, each taking turns giving him some, but the two brothers

Hiripan and Tangaxoan did not eat. Instead they held in their hands the roasted corn to give to Hiqugage and they ate only the weeds.

They had small, wooden lip-rings which held the weeds in their mouths. Noticing this, Hiqugage said: "Brothers, it seems that you do not eat corn, and that I am the only one who eats it. You are not eating anything." Upon hearing this Hiripan began to weep loudly, threw his arms around him and said: "Look, Lord Hiqugage, take heed not to leave us for if you did, what would your father think of us? If you are not content here, get permission for us and we shall take you to the village, for this is our customary way to eat." The two brothers continued weeping. Hiqugage noticed that their lips were covered with dirt and dust from the weeds and said: "Brothers Hiripan and Tangaxoan, cease crying for you make tears come to my eyes."

55 · DISCORD AMONG THE MASTERS

After they had been there awhile, they decided to cross the lake and take a gift to their uncle. When he saw them, Tariacuri extended a welcome and asked the boys about the place where they gather wood for the fires for the gods. They replied that they did nothing but gather wood and pile it there. Then Tariacuri said: "I want to give you a part of Curicaveri. Let me have one of your knives and you shall wrap a piece in blankets and take it back with you. You shall gather your wood for this piece and you shall make a shelter for him and an altar for this knife."

They departed taking their knife, crossed the lake and began to build a temple and a house for the chief priests. They also built a house called Eagle, and an ark for the knife which Tariacuri gave them. After it was all completed, the two brothers asked what they should do now since it was all done. One suggested that they go tell their uncle, but they could not decide who should go. Hiqugage objected inasmuch as he was not accustomed to being in his presence, and suggested that Tangaxoan go. But the latter dared not do so and suggested that Hiripan go. In the end they decided that they should go together so that they could all hear what he might have to say.

They crossed the lake and called on Tariacuri who extended a warm welcome to the boys, remarking that they seemed to be sad. He encouraged them to tell him quickly what they wanted or if something had befallen them. With this opening Hiripan told him how they had built a temple in the house of the chief priests, one for the Eagle which was the place where they made the salve to the Gods and the ark where their adornments were to be kept. All three were together when this was described to him, and when Tariacuri heard it, he became very angry and began to insult them, calling them stupid fools. "What pride has come over you, you snivelly smart alecks? Who told you to build temples? Now that you have constructed them, what will you sacrifice in them? It will probably be some shawls that you will put in the door. Is Curicaveri perchance a common god like the others? Is he as the first-born gods that you will give him wine in a cup and set it by the door for him, or some tamales which you will also put by the door as an offering, or pigweed bread? What pride has come over you? What will you do with the temples you have built for they have already been seen by the Gods of the Heavens, by those of the Four Quarters of the world, by the God of the Inferno, and by Mother Cueravaperi?"

Taking up his bow and arrows from near the entrance to his apartment, he said: "You fools, I have a mind to shoot all of you," and he put an arrow to the bow. (See Plate 34.) Seeing this they all got up quickly and rushed out of the house. The arrow shot after them, struck the wall and rebounded. Hiqugage looked back to see whether it had wounded him, and they all went home. They were very sad, not one spoke as Hiripan led the way. When they arrived at home they sat for a while with bowed and apathetic heads, then they went to get wood for the temples.

It was midnight now and Tariacuri was in a corner of the house of the chief priests doing his vigil when he called his old men, Chupitani, Tecaqua, and Nurivan, for a consultation. "What shall we do," he asked, "to redeem what my boys have

197

done?" Their respectful reply was, "You who are the Master must say." Tariacuri gave his verdict: "What shall I say, that my sons are not to blame, that they did not do it of their own accord but rather that I gave them that rock? Well, Chupitani, go to the Master of Pacandan Island, called Varapame, and tell him that we are old and tired now and that we are now willing to go to the God of the Inferno; ask him where we shall find people to take to the final death fray to be our death bed; tell him to choose the site for the fight and tell you; let it be in a green corn field on the bank; that if I should kill his people there, those who die shall be my dais and cover for my burial: that if he should kill my people they likewise shall be the dais for his burial; and where are we to get them to take to the fray?"

It was the custom among the lords and ladies when they died to kill many people to be buried with them, for it was believed that they took them to help along the road. Their bodies formed the dais or bed on top of which they would be buried in the sepulcher. The dead Master was placed on top, then more bodies on top of him, thus preventing the earth from touching him. Thus it was that they believed that the dead formed the dais or bed of the dying man.

It was for these reasons that Tariacuri sent the message to the Master of Pacandan, who was old, suggesting that their respective peoples fight each other for the purpose of having daises from among their people for the funeral. He also suggested it so that the Master might give him some of his people to be sacrificed in the temples that his nephews had constructed. The Master of Pacandan acceded and gave some either out of fear or because of that custom among the Masters. He also sent some of his people with an ulterior motive. By so doing Tariacuri's people would capture them for the sacrifice, thus preventing the killing of all of his people.

Accordingly, Chupitani departed and landed at midnight. When he arrived, all the people were asleep and the Master of the island was in the house of the chief priests holding his wake in a corner. Chupitani approached and began to feel his way, saying: "Awaken, for I have come to see you." Varapame wanted to know who he was and what he came for. Chupitani identified himself and recounted Tariacuri's message. Upon hearing it, he began to weep and said bitterly: "Tariacuri does great wrong for he does not take into account our misery; he wants us to be the first of those who are to be sacrificed in the new temple in Mechuacán, which to date has conquered no village, and I with my people are to be the premier sacrifice for the temples, and we are to be sacrificed in the temple of Querétaro. What can I do? Tariacuri has already informed the gods of the Heavens concerning the sacrifice he wants to make from among my people. Tell Tariacuri that I have an irrigated corn field on the bank of the lake and that I shall send one hundred men to work that field. I shall send across the lake with them a principal called Zipincanaqua, and when he and the oarsmen return, they will splash water upwards with their oars. This shall be a sign that the people are there irrigating the field and he may then capture some of my people."

Chupitani returned and reported the answer to Tariacuri, but the Master of the island repented of what he had said, exclaiming that he had been foolish to agree. Consequently, he sent the principal called Zipincanaqua to tell Hiripan and Tangaxoan, who were in Quereta and Chazicuyo, that he would send only sixty. Zipincanaqua, accompanied by others, departed and found Hiripan and Tangaxoan in their apartment and were required to identify themselves since it was dark. After they had done so, Hiripan and Tangaxoan demanded the purpose of the visit. Zipincanaqua and his companions explained their mission: "Sires, Varapame, the Master of Pacandan, sends us to tell Hiripan and Tangaxoan that he is in error, that he indicated one hundred but he meant only sixty." They replied in perplexity: "We do not know what you mean, we do not understand you, what is the truth?" To this Zipincanaqua answered: "Sires, I do not know; this is the way it was told to me," and they countered, "We know nothing of what you say about sixty; go to our uncle; perhaps he will know." Zipincanaqua objected to this: "Master,

I am not to go there; I was not told to go to your uncle; go your-selves and tell it to him." They retorted angrily, "Get away from here." Zipincanaqua took his leave, saying, "Sires, if we do not go tell him, it is enough that I tell you," and he left with his oar on his shoulder to go home.

Seeing the man go, Hiripan asked his brother, Tangaxoan, what they should do. He answered, "Let Hiqugage cross the lake and report to our uncle; you heard what he said." Hiqugage ob-jected, saying he was not the one who should go but that Tan-gaxoan should, and he in turn objected and said that Hiripan ought to go. The upshot was that all three decided to go together. They crossed the lake, went to Tariacuri, who at the moment of their arrival was listening to Chupitani's recounting of the an-swer of Varapame, the Master of the island of Pacandan. They immediately reported what Zipincanaqua had come to say and Tariacuri asked how they had answered him. "We said nothing to him," they replied. "He sent him so that he would report to you and we did not want to come." Then Tariacuri repeated his question: "Well, what did you tell them?" and they reiterated that they had said nothing. He commended them for their dis-cretion in coming and said: "I shall tell you what you are to do. These words you heard are mine. The Master of Pacandan in-dicated one hundred men and now it seems that there will be only sixty, as you have understood. Go to Araveni where it was indicated that they would irrigate a field, and Hiripan, you who are the oldest, listen to me: you shall go along the lake to a place called Patuquen and to another called Sivange, and there you will make a blind. Tangaxoan, you who are the youngest, will go the shortest way by Yvazi Xanchacuyo and will look out over the lake. You will see that principal on the lake in a canoe. When he splashes water upward with the oars, which is the signal that there are people on the bank, you will then capture them."

"It shall be as you say, Master," they replied and went back across the lake. In the morning they made arrows, and at night-fall they departed for the war, going the way Tariacuri had told them which was very rough and thick with brambles. They established themselves in their ambuscades and with the dawn came the people from the island to irrigate their field. All sixty men had passed, were on the bank and Zipincanaqua was returning across the lake with the canoes when he splashed water upward as had been agreed. Then everyone in the ambush arose with loud shouting, and since the Islanders had no place to go, they were all captured and taken to the new Querétaro temple. They made a great noise singing as they went along. Forty were taken to be sacrificed in the temples at Pázcuaro, while twenty were sacrificed in the dedication of the new temple. Thus was celebrated the feast of the dedication of that temple and they began anew to gather wood for the temples. They also began to capture others from the island, and they made a foray into a village of Coringuaro, Yzipanucu, and captured one hundred men.

56. THE DEATH OF TARIACURI'S SON

While they were busy about their numerous forays, their uncle Tariacuri sent for them, and when they came, he said: "Cross the lake and make a shelter for Curatame, at a distance from your own, fence it in with weeds and find some wine. This which is to be done is my order and mine are the words for I shall send word to Curatame to go meet you. Wait for him and you shall give him food. He will say to you, 'Brothers, have you not a little wine?' You shall answer, 'Yes, sir, there is some,' and you shall give him some to drink. When he has become drunk, you shall kill him."

All three left, crossed the lake and built a shelter. Tariacuri sent Chupitani to his son Curatame to tell him that his nephews came to him in great concern for they told him that there are two squadrons, one of Islanders from Pacandan and another from the island of Xaraquaro, and they are outnumbered by the Islanders. "Let him leave off the wine if he will, bathe himself and spend a night in the house of the chief priests. Let him depart the next morning, cross the lake, and on the third day, let him go help them. This you shall tell Curatame," said Tariacuri, "because there are many Islanders."

When Curatame heard the message from his father, he said it was only right, that he would be pleased to help them. He bathed himself, spent the night in vigil in the house of the chief priests, and at dawn went to his house to adorn himself. He put his quiver on his shoulder, fastened on his tiger skin, put his wreath on his head and hung many snake rattles that dangled by their tails from his temples, put on a rich necklace of sea fishbones, and crossed the lake. He was accompanied by servants, embarking at a place called Aterio and they all rowed along shouting. The Chichimecas stationed themselves at the foot of the high place where they had been. As Hiripan, Tangaxoan, and Hiqugage saw them coming, they said, "There they come, there he comes, brothers; which of us is to kill him? Remember that the Masters have two opinions for even though he ordered us to kill him he may repent later and punish us. Where did he find Curatame? Is he not his natural son?" Then they began to argue: "Hiqugage should be the one to kill him, not we. Let Hiqugage fight him and kill him." But Hiqugage objected: "Why should I be the one to kill him? Let Tangaxoan kill him for he is a valiant man." At this point Hiripan said: "What do you say, brothers, both of you shall kill him." By this time Curatame had reached the bank and was landing. They all, adorned in their best paint, went to receive him with their insignia of valiant men. Curatame was seated on a chair in his canoe wearing a blanket of duck feathers. When he reached the bank he jumped from the canoe, his servants placed themselves at his side and, escorted in this manner, he went toward the village. Hiripan received him and Tangaxoan went ahead leading the procession. Hiqugage talked with him as they went along and came to the shelter that had been made for him. They took him inside, took his quiver, placed it in another shelter, and he was seated there when they brought him food and placed themselves before him. He shared the food with Hiripan and the others and they all ate.

Then Curatame asked: "What shall we do, brothers, is there no wine that we might drink to rejoice?" They replied: "Of course there is, Sire; of course there is, we have wine here that was made in the very stump of the maguey," and they gave him some to drink. Tangaxoan was the one who gave him the wine; he gave him four cups and then four more, and he became drunk. He called Hiripan, who came and sat down at the entrance to the shelter. The two were talking while Tangaxoan gave him more wine and stationed himself at the door where he had hidden a club in the straw of the shelter. While he was drinking Tangaxoan handed him another cup which he held in his hand while he was talking. He raised the cup to his mouth to drink. Precisely at this moment Tangaxoan with a lightning-like motion jerked the club from the straw, hit him a blow across the neck, striking him in the nape, the blow causing him to fall over. He struck him again and very red blood flowed from several places on his body. (See Plate 35.) The servants, upon seeing this, arose and all fled. All the people who were there arose and wanted to run away. Hiripan got up and spoke to them, saying: "Where do you want to run to? Who is harming you? This is all among us Masters and only because we brook no evils. Calm yourselves and gather wood for the temples of Curicaveri and make your offerings of wood."

Curatame lay sprawled on the ground, all the plumes on his head soaked in blood, and they said, "Go and report to our uncle how we quarreled and killed him and see what he says." The messengers crossed the lake and informed Tariacuri: "Your nephews send us to report to you that they quarreled with Curatame," and Tariacuri asked, "Did they kill him?" When they replied in the affirmative he wanted to know which one killed him. They told him that Tangaxoan did and he said: "He is a valiant man; let the voluptuous fool die, they did well; throw him in the lake."

Once again they began to gather wood for the temples and Tariacuri returned to his first establishment at Pázcuaro [Pátzquaro] where his son Curatame had been Master.

57. THE GODS APPEAR IN VISIONS

While Hiripan, Tangaxoan, and Hiqugage were together in the place where their temple was, Hiripan approached his brother and suggested: "You stay here and fight with the people of Coringuaro, and I shall go to the mountain called Tariacaherio, which is here in Mechuacán. It is said that the people of the islands of Pacandan and Xaraquaro have stationed a battalion on them." For his part Tangaxoan answered: "Go brother, for the place you mention is not far from here, and I shall go to this other mountain called Pureperio for the people of Cumachen have a battalion there too who are going to enter the village of Tetepeo and I shall hold his road there. Let Hiqugage fight the people of Coringuaro," and they went their separate ways.

Hiripan made great fires and large clouds of smoke on the summit of the mountain called Tariacaherio. Tangaxoan did likewise on the highest part of the mountain called Pureperio. Both of these are mountains in Mechuacán. Hiqugage made his clouds of smoke in Querétaro where he had the new temple. After a few days Tariacuri sent for them and when they arrived, he complained of their actions: "Boys, you worry me greatly; where are you going now? Where are you making clouds of smoke? Who is making fires and smoke here on the summit of Mount Tariacaherio?" and Hiripan confessed. "And who makes them on Mount Pureperio, who makes the fires and the smoke there?" Hiripan answered for all three: "Tangaxoan and Hiqugage in Querétaro in the new temple for he fights with the people of Coringuaro." Then Tariacuri asked: "What will happen if they capture all of you?" Their reply was: "They will not take us for everything is calm and quiet." Then Tariacuri questioned: "Well, why do you climb up to the summit of the mountain, for that is the place which the Gods from the Heavens come down to touch. You must have had some dreams because you put wood in those places." They denied it and he spoke sternly: "You must have had dreams! Tell the truth, and if you did, explain what you dreamed." Hiripan insisted he had had no dreams but would not speak for Tangaxoan, and Tariacuri asked, "Is this true, Master Tangaxoan?" He answered affirmatively. Then Tariacuri ordered, "Let me hear you tell it." Tangaxoan agreed readily and went on: "I put wood on the fires, cleared a spot beside an oak and was lying at the foot of it. I took my quiver of arrows from my shoulder and put it and my tiger-skin wreath beside me. While sleeping I was transported and suddenly I saw an old woman coming whom I did not know; her hair was gray in spots, she wore a weed skirt and a coarse blanket, another similar blanket with which she covered herself, and she came to me. She touched me and said, 'Awaken, Tangaxoan, why do you say you are an orphan, yet you sleep? Awaken, look, I am Xaratanga; go ahead and clear the way to where I am to be. Go look at the foot of this mountain where the brambles are thickest and you will find there the seat of my temple. That is my house, called the House of Parrot Feathers and the House of Chicken Feathers. Look to the right where the ball game will be, there I must feed the gods at midday, and you will see the site of my baths which is called Ñuque Hurinquequa which is in the middle of the place where I must sometimes sacrifice to the Gods of the Left Hand, called Virambaneche, and to the Gods of the Hot Land. Clear the entire place where I was once before, and bring me back to Mechuacán which is no longer favored by me, my womb, for they do not fear me; no longer is there anyone there who will order wood gathered for my temples. Grant me this favor. Look at my back, the plumages that I have on my back and head, and look at my clothes; take care to renew my adornments and you shall be favored, for I shall make your house and your granaries, and they shall be filled with food. I shall cause you to have women enclosed in your house; there shall be old men in your house, and the population shall be large. I shall put golden ear-loops in your ears and golden bracelets on your arms and I shall give you all the insignia of the Masters.' This is what I dreamed, Father."

After listening to the foregoing, Tariacuri said, "Most fortunate one, where did you get the wood for the fire, did you leave any tree trunks? I, old as I am, would pull up the roots of that tree trunk because of its good powers, for it was because of it that you had your dream. All that I have done to gather wood for the temples, all has been to help you. That woman you mention is not an old woman but rather the Goddess Xaratanga. How can you bring her here? There are many dangers along the way. How will you go over there through that no man's land where there are endless numbers of people? Go clear her temples and her throne and place incense there, make fires and smoke in that place for she will smell them when she comes." Tangaxoan replied that already he had cleared that place and throne. Then Tariacuri asked Hiripan what he had dreamed and he, in turn, narrated his vision.

"I too had put off my quiver of arrows and was reclining against the foot of an oak. (See Plate 36.) I do not know who it was but a Lord appeared to me all covered with paint. He had a white hide for a wreath and a small lip-ring. He said to me, 'Awaken Hiripan, you say you are an orphan, why do you sleep? I am Curicaveri. Put plumes on your head and white heron plumages on your back and favor me, and I, in turn, shall favor you. I shall make your house, your arks and your granaries which shall have food in them. Your house shall be enlarged and you shall have slaves in your house and old men. I shall favor you. You shall wear golden ear-loops in your ears, plumes on your head, and necklaces around your throat. This is the way it will be, Hiripan.' This is what I dreamed, Father."

Having listened to this narration too, Tariacuri said: "Master Hiripan, according to all this you two are to be Masters. I have worked to gather wood for the temples only to help you. Where did you cut that wood for the temples, boys? Did you leave a few roots that I could dig up and burn? Go, boys, go back across the lake."

They departed and went back to where they were first, and they continued to make their fires and clouds of smoke as before.

58. THE OMEN OF YZIPAMUCU

Near where Tangaxoan was established, there was a settlement called Yzipamucu which was peopled by Coringuaros, and they saw the fires and smoke clouds that were being made in Pureperio. In this village there was a Master called Zinzuni, who feared the fires so much that he called his old men together and said to them: "Go to my nephews Cando and Huresqua, Masters of Coringuaro, for all together we are many, yet here in this village we are so few, and ask them whether it would not be advisable to select a few of us to station on a high place called Xaripitio to live there and to make fires and clouds of smoke. They should also make another temple, in a place called Hacumbapacicuyo, houses of the chief priests, and they should make fires and smokes there too. That way we could come to an understanding with each other because Hiripan makes clouds of smoke on the highest part of the mountain and Tangaxoan closer by on Mount Pureperio. You must watch Hiqugage's fires and smokes because they make them in one place to mislead while they go somewhere else, and because they want to conquer us. This you shall tell my nephews, and should they refuse to believe it, tell them the gate of my village of Yzipamucu will be opened. I and my people shall go away and pass beyond their boundaries to establish a new center if they do not believe what I am telling them. Tell them this last part at the time of departure."

In these words this Master is making a comparison with the gates made of boards tied together with cords which they usually have on their houses. He is saying that he will cease to be the door and lock of the pass which he defends and that he will make a foray and conquer them.

The messengers departed, going to the previously mentioned Masters, greeted them and were asked why they came. The old men recounted their mission and said, "This is what your uncle says." The Masters asked, "Who is he afraid of? Who will conquer us? What is all this business he is talking about? Is it not because he sees smoke clouds that he says this? Those who are making them may not be more than twenty all together in each case. Should we go after them, would each one of us have to get one of them? Of every hundred of us, not everyone would bring back his captive for there is a lack or scarcity of people here. Do we alone occupy the whole land? We are not very numerous. How long has Coringuaro existed? On the whole it is a divine community and it has the age of grey hair, of a most ancient population, and the homes have grown very deep roots here; who will come to destroy us? This is what you shall say." The messengers replied: "Yes, Sires, and for these reasons your uncle says that each hundred men shall go to take two settlements and they should make fires and clouds of smoke to the gods so that they may live awhile and that they should establish temples in Acumbapazicu, and there should be a hundred men there." "Old men, it can profit no one to come to destroy us." "So it is, Sires," they said, "that is why your uncle says the gate of his village of Yzipamucu will be opened, for he and his people are as a thick gate, that it will open and that he will go beyond your frontiers to establish a new settlement with his people." They replied: "What does our uncle say, to what purpose is he to go? Is he coming to destroy our villages?"

The messengers returned and when they had gotten back to Yzipamucu, the Master greeted them and asked: "Well, what do they say?" The old men answered: "Sire, they do not believe it." Zinzuni's only remark was, "What they have said is enough." He called for the tavern keeper and asked whether there was any wine left. Upon receiving an affirmative answer he said, "Bring it and we shall drink." Then he called together all the principals, all those who had charge of the war people and common people, women and children, and issued to them all the following instructions:

"Listen to me, you dwellers of Yzipamucu, kill the dogs, the chickens, and the large parrots and eat them all. You cannot take them with you on the flight. We are not to stay here, you and I, more than five days longer. Everyone shall gather dough or flour and dry it and anyone who wants to make up some other provisions may do so. You can not take all this with you. Listen, for I must go with you and move to some other place."

The people dispersed to their homes and began to get drunk, all of them. The Master called his majordomo and issued these orders: "Give me the green plumages with the long plumes that were brought from Pázcuaro as a ransom for Tamapucheca, Tariacuri's son whom we captured." From a granary they brought down an ark of green plumes and seized them by the handfuls, and he and all of the principals decorated themselves with golden anklets, earrings, turquoise necklaces, and rich plumages. Then he said: "Sires, you who dwell here in Yzipamucu, it is a great pleasure to drink and intoxicate ourselves; for a little while let us put on the plumages which are to be Hiripan's, Tangaxoan's, and Hiqugage's, for all that we have here will be theirs. Let us wear them a little while." They all began to weep and to make a great noise with their weeping. Wine was brought and they began getting drunk as a consolation.

No one knew who she was, but an old woman came wearing a coarse weed skirt and a blanket of the same material about her neck, and her ears were very long. She went into the house of Zinzuni's son, whose own son, Hopotacu, was being raised by his wife, and when his wife saw her, she said, "Come in Grandmother," for that is the way they speak to the old women. The old woman asked a strange question: "Lady, would you like to buy a mouse?" The wife answered, "What mouse is that?" to which the old woman replied, "A mole or a trollop." The wife asked for it, took it in her hand and noticed that it was all bright reddish in color, very large and long. "What do you ask for it, Grandmother?" she asked, and the old woman answered: "Lady, hunger brings me here, so give me a few ears of corn." The wife explained: "Grandmother, you bring it at a good time; I shall buy it from you for my husband is drinking, and I shall cook it for him to eat. In the meantime be seated." She was given food, a basketful of corn, and the woman took her leave saying, "I am leaving now, Lady," and she departed.

The wife singed the mole, washed it and put it in a pot, set it on the fire and cooked her son, the one called Hopotacu whom her husband had begotten, and arranged the blankets in the cradle to look as though the son were there. That afternoon her husband, Hopotacu, came home and, upon entering the house, he called his wife and said to her: "Wife, I am hungry, what have I to eat?" She replied quickly: "Sire, I have something special for you to eat for I bought you a mouse or a mole." Quickly she washed a gourd plate, set it before him, placed in it some tamales and from the pot she poured some soup in another gourd. When she served the cooked mole it looked much like his son which caused him to shout and weep. He threw the pot on the floor, and the baby was white from the cooking. He jumped to the bed, untied the cradle which was wrapped up and empty and, not finding the child, he was beside himself, and the mother began to cry out. Her husband asked what was the matter. Then he saw the baby again and said: "Oh stupid, evil woman," and as he was a valiant man, he seized his bow and arrows, put an arrow to the bow, pulled the string and shot his wife through the back and killed her. (See Plate 37.)

This took place at night and at dawn all the principals went to the Master's house and were told what had happened while they were drunk. Zinzuni, the Master, asked, "Who has done wrong during this drunkenness?" One replied he had, and another said he had done wrong, and each one told what had happened to him. Then the Master asked: "We got very drunk; which is more pleasure, to get drunk or to sleep with a woman? Why do they not do that way in Coringuaro?" Then he ordered the tavern keeper to make more wine of the large magueys for it would be a shame if the Chichimecas enjoyed them or made wine of them.

Full of remorse, Hopotacu spoke to his father, saying: "I do not know what has happened to me. Zinzuni, I have shot the mother of my son." Then the Master asked: "Why did you shoot her, what did she do to you?" Then Hopotacu explained the gruesome story: "Father," he said, "she cooked my son, the one you named for me. Some old woman wearing a coarse weed skirt and a blanket of the same material over her head brought a mole or a trollop to sell and said she wanted to sell it because she was hungry. Believing her story my wife bought it. But instead of a mole it turned out to be my son whom I begot and she cooked it. For this reason I killed her."

After listening to this explanation, his father said: "That was no old woman but an aunt of the Gods of the Heavens; her name is Avicanime, and by now all the gods without exception have died of starvation and we have lost our heads. The people will be likewise. Let us go somewhere." They stayed drunk for five days and then departed from the village.

When they suffered from some affliction, these people had the custom of saying "we have lost our heads," meaning that their enemies would capture them, sacrifice them and would put their heads on high poles. They merely imagined that they had already been captured, and for this reason Hiripamucu, the Master, said that they had lost their heads.

59 · MORALS AND MORE OMENS

Once more Tariacuri called his nephews and his son Hiqugage. When they had gathered he said to them: "What shall we do? Why do you not go to Master Hivacha, the son of my father-in-law, who gets so badly drunk every day, who eats no bread and whose only food is wine. Go to him, take this fish, tell him to eat first and that afterward he may begin to drink. He shall drink a cup and immediately afterward eat bread so that he will not die, for he will be killed while he is drunk. Go to him and warn him for I spoke to his father about this matter."

The two nephews and the son departed together and called upon Hivacha who had just finished bathing and was resting. He welcomed them as Chichimecas and they placed the fish before him. Before they could tell him Tariacuri's message, Hivacha thought to anticipate it and said: "What brings you here, brothers, if not to talk of war? Wait, we shall count the days; cane day, water day, the day of the monkey, and knife day, for I, Hivacha, do not fight with blankets. I buy my slaves."

The Mexicans have the custom of counting the months and days by means of figures painted on some papers: a cane, water, a monkey, and a knife together make up twenty figures, including in the same way a dog and a deer. By counting the days in this fashion they find their signs or omens for fighting and the interpretation of the birth of each one. This method of accounting seems to have been used by Master Hivacha but not by the Chichimecas. This is why he mentions counting the days of cane and water.

On hearing this, Tangaxoan could not contain himself and exploded: "Who told you to count the days. We do not fight counting the days that way, but we gather wood for the temples while the priest called Curichi and the sacrificer employ fragrances in the prayer to the gods. We spend two nights in our vigil to study the people and to dispatch them. With this preparation we fight," and they touched their bows.

Everybody sat down in the patio and food was served. The messengers were not given food but those who served went around them and served only their own people. They brought out blankets and short shirts and Hivacha granted favors, but to the brothers he gave nothing. Since no one paid any attention to them, they said, "Let us return to our village" and they took up their bows. An old man, who was Hivacha's majordomo, went to a granary and got out a very large giant fennell-tube that was full of plumes and followed after them with it, calling them and saying, "Chichimeca Lords, there is something I want to tell you." Tangaxoan turned to his brother and said: "Lord Hiripan, that old man who is coming, what is he saying?" "He says for us to wait here for he wants to talk to us a little; let him come, and we shall see what he wants." He caught up with them, they greeted each other with a welcome calling him Grandfather, which is the way they refer to the old men and priests. He broke the giant fennell-tube and took out many plumes, put them in Hiripan's hand and said to them: "Boys, take these plumes to your

212

God Curicaveri who uses this kind to make his adornments: there are eighty and they were brought from the islands of the lake as a ransom for the gourd plates. I beg you that they serve to save me and my relatives, that you set them free for what Hivacha said was not correct—that we have lost our heads—because your God Curicaveri will conquer the land with a heavy hand. I beg of you, set me free and separate me from the prisoners." When he had finished, Hiripan asked: "What is your name, Grandfather?" and the old man answered: "Sire, I am called Parangua, and a younger brother of mine is called Zipaqui." To this Hiripan answered: "All right, speak to all your people and separate all your relatives for it shall be as you say." They departed, went their way and came to Pázcuaro. They did not speak to Tariacuri, but in an angry mood, they went by a roundabout way to the new temple at Querétaro, where they had their settlement in Mechuacán.

Upon arriving they went to the mountain, they and the Islanders who were with them, to gather wood. Hiripan climbed a slender tree, seized the branches, bent them, and the tree, which was worm-eaten, gave way and fell with him so that he landed face down and was knocked unconscious. (See Plate 38.) Seeing him thus, his brother Tangaxoan began to weep, saying: "Oh, oh, my brother is dead," and he called Hiqugage. All the Islanders came and surrounded him; still he did not get up and remained sprawled on the ground. Tangaxoan went to him, took him by one arm, Hiqugage by the other, and they raised him to a sitting position and supported his back.

At this point Hiripan stood up and spoke most angrily of himself, saying: "Although I am of such small stature, even though I have a round head which is not characteristic of valiant men, I shall never forget that insult by Hivacha," and turning to his brother Tangaxoan he continued, "Has Hivacha as rough hands from breaking branches for the fires of the temples, look how calloused mine are! Are Hivacha's hands as rough from gathering wood and the fragrances that must be supplied, and how high must his piles of wood be? I shall never forget this insult."

213

These people had the custom of gathering wood for the temples, and fragrances, called *Andumucua*, would be used by the priests on the fires so that the gods would grant them victory over their enemies. In their prayer to the Fire God they would name all the Masters against whom they cast all the spells of the fragrances. This explains why Hiripan said that he had worked so hard to gather wood for the temples, that he had callouses on his hands which Hivacha did not have. Now, therefore, he deserved that the gods grant him the conquest for the sake of the great quantity of wood which he had brought to the temples. He had brought so much that he had enough callouses to deserve to conquer Hivacha and to show that he was a valiant man even if he were of small stature and had a round head, for those who are like this are not held to be valiant men. He explained that this is why they always flatten the heads of the lords and shape them to look like loaves or cakes. Tangaxoan said to Hiripan: "Brother, you are not as angry as I; I am angrier than you although I have small feet and a slender body. Let us go report to our uncle so he will not say that both Hivacha and I are to live. Although our uncle is still living, we shall die before he does for we have no desire to live. Let us go tell him what Hivacha told us."

They went to see their uncle Tariacuri, who by now was very old and tired. He was wearing golden ear-loops, a turquoise necklace, a wreath of clover on his head, and his wives were gathered around and holding him. When his nephews arrived, he said to the women, "Mothers, lift me up for my nephews are coming and they want to talk about something important." They lifted him, seated him on a chair with a back, and then he told them to go inside. When his nephews arrived, he greeted them warmly, and they returned his salutation. Then they broke that giant fennell-tube, took out the white plumes and put them in his hand, whereupon Tariacuri asked: "What is this, boys?" This was their opportunity to tell him what Hivacha, Master of Tariaran, had said to them. "Well, boys, what do you say?" asked Tariacuri. "Are you thinking about fighting?" "Yes, father," they answered, "since you are alive you shall see how we are going to die so you will not say afterward that we wanted to exist; to die is what we wish, and you shall see our death." Tariacuri objected, saying: "What do you mean, boys? Whom have you in your company to want to fight and make war against others?" They countered: "Why, father? We do not need company, we are many. There is a principal called Cueze, who almost killed Ycariqui, Quacangari, Aguanzique, and Cupavaxanci, who are valiant men among us and among the Islanders; there are also Zapivatame, Zangueta, Chapata, and Atachehucane." [These are the ancestors of Don Pedro who is now Governor and who made friends with the Chichimecas.] "We think we are enough." Tariacuri questioned them: "What do you mean, boys? You who so long ago began to want to make war, as it is said, it is a long time since you began and now you are experts. I do not mean to gainsay your words and change your opinions. First let me consult Huresta, the Master of Cumachen, who is most credible as a youth, for he will be on our side and will join us; and if this help suffices, we shall all arise and go together to a Master called Thivan, because he is indebted to us and is a most valiant man. Cross the lake again for I shall send you word tomorrow. The next day they will arrive, and we shall gather here in a place called Thivapu, on the highest part." Their reply was, "Let it be so, father," and they recrossed the lake.

60. THE DEFEAT OF HIVACHA

The messengers sent by Tariacuri to the Master of Cumachen returned, and three days later he sent for his nephews to inform them that the messengers had brought back good news and that he was willing to help them. His nephews came and, just before daylight, Tariacuri climbed a little mountain called Thivapu, cleared off a small space there, put three piles of dirt together, and on top of each a rock and an arrow. Then he removed himself a little distance from the spot and lay down. His nephews climbed the same little mountain, went to the summit, and came upon the spot where the piles of dirt were. Upon seeing them they asked: "What manner of thing is this? Who climbed up and cleared this place?" And they continued, "We do not know who did this or who piled up this dirt unless our uncle could have done it." They agreed that he might have, "But why did he put that dirt there?" Tariacuri, pretending that he was ascending the mountain, came to them and asked: "What is the trouble, boys, what have you done here? Why did you put these piles of dirt here?" They answered: "Father, we did not put it here, were you not the one who did it?" To this question Tariacuri replied: "Yes, boys, and you were wise not to destroy them. Listen to me boys: just like these three piles, so there are to be three Masters: you, Hiripan, will be on this pile in the middle, which is the village of Cuyacán; and you, Tangaxoan, will be on this pile, which is the village of Mechuacán; and you, Hiqugage, you will be on this one, which is the village of Pázcuaro. Thus you shall be three Masters." On the spot he drew the outlines of the village of the Master, called Hivacha Hirapan, and said to them: "Look, I want to show you the village; this line here is the way you are to go; this one here is a range, you are to go this way, and the people of Cumachen this way; those of Coringuaro, Hurichu, and Pichataro, will go by this road for they are on the way already. I appointed tomorrow as the day for them to come. So, go, boys." They agreed and said that it should be so done.

They departed with all the war people and by afternoon arrived at a village called Viramu Angaru. When night fell they took their god Curicaveri and traveled in separate squadrons to surround the entire village and get ready to destroy it. They established themselves in ambush, and as dawn broke Hiripan said to all of them: "Arise, everybody," and they all rose up, gave a great shout, and destroyed and burned all the houses. (See Plate 39.) They captured many enemies who made a great noise and shouted when they were taken. They hurriedly carried the wounded ones to Hivacha by the arms. When Tangaxoan approached, he struck Hivacha on the head with a club. They took all his wives, wherever they could capture them, and brought them to camp.

216

There were many natives living in the villages called Chun-engo. Zizupan, and Zicuvato, and many of the enemy fled to these villages shouting and making a great noise. But they were not received and had to return to their own village where they were captured and placed under guard for they were taken at night. All the next day the hunt went on, searching for those who had hidden, and they spent one night there. The next morn-ing all captives were counted. The news was brought by a prin-cipal called Zapivatame to inform Tariacuri how they had con-quered and captured. The messenger greeted Tariacuri and said to him: "Sire, Curicaveri has captured some prisoners." Taria-curi rejoined: "Are there any dead among our people to cause me sorrow?" Zapivatame replied in a happy tone: "Sire, the Master of the village did not fight, everything is calm again, we spent the night there and we captured them in one day by hunt-ing them down. In this fashion Curicaveri captured them." Tariacuri was overjoyed with the news. All the war people came with their captives, making a great noise. They formed a proces-sion with them and marched to Tariacuri's house.

Everybody was fed, then they chose those captives who were to be kept in jail for the sacrifices. They untied the old man called Parangua, who was Hivacha's majordomo, and he and his brother went to see Hiripan who said to them: "What is it, Grandfather?" They told him that he was the one who gave him the plumes. In view of this information, Hiripan said: "Let us tell our uncle." They appeared before their uncle who asked the reason for the visit, and they explained: "This is the one we told you about; he is the one who brought the plumes and is called Parangua. The one who comes with him claims to be his brother, he is called Zipaqui." Tariacuri countered: "What does Hivacha say?" And they replied, "What can he say, Sire?" Tariacuri cut them short: "There he is over there, what does he think? This is the manner in which Curicaveri punishes; this is what his par-ents in the heavens said, that he should conquer the land. Go and choose those whom you say," and they went and chose them. They freed four hundred and spent two days preparing the captives. They put plumes on them, silver miters, silver ingots like suns around their necks, and long hair on their backs. In the same manner they treated the Master, called Hivacha, and put tinkling bells on his legs. They held a vigil with all of them that night in the houses of the chief priests and danced with them. At midnight the trumpets were blown so that the gods would descend from the heavens and the next morning they placed their flour at the feet of the temples. Hiripan, Tangaxoan, Hiqugage, and the other lords, all dressed in their finest adornments, went up to the temples. Tariacuri was seated in a chair at the entrance to the houses of the chief priests, and they sacrificed all the captives. During one entire day they did nothing but sacrifice.

They wore bone necklaces called *Tarapu Uta* which were red and covered with the blood that splashed from the sacrificed victims. They washed them in the water in Don Pedro's house, governor of Pázcuaro, and Tariacuri named that place Carupu Uta, which it is called to this day. The common people still say that the water is not potable because of the washing of the bone necklaces at that early time.

61. HIRIPAN, TANGAXOAN, AND HIQUGAGE DIVIDE THE ENTIRE PROVINCE AMONG THE THREE OF THEM

After they had conquered Hivacha's village, they proceeded to the conquest of the people of Coringuaro, whom they destroyed (see Plate 40), then Atatepeo and Turipitio, all of which was accomplished in one morning. They also conquered the villages of Hetuquaro and Hoporo. Tangaxoan and Hiripan went on to the conquest of Xajo Chucandiro, Teremendo, and then came to Baniqueo where the men were so valiant that they could not be conquered. There was a momentary cessation of hostilities at midday. In view of the circumstances, Hiripan, Tangaxoan, and all their people sacrificed their ears in order to assure success in the conquest. They shamed each other for not having been more vigorous and brave. They all ate and then resumed the battle, slept there that night and took up the fight again the next morning. By midday they had conquered the village.

They conquered Cumachen, Naranjan, Zacapu, Cheran, Siviñan, and on their way back they also took Huriapa and the villages of the Navatlatos called Hacavato, Zizupanchemengo, Vacapu, and other villages called Tariyaran, Yuriri, Hepacutio, and Condenvaro. The people from all the villages fled to the mountains so Hiripan and Tangaxoan decided to go to Hurecho which they also conquered and then rested.

While they were engaged in these conquests, Tariacuri died and was buried in his place at Pázcuaro. Later, a Spaniard exhumed his ashes and found very little gold because it was at the beginning of the conquest.

Hiripan called Tangaxoan and Hiqugage and said to them, "Brothers, Tariacuri, our uncle, is now dead; Tangaxoan, you go to Mechuacán, I shall go to Cuyacán, and Hiqugage will stay here in Pátzcuaro for his house and his establishment are here." In Cuyacán they built a house for Hiripan and another in Mechuacán for Tangaxoan, and each one assumed the seigniory over his people so that there were three seigniories.

A few days later Hiripan called a meeting of Tangaxoan and Hiqugage and suggested to them: "Brothers, let us conquer Huripao," and they went on to the conquest of the following villages: Huripao, Charo, Thutiro, Tupataro, Vairisquaro, Xeroco, and Cuiseo. They returned from these conquests only to set out again and conquer Pevendro, Zinzimeo, and Araro before returning. Then Hiripan said to Tangaxoan and Hiqugage: "What shall we do, brothers? The people of the villages run away and carry off the plumes and jewels which made them Masters in the villages which we conquered. Wherever they have gone, go catch them; let the gods come back to their villages."

All those who had fled with the jewels, plumes, gold, and silver came and presented them all, arranging them in order. Seeing all the yellow gold and white silver, Hiripan said: "Look, brothers, this must be manure which the sun casts off, and that white metal must be manure cast off by the moon; and all these green plumages, white crests, and red plumages, what do you know about these? They are what the people ran away with and they have already brought them back to Curicaveri. This is what his parents told him in heaven; that he should take all the jewels away from everyone, that he alone should have them. The heavy piece of wrought stone, the gems and blankets, all these are to be his alone. Let all this remain with Curicaveri and Xaratanga. I shall take only red and green plumes, and let us not divide these jewels, but let them be kept in one place where they may be seen by the Gods in Heaven, by Mother Cueravaperi and the Gods of the Four Quarters of the world and of the Inferno. Let Hiqugage take them." But Hiqugage objected, saying: "I am not the one to take them, I want only the white plumes. Let the rest stay in one place and in one house; let it be guarded there where the gods may look at it."

Since no one wanted to take all this treasure that had been gathered from all over the province, they built a house in Cuyacán, and there they stored it in chests and placed guards around it. The guards planted their fields in order to make their offerings of bread and wine.

This entire treasure was carried off by Cristóbal de Olí [Olid] when he conquered this province, as will be indicated in greater detail below.[17]

All those who had remained in the villages were gathered together, and Hiripan addressed them: "Go, take possession of your villages, live in them as before; take possession once more of your fruit trees and your fields; it suffices now that our God Curicaveri has shown himself liberal and returns them to you. Gather wood for the temples, plant your fields for war and stand behind your god with your squadrons. Increase the quantity of your bows and arrows and set him free when he is in need." They all agreed that they would do so. The old women and the old men

---

17 This is as found in the *Relación*. However, the details are given in the first part. It appears that the first part of the original manuscript is lost, and perhaps further information was given on this subject in the lost portion.

wept for joy as did the boys, and they all returned to their villages.

They could not settle down in their villages as they had no aldermen or heads; they were all agitated and unsettled. They were constantly in fear and upset. Consequently, Hiripan and Tangaxoan held a consultation along with Hiqugage in which they decided to set up leaders. The Islanders took over one part on the right hand in Xenguaro, Cherani, and Cumachen, and in this manner every one was satisfied and a Kingdom was established. In the same manner they conquered Tacambaro, Hurapan, Parochu, Charuhetoquaro, and Curutupuhucacio. The women went along with those who went on the conquest and took all of their jewels. So Hiripan, Tangaxoan, and Hiqugage established themselves and did not intend to conquer any more of the Chichimecas or Islanders. The villages were divided among the Masters of the Chichimecas and Islanders as follows: The Chichimecas established themselves in Curupu Hucacio, Tiachucuque, Chaquaco, Zinguita, Tivitani, Zirimenga Varucha, Tavathacu, Acume, Varicha, and Terecho; and the Islanders, in the village of Hurapan. Another principal called Cupavaxanci settled in Quacanan; Zapivatame Zangueta settled in Parachoa, Chapata, and Achate; Hucaveti, who was a valiant man, took over Parapeo, Utame, Catugama, and Chupingo. Each and every one of these principals was engaged in the Conquest, and they conquered Casinda Agapeo, Puruhoato, Cavingan, Tucumeo, Marita Zangapeo, Hetuquaro, Haparendan, Zacango, and Cuseo, all of which villages are located in the Hot Lands; Xanoato, Angapeo, Quayameo, and another principal called Zangüeta, an Islander, conquered Apanoato. The conquest continued, taking in Vamuquaro, Hacuizapeo, Papazio, Hoata, Tetengueo, Puruaran, Cuzian, Mazani, Patacio, Camuqua, Hoata Yurequaro, and Sirasdaro. Chiefs were assigned to all these villages, even women were appointed chiefs. Cupavaxanei, who was the chief in Guacanan, did his part in the conquest taking the following villages: Caxuruyo, Sicuitaro, Tarimbo, Hazacuaran, Zicuitaran, Pamuchea, Cupeo, Yacoho, Ayaquda, Zinagua, Churumucu, and

Cuzaru. Furthermore, another principal called Utucuma, for his part, conquered the following villages: Parancio, Zinapan, Zirapitio, Taziran, Turuquaran, Urechu, and Amhaquetio, including a village of the Navatlatos called Copuan. He also conquered Charapichu, Paraquaro, Paqueshoato, Evaquaran, Taristaran, Pucahato, Tancitaro, Erucio, and Ziramaratiro. In this fashion the Chichimecas and the Islanders continued the conquest and took over the following villages: Visisdan, Haviriohoato, Hapanoato [Apanoato], Cuyacán, Hapazingani, and Pungarihoato, which are located in the Hot Lands; Ambecio, Tavengohoato, Tiringueo, Haracharando, Zacapuhato, Perachequaro, Vasishoato, Hucumu, Hacandicuao, Harroyo, Xungapeo Chapatohoato, Haciro, Havanio, and Taximaroa, which was an Otomi village; Pecuri, Ecuatacuyo, Maroatio, Hucario, Hirechuhoato, Acambaro, Hiramucuyo, Tevendao, Mayoo, Emenquaro, Cazaquaran, Yripapundaco, Cuypuhoato, Vangao, Tavequaro, Puruandiro, Zirapecuaro, Quaruno, Ynchazo, Hutaseo, Hacavato, Zanzani, and Verecan. Another Master, a son of Hiripan, conquered another village called Carapan; and the father and grandfather of the dead Cazonci conquered Tamazula and Capotlan and gave them to the others.

62. INSTRUCTION IN HISTORY

"You Chichimecas by the family names of Eneani and Zacapuheti, and you Lords by the name of Vanacace, scattered though you may be, for not all Chichimecas live in one place, yet each and every one is a Chichimeca: all you who live within the boundaries of this Province to supply the necessities of Curicaveri, hear what I have to tell you. (See Plate 41.) You who say that you are from Mechuacán, are you not newcomers? Where will more Chichimecas come from? They all have gone to conquer the frontiers so that you are newcomers from some part of Tangachuran, a god of the Islanders. You who claim to be from Mechuacán are from the conquered villages and are perfumed with incense, for that is the way they treat the captives; and we spared you to save our voices for we neither sacrificed nor ate you. Remember that you promised great things, such as planting the fields for our God Curicaveri; you promised the cinch and the ax to gather wood for his temples, that you would back him up with your battalions and help him in the battles, would take along reinforcements, that you would take his provisions to war, that you would increase his bows and arrows with the help that you would give him, and defend him in time of need. All this you promised in this manner, now you are ungrateful; you think you are Kings. You low class people of Mechuacán are all Lords and cause your thrones and seats to be brought along behind. You all think of yourselves as Kings, even those who are in charge of counting the people, called *Ocanvecha*, all of you are Lords; look how Curicaveri has made Kings and Masters. Why do you not look back over your shoulder to the past when you were slaves? Because you have now been conquered you do not keep your promises. You break up your battalions, for the fact is you have come from the captaincies of the war, and you do not keep up the supply of wood for the temples; you have not kept account of the wood which is brought by the community for his temples; your seedbeds for war are everywhere abandoned, for this you are knaves, you are serfs and slaves. All this you promised to do in exchange for not being sacrificed; that is the way you failed to keep your promises.

"You, people of the tribes; Curicaveri now has pity on himself in this the present year, and for this reason has you here to administer justice to you. You who have been delinquent, you who are two-faced witches and medicine men, you who cast spells and carry the images in your hands; for all this he who has us in charge has pity on himself; he who is King and Cazonci. You chiefs of the Four Quarters of the province and of the boundaries of the Kingdoms, you who are on the frontiers and have your captains; look, you chiefs, those who were Masters of the Chichimecas were raised in great poverty, they never tasted a piece of bread. The cinches with which they tied the wood were made of weeds, and for axes they used sharp stones in their bare hands in order to gather wood for the temples. The Masters, Hiripan, Tangaxoan, and Hiqugage, used very coarse thick blankets. They had no light ones. And as for the insignia of honor, such as the lip-rings, they had no access to gold. They used little sticks because they were Masters and their mothers say that they wore earrings made of roots of the maguey. That is the way the Masters lived in company with the Ladies, their Sisters. Remember that they ate weeds, the kind that are called *apupataxaqua, acumba, patoque coroche,* and *zimbico,* even one called *sirumata.* There were none that they did not eat. This is the way they increased the villages and dwellings, and they took blankets and food from the enemy for me. Now you are chiefs with large lip-rings which stretch your lips so that you seem more important. It would be better for you to put on masks, for you put on airs with such large lip-rings. You all wear skins, never leaving them off or undressing yourselves but always going about in skins. You will never take any captives. If you were the valiant men that you ought to be, you would take them off, and you would put some blankets on your naked backs when you work. You would take your bows and arrows, put on your war jackets, for that is the way your God Curicaveri does, and thus you would go to war to defend him in the battles, but you are not valiant men. You have all turned into chiefs and Lords, and you care for your bodies too much to make them work. Going to war you run away and come back lying to the Cazonci, saying thus and so is the village that you conquered. With your words you deceive the King who divided the people among you and made you chiefs. Oh, oh! This is all wrong, people, you who are all here. I have completed, on behalf of the Cazonci, what I was to tell you for these are his words. Take the wrongdoers and kill them for I so order." They all replied with one accord that it was well done. The priest ordered that those called *vazcata* be taken to jail, for they were some of the wrongdoers, who along with some captives, were to be sacrificed in the general feast of Cuingo. The others who were condemned to death were beaten lifeless with a club and then dragged and thrown to the weed patches, where they were eaten by the jackals, turkey buzzards, and carrion birds. They were dedicated to the God of the Inferno.

During the feast of Cuingo,[18] those who were in jail were blindfolded, each one was given a white blanket to cover himself with, a red-colored short skirt to dress in, two copper anklets and copper necklaces were put on them, clover-leaf wreaths with flowers were put on their heads, and they were given food and drink. They were caused to become intoxicated, and the priests of the sea god called Tupiecha played their kettledrums with them. After the clowns had fought mock battles with them, using their round shields and clubs, as was described in the feast of Cuingo, they sacrificed them, dressed themselves in their skins, and danced in them.

After the full day of general justice had been accomplished by administering the sentence of death by clubbing, the priest would go to the Cazonci's house where he was received warmly; he would thank him profusely and would offer the salve to the gods. Then food would be served to him and all those who were with him.

63. TARIACURI CONDEMNS A SON TO DEATH

Tariacuri had a son called Tamapucheca who has been mentioned before. He was captured in a village called Yzipamucu and was ransomed by the governesses who had raised him in exchange for a very rich plumage. The story is that Tamapucheca, going alone, went on a foray to the village, was captured by his enemies, and taken to the patio of the temples. They conducted him in a procession, as was customary with captives, and perfumed him with flour. The news of his capture was brought to his father Tariacuri who was greatly pleased and said, "Yes indeed, I am very pleased. I have given food to the Sun and to the Gods of the Heavens. I begot that head which satisfied them and that heart which they cut out of him. My son was as delicate

18 Caso, "The Calendar of the Tarascans," p. 28, dates this feast of Cuingo, March 14.

pigweed bread. Now I have given food to all the Gods in the Four Quarters of the world. This has been very good, what could be better? If he were here with me they would drag him through the streets on account of some woman; the people of Yzipamucu dared not sacrifice him for fear of his father Tariacuri."

The Master, called Zinzuni, said: "Let him go home, go; take him back because he is the son of a great Master," and they started him back, saying: "Sire, go home, let your servants take you," and Tamapucheca replied: "What do you mean? I cannot go because our God Curicaveri has thrown me out. The Gods of the Heavens already know that I am a prisoner and have already eaten me. Give me some wine for I want to get drunk," but they refused to give it to him and said: "Because you say this Sire, you have to go to your house." He then asked: "Do I have to go? What will my father say when he learns that I am returning, for he has already received the news? Bring the adornments that they put on captives and I shall sing to the Gods of the Heavens."

These people had a custom which prevented those who had been captured in war from daring to return to their villages because they would be killed. They believed that the gods had taken them for food from among their own. It also served the purpose of preventing them from giving information to their enemies should they return to their home villages.

Since Tamapucheca refused to go to his village, they gave him the adornments used by those who are to be sacrificed. They put a silver miter on his head, placed a small paper flag in his hand, a round silver shield on his neck, and he spent the entire day drinking.

At nightfall and without anyone knowing about it, the governesses who had raised him left Pázcuaro, taking with them a very large plumage of long, green plumes. Some old men took the plumage to Hizipamucu, the Master, and said to him: "Give us Tamapucheca, here is this plumage." This pleased the Master and he replied: "In truth, you shall take him." They put him in a hammock and, drunk as he was, brought him to a suburb of

Pázcuaro [Pátzcuaro] called Cutu, where he slept until day-break. When he came to, Tamapucheca asked: "Where am I?" and they explained that he was in Pázcuaro. Whereupon he asked: "What do you mean? Why did you bring me back?" They explained how they had gone for him and carried him back. He then asked: "What will my father say when he knows it?" His father did learn about it and began to scold because they had brought him back, and asked: "What pride is this? I condemn those who brought him back; go and kill him, his governesses, and the old men who brought him back. Let them take with them the cup in which they drank, for it was because they were drinking that they brought him back. Kill them all for they have done me wrong." He has to rule the people so he let them get drunk and they were all killed with a club. (See Plate 42.)

64. TARIACURI'S DAUGHTER KILLS A CORINGUARO LORD

One of Curicaveri's priests tells a story about a trip he made, when small, with a grandfather. They were traveling to the village of Coringuaro and, upon arriving at a certain point, the grandfather said: "One of the Lords of Coringuaro was killed here by a woman and it happened this way. Tariacuri, the Master of Pázcuaro, was at war with the nearby Lords of Coringuaro. He called a daughter of one of his women, dressed her with many adornments, and told her to go to Coringuaro and let herself be killed, for if she were a man she would die anyway in a war and be cast aside. It was the occasion of the feast of Hunis Pera-quaro[19] when it was customary to hold a wake with the bones of the captives in the houses of the chief priests. He gave her his adornments that she might put them on with a very good skirt and told her that if she should be taken she should not worry.

"She was to go to Parezaripitio and enter the house of the chief priests where the women are. The sacrificer would make

---

[19] Caso, "The Calendar of the Tarascans," p. 16–17, 28, gives the spelling as Unisperacuaro and states that it was April 3.

his entrance to tell the story of the bones, and they would all begin to sing. At this moment the women would appear and the brave men would begin to dance with them holding hands. 'Dance with whomever you can for there will be present the Lords called Uresqua, Cando, Sica, Zinaquambi, Quama, Quatamaripe, Equandira, and Chague. Look for one of them to dance with.' "
He gave her some stone knives wrapped in a blanket so that she might behead one of those lords. He also gave her some blankets and rawhide jackets to give to the one who should dance with her. The woman answered: "Sire, I want to go ahead and die before you do, because if I were a man I would die in battle anyway." Tariacuri continued his instructions: "Go, and you shall arrive tonight and perhaps it will please the gods for you to be taken by one of those Lords, and should he take you he will ask where you are from. Under no circumstances shall you let him know that you are from Pázcuaro, but say that you are from Tupataro, a village subject to Coringuaro, and you will say: 'A brother of mine brought a captive here to dance and weep with in order to make him go to heaven quickly. I did not find him here. I do not know where he has gone.' And if he should tell you that he was there or that he went to gather wood for the temples, no matter what he says, you shall say, 'Oh, Sire, it must be true that he has gone.' At dawn follow him, give him these blankets, which I have tied up for you, and you shall say to him, 'Sire, take these blankets and these jackets, this plumage for your head and this short shirt which you shall put on, and this cinch and the mats which I brought to my brother.' Then he will ask you: 'Lady, what shall your brother put on?' and you shall answer: 'I have other things he will put on; I must not take these back home. Perhaps he has gone far to the mountain to gather wood for the temples.' Come back any way you can and you will come as far as the mountain, and he will ask you, 'Lady, do you expect to come tonight?' and you will answer: 'Why not, Sire? Of course. Have we not come here to dance for five days?' He will then say to you, 'Oh, sister, will you not have to go home?' and

you will answer, 'Sire, I must return, I shall go tomorrow and tonight I shall sleep here.' This is what you shall say to him.

"When he goes outside with you, lead him aside from the road a little ways and there you shall sleep. While he is asleep, cut off his head with one of these knives."

The woman departed carrying the blankets on her back and arrived at Coringuaro at midnight. She lay down at the door to the houses of the chief priests, the sacrificer entered to preach his customary sermon, and they began to sing with the slaves.

The women came in and began dancing, men and women holding hands. When it was time for the feast of Hunisperaquaro, all the lords arranged themselves in order for the dance which was guided by one of them called Uresqua. He was followed by another lord called Cando, dressed in a white blanket, for he was one of the greater principals. They all wore clover-leaf wreaths on their heads, and Cando's wife came up to dance with him. They took a turn and then sat down next to the woman from Pázcuaro who was adorned prettily. She wore a turquoise necklace, strings of beads on her wrists, and a crimson shirt; she coiled her braids around her head, painted her teeth black, and put on the blankets she had brought with her. Then she joined the lord called Cando to dance with him, going between him and his wife, pushing her to one side. When Cando saw her, he took her by the hand, squeezed it, and everybody began to dance; they squeezed hands again, and he left her. He stood aside to look at the beauty of the women, then taking her by the hand, they began to dance again. The dance stopped and everyone returned to his place and sat down. Cando's brother Uresqua said to him: "Brother, who is that woman you are dancing with?" Cando replied: "Sir, she is a sister of my wife," and Uresqua remarked, "She is very pretty." They were all dancing and his wife came up to dance with her husband again, but the woman from Pázcuaro [Pátzcuaro] would always come between them. Cando would always leave his wife to dance with the other woman. He danced with her four times, then everyone had a drink called *Puzquan*. While this was taking place Cando took the woman by the hand and led her out to the portal of the houses of the chief priests where they sat down together.

"Where are you from, lady?" He asked her and she replied: "Sire, from Tupataro, a village subject to this one," and Cando asked her why she came here. She explained: "I came because a brother of mine left a slave here. We both came to weep for him and make him go to heaven quickly." [This was according to the usual custom, for, when these people take a captive who is to be sacrificed, they dance with him and say that the dance is to express sorrow for him and make him arrive in heaven quickly.] Cando then asked: "Is your brother not married?" She explained that he was not yet married and Cando asked whether both were dancing here. When she replied in the affirmative, Cando said: "He was here and went to gather wood for the temples." She agreed that this must be what happened and said she would go back to her house. Cando reminded her that it was midnight and asked whether she were not afraid. She replied that she was not, that she would rather go for she had nothing to do here. Cando then indicated that he wanted to go with her and she asked him why. Cando made up an excuse, saying: "I will go a ways with you and get some wood for the temples." The woman agreed, went for the blankets she had brought along to give to him, and he went for his short shirt, for they had danced naked with nothing but a blanket on their backs. The woman came out with Cando following.

The people were all drinking a beverage called *Puzquan*. He took her by the hand and they went through the patio of the temples, through the wooden fence and out to the road where they entered some weed patches, where Cando said: "Come this way lady, and let us talk a little while." They left the road but the woman objected: "We are too close to the road, maybe people will come by, there is a better place down there (to get him away from the road)." They went a little farther to where she suggested that they stop, because she recognized a large crag there, a familiar spot.

When Cando fell asleep on his back the woman got up very

quickly, held her skirts very tight and cut them off at the knee so that she would be able to move quickly, untied the knives which were wrapped in the blanket and took one in one hand. With the other hand she turned his head so as to stretch his neck a little more and put the knife against his throat. She drew the knife with a lightninglike motion, cut off his head, and did it all so quickly that he was unable to cry out. Then, putting one hand on his chest, and, as if slaughtering an animal, she finished cutting his head off cleanly so that only the torso was left. Carrying the head by the hair, she took it to her village at the edge of which there was an altar, where they usually placed captives which they brought back from the wars. (See Plate 43.) She put the head there in a place called Piruen. Then she went home to Tariacuri and reported to him what had happened. Everybody rejoiced and Tariacuri said to her: "Now you have given food to the gods; let the Coringuaros blame whomever they wish, it makes no difference to us. Let them attribute it to whomsoever they wish."

According to these people this is what happened in Coringuaro, a village of their enemies, and it is related here in accordance with their narration and the way they told it.

65. THE DEATHS OF HIRIPAN, TANGAXOAN, AND HIQUGAGE

It has been told how Tariacuri divided Mechuacán into three seigniories. (See Plate 44.) Hiripan was the Master of Cuyacán, which was the seat of government, for that was the location of his god Curicaveri, that piece of rock which they said was Curicaveri himself. Hiripan had a son called Ticatame who became Master of Cuyacán after the death of his father. In Pázcuaro, the Master was Hiqugage, who had many sons. Because they got drunk and killed people by sticking knives in their backs, he ordered his sons killed. Hiqugage had another son by the same name who they say was struck and killed by lightning. They embalmed him and the people of the lake held him to be a god until the Spaniards came to this province and took him away.

Hiripan had a son called Ticatame, who was the Master in Cuyacán, and he in turn had a son called Tucuruan, who also had a son. The latter was called Paguingata, the father of Doña María who is married to a Spaniard.

Tangaxoan had sons among whom was one called Zizispanda-quare who was the Master in Mechuacán at the time when Tica-tame was the Master in Cuyacán. The seat of government passed to Mechuacán. He put part of it on some islands in the lake and kept part in his house.

Zizispandaquare had another son called Zuanga [Zuangua] who was the Master in Mechuacán when the Spaniards came to Taxcala [Tlaxcala], but he died before they came to the province of Mechuacán. Zuangua left the following sons: Tangaxoan, otherwise known as Zincicha, the father of Don Francisco and Don Antonio; Trimaransco, Cuini, Sirangua Aconsti, Timage, Tagani, Patamu, Chuicico, and many daughters.

After the Spaniards came to the land, Tangaxoan, alias Zin-cicha, was raised to the office of Master. He killed four of his brothers because of the accusations of another brother, Timage, who claimed that they were plotting his overthrow, as was explained elsewhere.

There was no further seigniory in Pátzcuaro after Hiqugage died because his sons had Hiripan killed. They buried him in Cuyacán, but he was disinterred later by a Spaniard who took all the gold that had been buried there with him. Tangaxoan, Zizis-pandaquare, and Zuangua were buried in Mechuacán. Zizispan-daquare made a few forays toward Toluca and Xocotitlan, and on two occasions they killed 16,000 men for him; other times he brought the captives back.

On one occasion the Mexicans came to Taximaroa and destroyed it during the time of the father of Montezuma called Hacangari. Zizispandaquare resettled it and made his conquests in the direction of Colima and Zacatula, among other villages. He was a great Master, and after him his son Zuangua enlarged the seigniory considerably.

PLATE 1: Presentation of the manuscript to the Viceroy Don Antonio de Mendoza.

PLATE 2: Concerning their government.

PLATE 3: Concerning their government.

PLATE 4: The priests of the temples.

PLATE 5: Forays into the villages of their enemies. *In the Morelia edition this sketch is captioned "Sicundiro," an obvious error. The caption used here is taken from the Escorial Manuscript C–IV–5.*

PLATE 6:   How they destroyed a village.

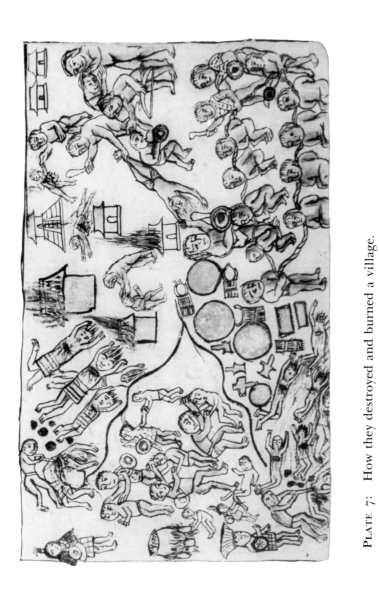

PLATE 7: How they destroyed and burned a village.

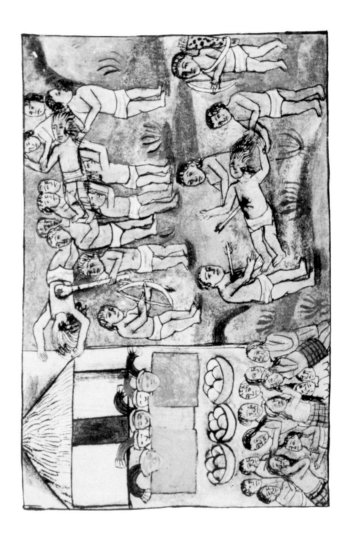

PLATE 8: Concerning those who died at war.

PLATE 9: Concerning the justice administered by the Cazonci.

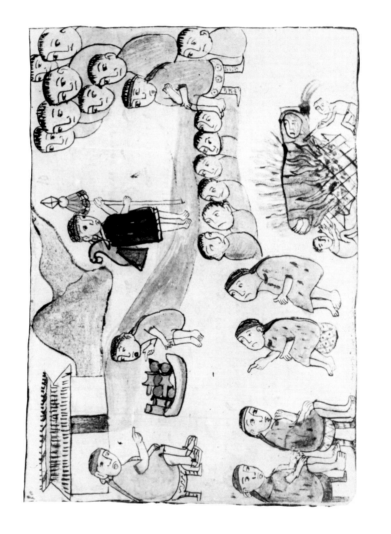

PLATE 10: Concerning the deaths of the chiefs and how they were replaced.

PLATE 11: Concerning the manner of the marriage of the lords.

PLATE 12: The manner of marriage among the lower-class people.

PLATE 13:   The death of the Cazonci and the burial ceremony.

PLATE 14: How another Master was selected.

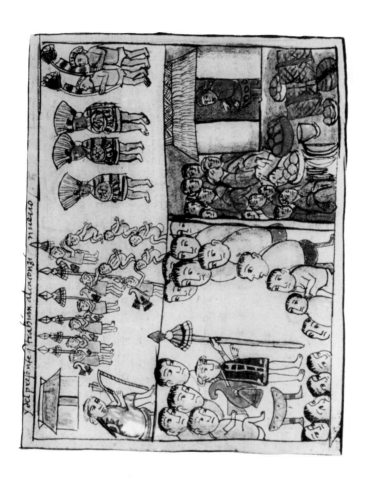

PLATE 15: The speeches of the chief priests and the presentation made to the Cazonci.

PLATE 16: Concerning the dreams and omens of these people before the Spaniards came.

PLATE 17: How Montezuma, Master of Mexico, sent a request for help to the Cazonci Zuanga [Zuangua].

PLATE 18: How the Cazonci and other lords tried to drown themselves.

PLATE 19:   Concerning the general administration of justice.

PLATE 20:   How the Masters of the Chichimecas took the daughter
of a fisherman and married her. (*Caption from C–IV–5.*)

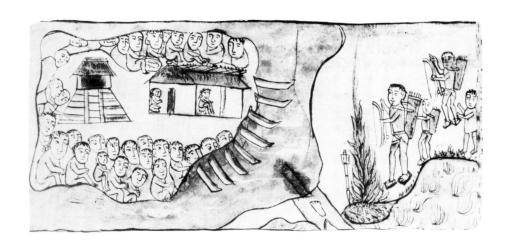

PLATE 21: Lord Caricaten asked Zurumban for help against Tariacuri, for he was surrounded on his island. (*Caption from*
C–IV–5.)

PLATE 22: How Quariacuri warned Tariacuri and he was able to
capture the priest Naca in an ambush. (*Caption from*
C–IV–5.)

PLATE 23: How Tariacuri had Naca cooked and eaten by his enemies.

PLATE 24: Zurumban ordered the destruction of the houses of Tariacuri's people, and the lords who were the cousins of Tariacuri were shot and his sisters were sacrificed. *(Caption from C–IV–5.)*

PLATE 25: Concerning the marriage of Tariacuri with the daughter of the Master of Coringuaro, and she was a bad woman. *(Caption from C–IV–5.)*

PLATE 26: How the friends of Tariacuri's wife came and got drunk with her, and Tariacuri's grief over his wife's infidelity.

PLATE 27:   The enemies of Tariacuri are sacrificed. *(Caption from C–IV–5.)*

PLATE 28:   How the brothers-in-law of Tariacuri, through his first wife from Coringuaro, sent a message asking for rich plumages, gold, silver, and other things.

PLATE 29:   Tariacuri finds his lost mother and nephews.

PLATE 30: Tariacuri sent a messenger for his son Curatame, and they disagreed. (*Caption from C–IV–5.*)

PLATE 31:   Tariacuri advises his nephews and son that they are to be Masters. (*Caption from C–IV–5.*)

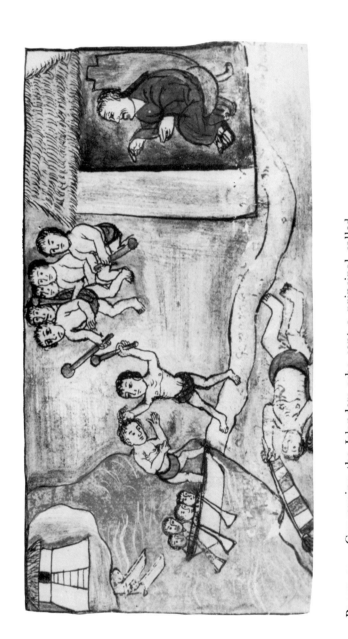

PLATE 32: Concerning the Islanders who sent a principal called Zapivatame to place himself under the orders of Taria-curi, and how he was imprisoned. (*Caption from C–IV–5.*)

PLATE 33: Curatame sent for Hiripan and Tangaxoan, who were doing penance in a cave.

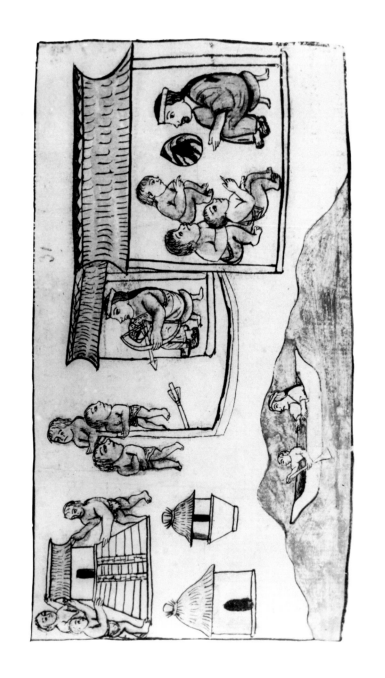

PLATE 34: Tariacuri gave a part of his God Curicaveri to his nephews and his son, then tried to shoot them because of some temples they made.

PLATE 35: Tariacuri ordered Hiripan and Tangaxoan to kill his son Curatame because he was a drunkard, and they killed him while he was drunk.

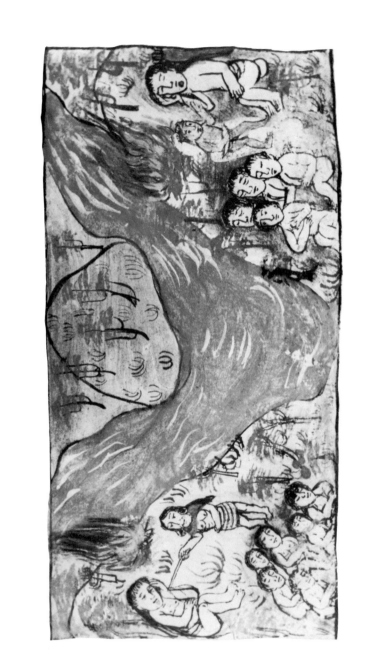

PLATE 36: In dreams the goddess Xaratanga appears to Tangaxoan (*left*) and the god Curicaveri to Hiripan (*right*). (*Caption by translators.*)

PLATE 37: The people of the village of Yzipamucu asked the people of Coringuaro for help.

PLATE 38: Tariacuri sent his nephews to warn and advise a brother-in-law not to get drunk. While returning, a strange thing happened to Hiripan connected with a tree on the mountain.

PLATE 39: Tariacuri showed his nephews and his son how to carry on the war.

PLATE 40: How Hiripan, Tangaxoan, and Hiqugage conquered the entire province.

PLATE 41: Speeches and reasoning of the chief priests regarding the history of their ancestors.

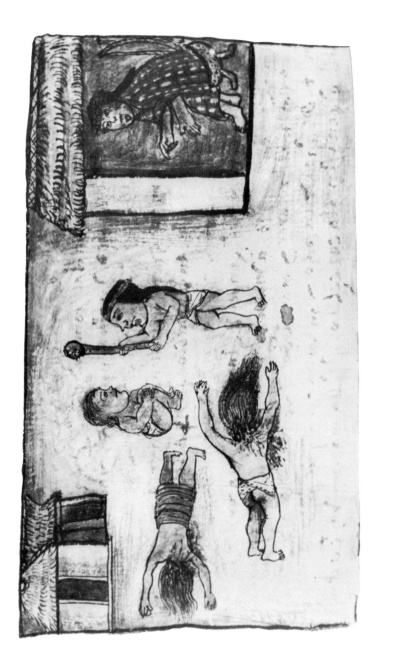

PLATE 42: One of Tariacuri's sons called Tamapucheca was captured, and his father ordered him killed.

PLATE 43: A lord of Coringuaro was killed by a daughter of Tariacuri.

PLATE 44: The Masters who followed Hiripan, Tangaxoan, and Hiqugage.

DRAWN BY JOHN RAY

Map of Michoacán

233

Glossary of Terms

APPENDIX A

Acacecha: Tarascan name for the Spaniard. Means people who wear caps and hats.

Acipecha: A type of fruit grown in Michoacán.

Acumarami: A type of fish.

Acumba: A type of weed.

Andamuqua: A fragrance used by individuals while giving prayers. Apparently not worn but used to make the air pleasant for the gods.

Andumucua: A fragrance used by the priests in the temples for various ceremonies.

Angoruti: A miter of fine silver.

Apupataxaqua: A type of weed.

Ariven: A dance.

Banacaci: Tarascan family name.

Cacagueo: Enemies of the Tarascans.

Cacapuhereti: People of the lineage of the god Curicaveri.

Caheri: Used as a prefix and means big.

Carupu Uta: Name of the place where the bones and shells that were splashed with blood, as a result of sacrifices, were washed.

Cazangari: One of the richest kinds of blankets.

Cazaretaqua: A necklace of gold.

Chaperi: A chest, usually filled with gold or silver.

Charoel: A type of fish.

Chatani: A type of feathers.

Chereque: A dance.

Cu: Temple.

Cuaro: Means in time of or in the place of. Usually used as a suffix.

Cuchahecha: Indian name for the Castilian women. It means ladies and goddesses.

Cuerapan: Enemies of the Tarascans.

Cuerepu: A type of fish.

Cuinequen: Some type of small animal.

Cuitlatecas: An Indian tribe.

Curice: A type of blanket

Curinda: Round loaves.

Curuzegro: Jail.

Echereatancata: A type of blanket.

Eneani: Chichimeca family name of the lineage of the god Curicaveri.

Escomaechas: An Indian tribe.

Feasts: See Appendix C.

Grandfather: Term of respect used when speaking to a priest or very old man.

Grandmother: Term of respect used when speaking to a priestess or very old woman.

Guacana: Enemies of the Tarascans.

Hacumaran: A type of fish.

Haparicha: A family lineage and an island group.

Hapupata Xaguay: A type of weed.

Henditare: Word meaning he is a lord.

Heneani: Tarascan family name.

Hurechu: Enemies of the Tarascans.

Huren de Tiechan: Name of those who lived on the island of Hacia-curuin.

Hurespondi: Arrows that have black, white, red, and yellow flints.

Mayordomo: Steward of a sodality.

Miecua Ageva: Name of one of the rocks at the temple site near Pázcuaro.

Moon: Time. Twenty days.

Nuguatatis: A group of people who lived on the mountain Zacapuha-cuzua.

Ocanvecha: Lords in charge of counting the people. Census takers.

Patoque coroche: A type of weed.
Patos: A type of fish.
Principal: Indian of noble status.
Puruaten: The high part of a temple.
Puzquan: A drink.

Quapimequa: Large blankets used as offerings to the gods.
Quatatos: A group of early Mexican peoples.
Quierequaro: A type of plant.

Sescuasecha: Name for the dancers at the feast of Sicuindiro.
Sirumata: A type of weed.

Tamemes: Bearers, carriers.
Tarapu Uta: Name of necklaces made of bone.
Tarascue: Son-in-law. Name the Indians gave the Spanish because they took the Indian girls. The Spanish misunderstood the name and thought they were saying that they were Tarascue's, and thus the name Tarascans was derived.
Tecohecha Xungada: The name for a green-painted arrow.
Teparacha: The Indian name for Spanish men. It means big men and was also used to mean gods.
Terapaquaebahecha: The name for slaves, both men and women, who had not been sacrificed.
Thira: A type of fish.
Thiron: A type of fish.
Tingarata: The name for one of the rocks at the temple site near Pázcuaro.
Tintivapema: Carrion birds.
Tucupacha: The name the Indians gave the Spanish when they saw what strange people the Spanish were and that they did not eat the same foods. The word also means gods.
Tupiecha: Sea-god.

Tuycen: A bread made in the shape of deer and used at feasts. Also the name used by the Tarascans for the horses of the Spanish.

Ucatatataze quequenezza: The name for the shirt worn by the chief priest who was called Petamiti.

Vacuesecha: Name for one of the rocks at the temple site near Pátzcuaro. Also, the eagle.

Vacuseecha: Name for the group we call the Chichimecas.

Vanacacin: Chichimeca family name of the lineage of Curicaveri.

Vanaonciquarecha: The name for slaves whose task it was to amuse and entertain the Cazonci.

Vazcata: The name for those who had committed any type of crime—evildoers. They were tried the day after the feast of Yzquatacons-cuaro. If they had transgressed four times, they were sacrificed.

Viriquareni: A ceremony of blacking the body with soot out of love for the god Curicaveri.

Vonaquaro: A seat.

Vrani Atari: Painted gourd plates.

Vrapeti: A type of fish.

Xupaquata: A tent-type pavillion.

Yurapeti: A type of fish.

Zacapuhiretin: Chichimeca family name of the lineage of the god Curicaveri.

Zacapuirio: Tarascan family name.

Zapi: Suffix meaning little.

Zeritacherengue: Name of one of the rocks at the temple site near Pátzcuaro.

Zimbico: A type of weed.

Zizamba: Kettledrummer.

Ziziquivaraquan: A dance.

Zizupa: A type of blanket.

Zuecepu: A type of fish.

Glossary of Gods and Goddesses

GODS

Achurihiepe*

Acuiecatapeme*

Carocuchango: One of the gods of the island of Xaraquaro.

Caroen: A child of the god Hacuizecapeme.

Chupitiripeme: A god of the island of Pacandan.

Cupanzieri*

Curicaveri: Nephew of Tiripanienquarencha and Curitacaheri.

Curitacaheri: Brother of Tiripanienquarencha. A messenger of the dieties.

Hacuizecapeme: Principal god on the island of Varucaten Hacicuruin.

Huren de Quevecara*

Manovapa: Son of the goddess Xaratanga.

Nurite: A child of the god Hacuizecapeme.

Nuriti: One of the gods of the island of Xaraquaro.

Pungarancha: god of the runners.

Pungarecha: A war-god.

Puruaten*

Querenda Angapeti [Agapeti]: god of Zacapu.

Siratatapeci: Son of the god Achurihirepe.

Sirunda Aran: Messenger of the god Querenda Angapeti.

Tangachuran: A god of the Islanders.

Tangachurani: A child of the god Hacuizecapeme. One of the gods of the island of Xaraquaro.

Tares Upeme: The god of the village of Cumachen.

Tiripanienquarencha: Brother of Curitacaheri.

Tiripeme Caheri*

Tiripemecha: Collective name of the gods who were brothers of Curicaveri.

Tiripenie*

Tiripenie Xugapeti*

Turesupeme: god of the village of Cumachen.

Unazihicecha: A god on the island of Pacandan.

Uquare: A child of the god Hacuizecapeme.

Uredecuavecara: God of the Morning Star [Also Uren de Cuavecara?] [Huren de Quevecaro].

Varichu Uquare: One of the gods of the island of Xaraquaro.

Vazoriquare: God of the village of Naranjan.

Vinturopatin*

Virambaneche: Gods of the Hot Lands. Gods of the Left Hand.

Viranecha: Collective name for gods.

Viravanecha: Gods on the Left Hand of Curicaveri.

Xarenave: One of the gods of the island of Xaraquaro.

Xarenivarechu: A child of the god Hacuizecapeme.

Zinziviqxo: Claimed by the Indians to be the god who named Mexico City.

Zizambanacha: Gods on the mountain near the village of Zacapo Lacanenden.

GODDESSES

Avicanime: Aunt of the gods of the Heavens.

Camavaperi: Sister of the god Unazihicecha.

Cueravaperi: Mother goddess of all the gods. In charge of clouds of vapor from hot springs which were believed to produce rain.

Pevame: Wife of Querenda Agapeti [Angapeti].

Purupe Cuxareti: Sister of the god Hacuizecapeme.

Xaratanga: A major goddess with temple and priests in the city of Mechuacán. Her priests were called Vatarcha.

* The *Relación* gives no identification other than to speak of a god by this name.

List of Tarascan Feasts

Throughout the *Relación*, references are made to definite time periods indicating that, as with other Mesoamerica groups, the Tarascans knew and understood a calendar. In Mesoamerica most of the organized societies used a twenty-day month and ended the month with a feast. Modern scholars have, therefore, given the months the same name as the feast which ends that time period. The *Relación de Michoacán* is the only known source for reconstructing the calendar of the Tarascans. In the *Relación* fourteen feasts are named by the priest-interpreter; he gives the Christian month name and day number for four of them in direct relationship to the Tarascan feast and states that another was held on November 14 but does not give the feast name of that date. Four men have worked on the problem of the Tarascan calendar: Caso,[1] Troncoso,[2] Leon,[3] and Seller.[4] As a result of these labors, Caso has been able to identify and establish a calendrical name and time order which lacks only four month names.[5] The feast [month] names are listed here in alphabetical order with the spelling and dates as found in the Morelia edition. The spellings within the brackets represent the orthographic changes that have

[1] Caso, "The Calendar of the Tarascans," *American Antiquity*, Vol. IX (July, 1943), 11–28.

[2] Francisco Del Paso y Troncoso, "Calendario de los Tarascos," *Anales del Museo Michoacano*, Vol. I (1888), 85–96.

[3] Nicolás León, "Los Tarascos," *Anales del Museo Nacional de México*, Segunda Epoca, I (1903), 484–90.

[4] Eduard Seler, "Die alten Bewohner der Landschaft," *Gesammelten Abhandlungen zur Amerikanischen Sprach-und Altertumskunde*, Vol. III (1908), 33–156.

[5] Caso, "The Calendar of the Tarascans," *American Antiquity*, Vol. IX (July, 1943), 28.

been made by scholars who have made linguistic studies of the feast names.

Caherivapansquaro [Caheri Uapanscuaro]
Charapuzapi [Charapu Zapi]
Cohora Cosquaro [Caheri Conscuaro] July 17
Corindaro [Curindaro]
Cuingo
Hazinas quaro [Hancinascuaro]
Hicuandiro
Hunis Peraquaro [Unisperacuaro]
Mazcoto [Mazcuto] June 7
Puracotacuaro [Peuanscuaro]
Purecoraqua [Purecoracua or Phurecutacuaro] February 23
Sicuindiro
Vapamquaro [Uapanscuaro] October 25
Yzquataconscuaro [Uazcuata Conscuaro]

Suggested Readings

Arriaga, Antonio. *Organización social de los tarascos.* Morelia, México, 1938.

Beals, Ralph L. *Cherán: A Sierra Tarascan Village.* Smithsonian Institution, Institute of Social Anthropology, Publication No. 2. Washington, Government Printing Office, 1946.

Beaumont, Pablo de la Purísima Concepción. *Crónica de la Provincia de los Santos Apóstoles S. Pedro y S. Pablo de Michoacán.* México, Imprenta de Ignacio Escalante, 1874.

Brand, Donald D. "An Historical Sketch of Geography and Anthropology in the Tarascan Region: Part #1," *New Mexico Anthropologist,* Vols. VI, VII, No. 2 (April–May–June, 1943), 37–108.

Bravo Ugarte, José. *Historia succinta de Michoacán,* 3 Vols. México, Editorial Jus, 1962–64.

Carrasco, Pedro Pizana. *Tarascan Folk-Religion, An Analysis of Economic, Social, and Religious Interactions.* New Orleans, Middle American Institute, Tulane University, 1952.

Caso, Alfonso. "The Calendar of the Tarascans," *American Antiquity,* Vol. IX (July, 1943), 11–28.

Covarrubias, Miguel. *Indian Art of Mexico and Central America.* New York, Alfred A. Knopf, 1957.

Foster, George F. and Gabriel Ospina. *Empire's Children: The People of Tzintzuntzan.* Smithsonian Institution, Institute of Social Anthropology, Publication No. 6. Washington, Government Printing Office, 1948.

García Manzanedo, Héctor. *Informe sobre la cerámica de Tzintzuntzan.* México, Instituto Nacional del Indigenista VII, 1955.

Kelly, Isabel Truesdell. *Excavations at Apatzingan.* New York, Viking Fund, 1947.

León, Nicolás. "Los Tarascos," in *Anales del Museo Nacional de México,* Segunda Epoca. México. Vol. I (1903), 484–90.

Mendieta, Fray Gerónimo de. *Historia Eclesiástica Indiana.* México, Antigua Librería Portal de Augustinos No. I, 1870.

Mendieta y Núñez, L., González F. Rojas, and others. *Los Tarascos: Monografía histórica, etnográfica, y económica.* México, Instituto de Investigaciones Sociales de la Biblioteca Nacionál de México, 1940.

Rea, Fray Alonso de la, *Crónica de la Orden de N. Seráfico P. S. Francisco, Provincia de San Pedro y San Pablo de Mechoacán en la Nueva España.* Querétaro, México, Ediciones Cimatario, 1882.

Stanislawski, Dan. "Tarascan Political Geography," *American Anthropologist,* New Series, Vol. 49, No. 1 (January–March, 1947), 46–55.

Troncoso, Francisco Del Paso y. "Calendario de los Tarascos," *Anales del Museo Michoacano.* Vol. I (1888), 85–96.

Index

zeguempare [Quezecuapare] [Queze-
quampare], 70, 73; Xamando, 73;
Aniniarangari, 76; Caycido, 89;
Ortega (Spaniard) , 89 & n., 90; Antonio de Godoy, 90 & n., 91, 95; An-
dres de Tapia, 90, 91; Tareca de
Xenoanto, 91; Abalos, 92, 93; Pilar,
92, 93, 94, 95; Father Martin, 96; Juan
de Ortega, 96; Alboronoz, 99; Brother
Francisco de Bolonia, 100; Brother
Jacobo de Testera, 100; Vanacace,
103; Ziranzirancamaro, 104; Sicuirancha, 106, 107, 108, 109, 110; Zimzamban, 106; Oresta, 108; Tariyaran,
111; Turepupanquaran, 112; Ude-
cavecara, 112; Ypinchuani, 112; Mahicuri, 113; Caricaten, 115, 119, 132, 133,
143, 145, 181; Curipajan [Curiparax-
an] [Curiparancha], 116, 117, 118;
Curuzapi, 123; Aramen, 129, 130, 131,
137, 139, 142, 143, 144–45, 169, 170;
Cetaco, 129, 130, 131, 137, 139, 142,
143, 144, 169, 170; Canagecua, 133;
Uxuriqua, 133; Quaracuri, 134–36,
138, 140, 141; Naca, 134–42; Perapaqua, 136; Cuta, 141; Chanhori, 145,
181; Mahiquisi, 145, 146; Huresqua,
149, 207; Tareqüesinguata, 152, 153;
Xoropeti, 152, 153; Zinzuni, 154, 164,
165, 207ff.; Huyana, 161; Atapezi, 165;
Anachurichenzi, 165; Hapariva, 165;
Uresqua, 166, 167; Curatame, 169;
Niniquaran, 170, 171; Chapa, 171,
181, 182; Cuyuva, 171, 172; Zirutame,
173; Tariachu, 177; Cando Huresqua,
181; Aristaquata, 181; Cuynzurumu,
181; Quanto, 181; Sica, 181; Utume,
181; Varapame, 181, 198, 199, 200;
Zinacuabi, 181; Zizito, 181; Hozeti,
182; Hucaco, 182; Quanirescu, 182;
Quata Maripe, 182; Vacusquazita,
182, 184; Xaracato, 182; Carata, 184;
Cocopa, 184; Hencivan, 184; Sicuindi-
cuma, 184; Tangaxonondo, 184;
Thiacani, 184; Ticuricaia, 184;
Chicuircata, 184; Caracomaco, 185,
186; Quenomen, 187; Zapivatame,
188; Zipincanaqua, 199; Cando, 207;
Hivacha, 211, 212, 213; see also
Tecaqua, Chupitani, Zuangua, Pedro,
Nurivan, and Guzmán

Petamiti (chief priest) : 17, 42, 102–
103; relates history, 103–111; see also
priests
Pilar (Guzmán's interpreter) : 92, 93,
94, 95
Pirovaquenvandari: see under govern-
ment, titles of office
Place of the Gods: see under gods
Priests: Baricha (priest of Araro) , 58;
Indian name for, 88; Indian concept
of Spanish, 88; Bolonia, Brother
Francisco de, 100; Testera, Brother
Jacobo de, 100; Hoatamanaquere (of
Xaratanga) , 113; Mizivan, 126, 127,
129 & n.; Tecaqua, 126, 127, 129 & n.;
Chupitani, 126, 127, 129 & n.; Naca,
133–42; Curiti, 160; see also Petamiti
Priests, titles of: Huaripiapecha [Hauri-
piupecha], 15; Axamiecha, 17; Curipecha [Curicitacha], 17; Curitiecha,
17, 20, 32, 33; Hiripacha, 17, 21;
Opitiecha, 17, 22; Pasantiecha [Pasar-
tiecha], 17; Quiquiecha, 17; Tininie-
cha, 17, 20, 21; Hiripati, 20, 21; Curi-
pecheo, 21; Curitecha, 22; Pirimu
(chief priests) , 77; Vatarecha, 111;
Vatarecha (of Xaratanga) , 111, 112,
117; Cuahuen (of Xaratanga) , 112;
Camejan (of Xaratanga) , 112; Cuyu-
puri (of Xaratanga) , 113; Tucime,
183
Prisoners (vazcata) : 101, 103, 224
Prisons: 37
Prophecy: 53–60; see also omens and
augury
Provinces: 59; Uruapán, 81, 89
Pucuricuari: see under government,
titles of office
Pumeo: see under hunting places
Pungarancha: see under gods
Pungarecha: see under gods
Punishment: see crime
Puruaten: see under gods

Quahueyucha Zequaro (landing on
lake shore) : 112
Quangariecha: see under government,
titles of office
Quanicoti: see under government, titles
of office

of which *The Chronicles of Michoacán* is the ninety-eighth volume, was inaugurated in 1932 by the University of Oklahoma Press, and has as its purpose the reconstruction of American Indian civilization by presenting aboriginal, historical, and contemporary Indian life. The following list is complete as of the date of publication of this volume.

1. *Forgotten Frontiers:* A Study of the Spanish Indian Policy of Don Juan Bautista de Anza, Governor of New Mexico, 1777–1787. Translated and edited by Alfred Barnaby Thomas.
2. Grant Foreman. *Indian Removal:* The Emigration of the Five Civilized Tribes of Indians.
3. John Joseph Mathews. *Wah'Kon-Tah:* The Osage and the White Man's Road.
4. Grant Foreman. *Advancing the Frontier, 1830–1860.*
5. John H. Seger. *Early Days Among the Cheyenne and Arapahoe Indians.* Edited by Stanley Vestal.
6. Angie Debo. *The Rise and Fall of the Choctaw Republic.*
7. Stanley Vestal. *New Sources of Indian History, 1850–1891:* A Miscellany. Out of print.
8. Grant Foreman. *The Five Civilized Tribes.*
9. *After Coronado:* Spanish Exploration Northeast of New Mexico, 1696–1727. Translated and edited by Alfred Barnaby Thomas.
10. Frank G. Speck, *Naskapi:* The Savage Hunters of the Labrador Peninsula. Out of print.
11. Elaine Goodale Eastman. *Pratt:* The Red Man's Moses. Out of print.
12. Althea Bass. *Cherokee Messenger:* A Life of Samuel Austin Worcester.
13. Thomas Wildcat Alford. *Civilization.* As told to Florence Drake. Out of print.
14. Grant Foreman. *Indians and Pioneers:* The Story of the American Southwest Before 1830.
15. George E. Hyde. *Red Cloud's Folk:* A History of the Oglala Sioux Indians.
16. Grant Foreman. *Sequoyah.*

17. Morris L. Wardell. *A Political History of the Cherokee Nation, 1838–1907*. Out of print.
18. John Walton Caughey. *McGillivray of the Creeks.*
19. Edward Everett Dale and Gaston Litton. *Cherokee Cavaliers:* Forty Years of Cherokee History as Told in the Correspondence of the Ridge-Watie-Boudinot Family.
20. Ralph Henry Gabriel. *Elias Boudinot, Cherokee, and His America*. Out of print.
21. Karl N. Llewellyn and E. Adamson Hoebel. *The Cheyenne Way:* Conflict and Case Law in Primitive Jurisprudence.
22. Angie Debo. *The Road to Disappearance.*
23. Oliver La Farge and others. *The Changing Indian*. Out of print.
24. Carolyn Thomas Foreman. *Indians Abroad*. Out of print.
25. John Adair. *The Navajo and Pueblo Silversmiths.*
26. Alice Marriott. *The Ten Grandmothers.*
27. Alice Marriott. *María:* The Potter of San Ildefonso.
28. Edward Everett Dale. *The Indians of the Southwest:* A Century of Development Under the United States. Out of print.
29. *Popol Vuh:* The Sacred Book of the Ancient Quiché Maya. English version by Delia Goetz and Sylvanus G. Morley from the translation of Adrián Recinos.
30. Walter Collins O'Kane. *Sun in the Sky.*
31. Stanley A. Stubbs. *Bird's-Eye View of the Pueblos*. Out of print.
32. Katharine C. Turner. *Red Men Calling on the Great White Father.*
33. Muriel H. Wright. *A Guide to the Indian Tribes of Oklahoma.*
34. Ernest Wallace and E. Adamson Hoebel. *The Comanches:* Lords of the South Plains.
35. Walter Collins O'Kane. *The Hopis:* Portrait of a Desert People.
36. *The Sacred Pipe:* Black Elk's Account of the Seven Rites of the Oglala Sioux. Edited by Joseph Epes Brown.
37. *The Annals of the Cakchiquels,* translated from the Cakchiquel Maya by Adrián Recinos and Delia Goetz, with *Title of the Lords of Totonicapán*, translated from the Quiché text into Spanish by Dionisio José Chonay, English version by Delia Goetz.
38. R. S. Cotterill. *The Southern Indians:* The Story of the Civilized Tribes Before Removal.

The paper on which this book is printed bears the watermark of the University of Oklahoma Press and has an effective life of at least three hundred years.

UNIVERSITY OF OKLAHOMA PRESS

NORMAN